Monetary History, Exchange Rates and Financial Markets

Monetary History, Exchange Rates and Financial Markets

Essays in Honour of Charles Goodhart,
Volume Two

Edited by

Paul Mizen

*Reader in Monetary Economics and Deputy Director,
Experian Centre for Economic Modelling, University of
Nottingham, UK*

Edward Elgar
Cheltenham, UK • Northampton, MA, USA

Published by
Edward Elgar Publishing Limited
Glensanda House
Montpellier Parade
Cheltenham
Glos GL50 1UA
UK

Edward Elgar Publishing, Inc.
136 West Street
Suite 202
Northampton
Massachusetts 01060
USA

A catalogue record for this book
is available from the British Library

Library of Congress Cataloguing in Publication Data

Monetary history, exchange rates and financial markets: essays in honour of
Charles Goodhart, volume two/edited by Paul Mizen.
      p.   cm.
    'This volume and its companion have been compiled from the proceedings of
a two-day Festschrift conference in honour of Charles Goodhart at the Bank of
England, 15–16 November 2001'—Preface.
    1. Foreign exchange rates—Congresses.   2. Monetary policy—History—
Congresses.   3. Finance—Congresses.   I. Title: Essays in honour of Charles
Goodhart: volume two.   II. Goodhart, C.A.E. (Charles Albert Eric).   III.
Mizen, Paul.
HG3821.M67   2003
332—dc21   2002034704

ISBN 1 84376 086 X (cased)

Printed and bound in Great Britain by MPG Books Ltd, Bodmin, Cornwall

Contents

Figures

Tables

Contributors

Michael Artis, European University Institute, Florence, Italy
Michael D. Bordo, Rutgers University, New Brunswick, USA
Forrest Capie, City University Business School, UK
Elena Carletti, University of Mannheim, Germany
Andrew Crockett, General Manager, Bank for International Settlements, Switzerland
Barry Eichengreen, University of California, Berkeley, USA
Mintao Fan, University of California, Berkeley, USA
Michael Foot, Managing Director, Financial Services Authority, UK
Charles Goodhart, London School of Economics and Bank of England, UK
Philipp Hartmann, European Central Bank, Germany
Takatoshi Ito, Hitotsubashi University and the University of Tokyo, Japan
David Laidler, University of Western Ontario, Canada
Richard K. Lyons, University of California, Berkeley, USA
Jacques Melitz, Strathclyde University, UK
Marcus Miller, University of Warwick, UK
Richard G. Payne, London School of Economics, UK
Dirk Schoenmaker, Ministry of Finance, Netherlands
Anna J. Schwartz, National Bureau of Economic Research, USA
Andrew Sheng, Securities and Futures Commission, Hong Kong
Tan Gaik Looi, Securities and Futures Commission, Hong Kong
Mark P. Taylor, University of Warwick, UK
Jose Viñals, Director General, Banco de España, Spain

Preface

This volume and its companion have been compiled from the proceedings of a two-day Festschrift conference in honour of Charles Goodhart at the Bank of England, 15–16 November 2001. The conference would not have been possible without the participation and efforts of a large number of people. The contributors of papers are listed on page ix and my thanks are extended to each and every one of them for producing exceptionally high-quality papers. My thanks must also be extended to all those who chaired the sessions: Mark Gertler, Roger Alford, Leslie Dicks-Mireaux, Sushil Wadhwani, Anna J. Schwartz, Lord Desai, Peter Cooke, and David Webb, the discussants and those who provided comments from the floor. In some cases contributors and discussants went to considerable lengths to attend despite the commitments they were obliged to keep to other events on different continents the following day. My thanks are extended to them all.

As with all great enterprises there is a large number of people whose time and energy has been devoted to the task of putting the arrangements in place. I would particularly like to mention a few who took on the greater part of the task. The organisation of the conference at the Bank involved a number of people including Charles Goodhart, Mervyn King's office and especially his two Personal Assistants at the time, Mark Cornelius and Phil Evans, and the conference organisers, Debbie Nyman and Maureen Black. Ryan Love and Raoul Minetti undertook the task of writing detailed notes summarising the presentations and the subsequent discussion, for which I am very grateful. My own secretary, Jill Brown, at the University of Nottingham took on much of the administrative work and Tara Lehane at the Financial Markets Group, London School of Economics, handled the financial affairs. We are most grateful that the conference was generously supported by the Bank of England and the Financial Markets Group, London School of Economics. The publication of the two-volume set has been organised by Edward Elgar under the oversight of Dymphna Evans and Caroline Cornish who have been supportive and encouraging as always. My thanks are extended to them all for their patience and help.

Paul Mizen

Introduction

He accumulated a vast and various collection of learning and knowledge, which was so arranged in his mind as to be ever in readiness to be brought forth. But his superiority over other learned men consisted chiefly in what may be called the art of thinking, the art of using his mind – a certain continual power of seizing the useful substance of all that he knew, and exhibiting it in a clear and forcible manner; so that knowledge, which we often see to be no better than lumber in men of dull understanding, was in him true, evident and actual wisdom . . . His maxims carry conviction; for they are founded on the basis of common sense, and a very attentive and minute survey of real life . . .

(James Boswell's *Life of Samuel Johnson*, p. 511)

Ben Friedman refers in the first volume to Charles Goodhart as the Samuel Johnson of Monetary Policy – and how true a statement that is. The extract quoted above was written by James Boswell of Johnson at the end of his life in 1784 but could equally have been written of Charles's academic career in 2002. Like Johnson, Charles Goodhart has written extensively in many styles and has become synonymous with his subjects of monetary economics and central banking. Although I am not aware that Charles has ever produced a dictionary, he has made substantial contributions to the literature in his field and has on many occasions been the influence that has altered its direction at crucial junctures. He has also been a helpful critic and commentator on other authors' work, an encouragement and a source of wisdom to many younger colleagues. He has combined these features with a great deal of wit and amusement, and I am sure Charles would not mind if I continue to quote from Boswell, who states, quite accurately I believe, that 'Though usually grave, and even awful in his deportment, he possessed uncommon and peculiar powers of wit and humour; he frequently indulged himself in colloquial pleasantry; and the heartiest merriment was enjoyed in his company.'

This volume and its companion are a testimony to the high regard and good will that exist among his fellow economists. Not every economist deserves a Festschrift upon retirement from academic life, since a Festschrift is a mark of distinction reserved for the outstanding academics of their generation. It is an indication that they have made a significant contribution to the development and understanding of their subject. The quality of the economist can be judged by the excellence of the contributions, and there is no doubt that this volume and its companion, that have arisen from a two-day conference held at the Bank of England on 15 and 16 November 2001, have a stellar quality about them. It was a delight to find that the Governor of the Bank of England, Sir Edward George, was able to make time in his diary to open the conference, despite its close proximity to the IMF–World Bank meetings the following weekend. His opening address summed up this point exactly when he said 'I hope the MPC – and the Bank staff who provide us with such wonderful support – will not misunderstand me when I say that I cannot remember ever before having had such a galaxy of academic economist and central banking superstars gathered together under one roof!' As the Governor went on to say 'that is just how it should be as we meet to pay tribute to Charles who has given such a huge amount to his twin professions throughout his working life'.

The comments of the contributors, discussants and members of the audience all confirmed this view. Those who attended the conference were given privileged access to some of the outstanding minds in the vast fields of monetary economics, central banking, financial regulation and exchange rate economics. In view of the outstanding quality of the contributions it was a high priority to make them available to the wider profession. For this reason the original conference papers have been drawn together into two volumes with the help of Edward Elgar to ensure that they reach a broader group of professional economists, central bankers, academics and students of monetary economics.

It has been difficult to know how to divide up the contributions by the various authors into two volumes. All the chapters refer to subjects that have been major research topics in Charles's wide-ranging portfolio, and all are interconnected. It would have been possible to reorganise the chapters in many other ways, and no doubt there will be some who would wish that chapters on certain subjects had been put in the same volume. Indeed the order of the presentations in the conference was different from the order that the chapters now appear, but the timing of the chapters in the conference was driven by the diaries of many busy people. The printed volume is free from these constraints and we have sought to draw together the chapters that have the most in common with each other. All the chapters highlight the contribution that Charles has made to their field whilst also offering a contribution of their own in terms of a summary of current thinking and insights into the latest controversies. The benefit that this volume offers the reader is a summary of subjects from the full range of modern monetary economics. Hardly a single issue is omitted and all the topics blend the clarity of academic thinking with the practicalities of policy; whether that falls into the realm of central banking, financial regulation or international finance. We encourage the reader to read beyond his or her own interests and draw the full benefit from this collection of chapters by economists who are eminent in their field. It is to be hoped that the readers will appreciate them as much as those who heard the presentations at first hand.

The contents of this volume refer to monetary history, crises and exchange rates. The opening contributions are written by some of the most lucid and articulate members of our profession. They have taken as their theme a matter of general application to the economics profession: the role of the history of the subject in the education of economists. The first chapter is written by David Laidler of the University of Western Ontario who provides a delightfully controversial appraisal of 'The role of economic thought in modern macroeconomics'. Laidler stresses that interest in the history of economic thought has progressively declined, and teaching in the subject at the graduate level is now the exception rather than the rule. On the one hand this appears a stylised fact of every discipline. In particular, it is generally argued that there exists a negative correlation between the development of a discipline and the history of that discipline, and as Jean Baptiste Say put it (quoted by Jacques Melitz) 'The more perfect the science, the shorter the history'. However, Laidler stresses the importance of keeping the history of economic thought alive since it has an influence on the development of the subject and policy debates. In particular, he mentions a number of interesting examples in which a better knowledge of the history of economics would have helped in formulating more suitable policy actions. This was a theme that excited some interest. In the reaction to this paper when it was originally given, it was argued that the decline of the history of economic thought cannot be dissociated from the capacity of the scholars to stimulate the profession to take what they have to offer as a serious contribution to knowledge and economic education.

Jacques Melitz's discussion brings out the comparison between Mark Blaug's 'No history of ideas, please, we're economists' published in the winter issue of the *Journal of Economic Perspectives* 2001 and the contribution of David Laidler from the perspective of someone who is in substantial agreement with what both authors have to say. Melitz points out that we need to re-assess the state of the subject in relation to its history, and in so doing we may conclude that the history of economics is not uniform across the sub-disciplines. Macroeconomics may need its history more than, say, microeconomics or econometrics. His conclusion from reading Laidler's chapter is that macroeconomics has great difficulty in distinguishing the subject from the history of the subject. Monetary history and our knowledge of monetary economics are hard to disentangle, not least because some key developments have been made by a careful examination of the monetary history.

The next two chapters are based on monetary history. This was the subject of Charles Goodhart's doctoral dissertation at Harvard completed in 1962, and no better exponents can be found than the authors, Anna J. Schwartz of the National Bureau of Economic Research and Barry Eichengreen of University of California, Berkeley, who both co-author their chapters with Michael D. Bordo of Rutgers University. Michael D. Bordo and Anna J. Schwartz's chapter is entitled 'Charles Goodhart's contributions to the history of monetary institutions'. The chapter first discusses Charles's investigation of US central banking history from 1900 to 1914 and then the equivalent exercise for the United Kingdom, where he examined the adjustment mechanism by which the balance of payments equilibrium was achieved under the gold standard in Britain from 1891 to 1913. The standard view at the time was that if the Bank of England's gold reserves became threatened then it should increase its bank rate inducing a short-term capital inflow and reduce domestic economic activity. However, Goodhart suggested a different mechanism. An increase in economic activity that led to increased bank lending and deposits would maintain stable reserve ratios, if the Bank of England supplied the extra reserves by reducing other assets. This would reduce the gold reserve ratio and would lead to a higher bank rate. This resulting inflow of gold would restore the Bank of England's gold reserve ratio.

The chapter goes on to discuss Goodhart's beliefs about central banking activities. For example, Goodhart believes there to be a need for a central bank since commercial banks are inherently unstable (due to incomplete/asymmetric information and the herding behaviour of banks). Although he has studied systems without central banks, such as currency boards, and free banking, his conclusion has been that central banks are necessary to deal with commercial bank instability. Bordo and Schwartz argue that the instability in the banking sector is the result of unstable monetary policy and ill-advised regulation originating in the central bank. On this matter they agree to differ even after over thirty years of discussion.

Bordo's second chapter is with Barry Eichengreen and refers to 'Crises now and then: what lessons from the last era of financial globalization?'. This considers the differences between the financial crises of a hundred years ago from those of today. Bordo and Eichengreen use data from 32 crises in 21 countries from 1880 to the present day to make comparisons with the analysis of Delargy and Goodhart's *Financial Markets Group Special Paper* of 1999. Their findings are that crises are twice as frequent today compared to pre-1914 and this is due to the greater incidence of currency crises (banking crises have remained just as frequent). They also find that the output loss due to crises is similar now compared to pre-1914 and the recovery time is again similar, although Delargy and Goodhart suggest that the recovery time was quicker in the 19th century than in the 20th century, and this is confirmed in this chapter for banking and for twin crises. An important difference between the crises in the two periods is that banking crises did not previously spill over into currency crises. The reason for this, according to Eichengreen and Bordo, is that there was not a particularly close connection between banking crises and monetisation and thus no expectations of a spillover from the banking sector to create a currency crisis. To some degree this was enforced because the option of devaluing from a hard peg was not available. The conclusion of the chapter is that crises are becoming more common but not more severe in their nature, and in agreement with Delargy and Goodhart, the authors suggest that we have become more prone to twin crises, which the pre-1914 system was better able to handle than our present system.

The discussant of these chapters is Forrest Capie of City University, London. When reviewing Bordo and Schwartz's chapter he emphasises the differences of opinion between the authors and Goodhart. If Goodhart is right, he asks how was it that the banks emerged through their own self-imposed prudent behaviour before regulators were invented? And asks whether Charles is having second thoughts about the view that banks need complex regulation following the enlargement of his views in the recent speech in Brussels (Goodhart, 2001). Capie welcomes the American perspective from Bordo and Schwartz, but asks whether Charles, whose forebears, early life and graduate education were all American, is really British after all. His familiarity is with British institutions, for sure, and the Bank has a prominent place in his thinking but his conclusions are not those that accord with the British experience. When discussing Bordo and Eichengreen's chapter, Capie raises the issue of data quality. UK data in the 19th century is notorious for being suspect, so for the twenty-one countries for which data was available pre-1914, the data is likely to be very unreliable. His 'quibbles' about the dates of peaks and troughs, crises and turmoil, may be the basis for progress when the issue of whether crises are worse now than one hundred years ago is debated in the light of Asia 1997, Russia, 1998, Argentina 2001 and so on.

The topic of international monetary stability for the present day is one that has received some considerable attention from Charles. The following four chapters begin with the 'big picture' of the choice of exchange rate regimes with a chapter by Andrew Crockett, the General Manager of the Bank for International Settlements, which follows naturally from the chapter by Eichengreen and Bordo. The next three chapters work progressively through issues relating to foreign exchange rate intervention discussed by Takatoshi Ito, to the microstructure and high frequency data questions presented by Rich Lyons and Richard Payne.

Andrew Crockett's chapter, 'Exchange rate regimes in theory and practice' discusses the possible stable exchange rate regimes that were initially suggested, separately by Larry Summers at the policy institution end of the spectrum and Geoff Frankel at the research economist end. These were currency unions, currency boards, fully fixed and free float regimes. Crockett argues that since adjustable pegs are considered unstable, so too must currency boards, witness Argentina in 2001–02. Therefore he suggests that only the extreme cases of currency unions and free floats are stable, but the choice of the most appropriate exchange rate arrangement for a particular country is conditional upon a specific set of attributes that the country possesses in relation to its trade patterns, investment and portfolio flows and inflationary policies. Nor are these patterns likely to remain fixed for long, but they will change over time. Crockett notes that a number of countries have opted in favour of exiting from a pegged exchange rate in order to move in the direction of a more flexible exchange rate. He asks the question: how does one exit from a fixed exchange rate at the right time and in the right manner to avoid destabilising the economic and political environment? The answer is to exit while the currency is strong, and the economic conditions are unlikely to cause substantial changes to the prevailing rate. In addition, exit should be gradual, with the appropriate institutional and supervisory mechanisms brought into place before the exit occurs. Last of all an alternative nominal anchor needs to be identified. The move in the other direction is exemplified in the convergence criteria of the Maastricht Treaty for European monetary union. When speculating on future foreign exchange developments, Crockett suggested that only three major currencies might survive: the dollar, the euro and the yen. Smaller currencies may decide to link to one of these currencies, and therefore he implies that more currency unions are likely to emerge.

The discussant, Jose Viñals (Banco de España) talks about the disappearance of the middle between the extremes of free float and currency unions, suggesting that, due to the existence of many managed float regimes, it is in fact only the fixed part of the middle that is disappearing. He also talks about possible non-linear mean reversion when an exchange rate is allowed to move within a band quite freely but is forced back within the band if market forces threaten the existing peg.

The next chapter is by Takatoshi Ito of Hitotsubashi University and the University of Tokyo who asks the question 'Is foreign exchange intervention effective?' He acknowledges up front that the process of foreign exchange intervention is one of the most secretive activities of central banks and a great source of controversy. Some commentators imply that the central bank, as a relatively small player in the market, is therefore unlikely to be able to effectively alter the exchange rate. Others point to the importance of signalling to alter the market's perception of the future direction of exchange rate movements.

This chapter examines the effectiveness of the foreign exchange intervention by the Japanese ministry of finance using a ten-year dataset from April 1991 to March 2001. Ito presents a summary of the data on the size and timing of the intervention and shows that the cut off exchange rate above which the Ministry of Finance bought yen (sold dollars) and below which it sold yen was 125 yen/dollar. This policy, Ito argues, of buying yen low and selling it high resulted in realised profits of approximately 1 trillion yen. When considering the fact that more dollars were bought than sold over this period and since the Ministry of Finance borrowed yen by issuing low-interest bonds and invested in higher-interest-earning US debt, the total gains from the intervention were estimated to be approximately 2 per cent of GDP. Thus the central bank has engaged in effective, stabilising, intervention that has yielded considerable profits, with the intended influence over the direction of the yen that was desired.

Marcus Miller of the University of Warwick evaluates the options proposed by Andrew Crockett for international monetary arrangements. Crockett's four feasible options are contrasted with Morris Goldstein's view that there are 'five horses' in the exchange rate race in his Institute of International Economics article *Managed Floating Plus*. Both Crockett and Goldstein agree that adjustable pegs and crawling bands are too fragile for the present system with large capital flows and sometimes stuttering policy reforms. Miller muses that if Goldstein can add extras what would we like to add to the present floating rate system? His identifies two options – capital controls and soft margins. Capital controls, he argues, are a useful supplement to currency boards, for example Argentina, and to bands, baskets and crawls (the category he labels BBC). Soft margins to target zones as proposed by John Williamson could ensure the expectation of mean reversion even in the midst of a crisis – a feature of the gold standard's stability identified by Charles in his article with Delargy. Last of all, Miller turns to the issue of asset bubbles. Recent research has shown that monitoring bands and 'leaning-into-the-wind' strategies may create non-linear mean reversion but they cannot rule out bubbles. A wider backstop is required, and Takatoshi Ito's article presents evidence that sterilised intervention has fulfilled this role. Miller indicates that how and when sterilised intervention is likely to succeed is of significant interest and will command attention.

Research into the behaviour of high frequency foreign exchange rate data is another theme that has interested Charles Goodhart, and the next two chapters lie within this field. The first is prepared by Mintao Fan and Richard K. Lyons of University of California, Berkeley on 'Customer trades and extreme events in foreign exchange'. They describe the research into the trading of foreign exchange customers – as opposed to 'interdealer' trades – as an expanding frontier for the understanding of how information, which is often dispersed and diffuse, filters into the market. Although inter-dealer trades are the largest part of the market, the customer trades are the underlying demand of the market, and therefore potentially the most inter-esting. Fan and Lyons start by stressing the traditional difficulty in captur-ing the dynamics of the exchange rate, with sophisticated exchange rate models notoriously out-performed by a random walk. They have a model based on earlier work by Evans and Lyons in the *Journal of Political Economy* with an interesting description of the microstructure of the foreign exchange market where the crucial innovation is the presence of proprietary traders in between market makers and the public. They focus on a case study of the 10 per cent drop in the yen–dollar exchange rate in October 1998 during a single day. The customer order flow over this data set shows little evidence of mean reverting behaviour, and aggregate customer flow tracks the exchange rate movements at lower frequencies. They show that hedge funds were not responsible for the drop (despite the collapse of the massive Long-Term Capital Management) since they were net providers of liquid-ity, but rather that the institutional investors such as pension funds, insur-ance companies and mutuals were responsible. Therefore a chain of liquidity provision arises with the key players being dealers (high frequency liquidity providers), proprietary traders and mutual funds. These same insti-tutions are responsible for creating the large net flows that are associated with the high-frequency exchange rate movements.

Richard G. Payne of the London School of Economics follows with a presentation of the microeconomic determinants of liquidity demand and supply in the foreign exchange market. Liquidity, he notes, is an oft-used but rarely defined concept. The chapter considers the dynamic interactions between trading activity, return volatility and bid-ask spreads at hourly fre-quencies. There is a great deal of similarity between this chapter and the previous one by Fan and Lyons, and the investigation of the 'order flow', the difference between aggregate number or volume of buyer and seller ini-tiated trades is important. Three questions are raised: 'Is the order flow destabilising?', 'How is market liquidity affected by prior trading and return volatility?' and 'Does liquidity feedback on volatility and transac-tion frequency?' Payne stresses that the interaction between transaction fre-quency and order flow are crucial in capturing liquidity demand whilst on the supply side the bid–ask spread and market depth are crucial for deter-mining the supply of liquidity. The data used in the empirical analysis were drawn from transactions in the sterling–dollar exchange rate market. Payne particularly emphasises the importance of testing whether both supply and demand of liquidity are well behaved or exhibit anomalous patterns due to agents' speculative behaviour.

Mark P. Taylor of the University of Warwick discusses both chapters. He notes that Charles Goodhart's inaugural lecture was a major spur to the development of research on the microstructure of foreign exchange markets. Recognising Lyons, Fan and Payne as major contributors to this literature from either side of the Atlantic, Taylor suggests that the findings of these papers on the relationship between customer order flows and exchange rate movements are of considerable significance. The most noticeable result of the first paper is that it appears to contradict the Evans–Lyons model published in the *Journal of Political Economy*. Taylor suggests that the Evans–Lyons paper need not be taken as axiomatic, and further empirical research should be undertaken to investigate the Fan–Lyons chapter presented here. Likewise the chapter by Richard Payne offers intriguing empirical results which could be compared with earlier research on technical analysis. Taylor has in mind a comparison between Payne's findings and those of Allen and Taylor published in the *Economic Journal* which uncovered activity in the foreign exchange markets that was related closely to indicators of overbuying and overselling. Both chapters are regarded as likely to stimulate future research on the drivers of exchange rate movements based on micro analysis of the market structure.

The final chapters in this volume relate to the issue of banking, financial stability and financial regulation. The first chapter in this section by Philipp Hartmann of the European Central Bank and Elena Carletti of the University of Mannheim explains the wave of consolidation that has occurred in the financial sector in recent years. They present a theoretical model on the impact of bank mergers on competition and financial stability. The impact of mergers on the efficiency of the financial sector is debatable, since bank mergers have ambiguous effects on both lending rates and financial stability. Bank mergers reduce competition but at the same time potentially enhance cost efficiency. Regarding financial stability, the impact of bank mergers is related to the changes in the size of balance sheets resulting from competition effects and to the structure of liquidity shocks.

The discussant, Michael Artis, stresses the difficulties of capturing the impact of bank mergers on phenomena like financial instability. He demonstrates that within the European Union at least, there has been less banking competition than we might have expected. The widely expected European arbitrage has only been partial, strengthening the capital markets but not the banking sector, despite the documented differences in efficiency. Artis points out that banks are special, and are not therefore comparable to any other industry, but asks whether this is the whole reason for the sluggish, or even glacial, speed of integration. The illustrations, taken from his adopted home of Italy, point to the common problem of national interests in financial regulation and surveillance which act as barriers to mergers, takeovers and increasing competition from abroad.

Although Charles engaged in research on financial regulation late in his career, he quickly established his position as a key commentator on this issue. The following chapter by Andrew Sheng and Tan Gaik Looi of the Securities and Futures Commission of Hong Kong documents Charles's contribution to financial regulation and asks 'Is there a Goodhart's Law in financial regulation?' Sheng and Tan Gaik Looi draw parallels between the approach that Charles Goodhart applied to an assessment of monetary policy making in Goodhart's Law. They seek to determine whether the same issues apply to the financial regulator seeking to apply regulatory rules 'for control purposes'. They begin by surveying the difficulties encountered by regulators during the recent financial crises and stresses that neither South-East Asia nor Russia had sound financial regulation before their respective problems. Both countries underwent a process of overlending and asset price inflation and deflation facilitated by the lack of adequate scrutiny on the part of regulators – but more regulation by the application of rules is not necessarily the answer. According to Sheng and Looi regulation of the financial system should be pushed too far, in that regulation itself implies costs (not only the cost of resources but also risk of moral hazard). Sheng and Looi argue that there must always be a cost–benefit analysis behind regulatory decisions.

Michael Foot, the Managing Director of the Financial Services Authority presents a chapter on the issue of 'Working with market forces'. Foot stresses that the regulator should always have three targets in mind: the protection of depositors, the prevention of systemic instability and the prevention of money laundering. The regulator should pay attention to a number of 'obvious' market signals like share prices, bond prices and ratings, but also to a number of less obvious market signals like the liquidity of Certificates of Deposit and the cost of funds (both retail and wholesale). In turn, the market itself places constraints on financial institutions, (such as market-based capital requirements) and some market disciplines are progressively developing, like market-based pricing of deposit insurance, a public pre-commitment of the bank not to take excessive risks and the adequate treatment of subordinated debt.

The discussant, Dirk Schoenmaker from the Ministry of Finance, the Netherlands, praises both chapters for their clarity in stressing the pros and cons of a strict financial regulation. He notes that the capital adequacy requirements – known often as Cooke ratios after the chairman of the session – have become important policy variables in the hands of the regulator. This puts in place at least the preconditions for a Goodhart's law of financial regulation. He also points out in passing that there are many parallels between monetary policy and financial regulation, for example time inconsistency of actions, rules versus discretion debates and so on. In dicussing Michael Foot's chapter Schoenmaker analyses the concept of risk in the numerical meaures such as Value at Risk, and the effectiveness of market discipline in financial regulation. He focuses his discussion on the dangers implicit in the new proposals for capital requirements (the so-called Basle II) since they vary with the level of risk, and he points out that for internationally active banks the procyclicality of capital regulation could lead to adverse macroeconomic effects.

The final contribution is by Charles Goodhart. This postscript offers his views on three topics worthy of further study that arise from the contributions of various authors in the two Festschrift volumes. The first topic relates to the treatment of volatility in foreign exchange markets following a major shock. Charles's objective is to seek out a theoretically plausible and institutionally robust explanation for volatility measures such as GARCH. The second topic amounts to a difference of opinion between Charles and Lars Svensson over the shape of the loss function. Charles contends that at the crucial point where a threshold is about to be breached the loss function is very steep, but thereafter it is flat. The fact that this does not correspond to a quadratic loss function raises the issue of how to characterise the authorities' loss function in monetary theory. The final topic relates to monetary history and the gold standard. Charles points out that the historical importance of the inflow and outflow of capital (gold) following a rate rise was an important link in the transmission mechanism. The fact that this is now regarded as unreliable, or even reversible, is a matter of concern and worthy of more research. It is no surprise to find that each of these research 'ideas' lies in a completely different field of monetary economics. Such is Charles's breadth of knowledge and interest!

1. The role of the history of economic thought in modern macroeconomics[*]

David Laidler

1. INTRODUCTION

I intend it as a compliment to say that I do not regard Charles Goodhart as a modern macroeconomist. From the very beginning of his career, with his 1962 PhD thesis on the activities of the New York money market at the beginning of the last century (Goodhart, 1969) until now, with his work on the Wicksellian nature of modern monetary systems (Goodhart, 2002), Charles's economics has been informed by a deep understanding of the history of monetary institutions and policy, and of the economic ideas that have underlain that history. It might appear paradoxical that this very characteristic of his intellectual equipment, which to many would seem to have suited him only for a life in the ivory tower, has also made him an important and effective policy advisor. But, as I hope to show, an approach of the type that Charles has always taken to economics is as productive and practical as it is unfashionable

2. THE STATUS OF THE HISTORY OF THOUGHT WITHIN ECONOMICS

The title of a recent article by Mark Blaug (2001) succinctly and accurately describes the current status of the History of Economic Thought among economists: 'No History of Ideas Please, We're Economists'. One of the most distinguished of the younger generation of macroeconomists, Paul Romer, expresses the attitude that prompted Blaug's title in the following way: 'I guess I would describe ancestor worship as a research strategy as probably an unproductive one (*laughter*). But as a consumption activity it is something that can be fun' (Snowdon and Vane, 1999, p. 304). He explains his attitude as follows:

> it is very hard to tell, quite frankly, when you go back and read economics that is stated in purely verbal terms. There is always the danger that you read between

the lines and say, oh, they had it exactly right – here is this mathematical model which shows what they were thinking. But that is usually based on a charitable reading and one that ignores some of the ambiguities and confusions. I wrote a paper like that at one time interpreting Allyn Young's paper . . . (p. 304)

Romer takes it for granted that anyone can read older literature without help or training, and that the only productive role for such an activity is as a source of ideas for mathematical formulation. Both presumptions present serious pitfalls, as some of Romer's own work (1991), illustrates.[1] In discussing the historical background to modern endogenous growth theory, he begins by telling his readers that:

Adam Smith put two propositions at the center of economic theory. The first was that competition allocates the preexisting stock of productive inputs in a way that is wealth maximising. The second was that an endogenous process of accumulation and investment was the fundamental force that led to increases in the stock of these inputs, and, therefore, to growth in income and wealth. (p. 83)

Now these two propositions, and their reconciliation, are certainly central to Romer's own work but it is unlikely that Adam Smith would have summarised the message of the *Wealth of Nations* in quite this way.

Older texts were not written for us, but for their authors' contemporaries. Words and phrases change their meaning over time, knowledge that we now take for granted, and in whose light we might be tempted to interpret works, has not always been current, while commonly held ideas that once provided a context for the discussion of economic issues have got lost, and so on. Reading older texts is tricky even for the specialist, let alone the economist whose primary interest lies elsewhere. That is why it was once thought essential to train all economists in this skill. Furthermore, though modern economists sometimes revisit old themes unaware, to suggest that there is no point in studying the subject's history unless it provides insights for further theoretical development is to adopt an extremely narrow point of view.

In this chapter I shall consider two other uses to which the history of thought is more frequently put. I shall discuss the rhetorical use that certain modern monetary economists make of the older literature when they expound their own ideas, and then I shall take up the part played by the history of economic thought in interpreting the experience which forms the empirical basis of our subject. I shall conclude that mainstream economists fail to appreciate the importance of the History of Economic Thought as a sub-discipline in its own right, and that this has a debilitating effect on economics as a whole.

3. THE HISTORY OF ECONOMIC THOUGHT AS A RHETORICAL WEAPON

The History of Economic Thought has received more than passing attention from those who have developed the most influential strand in modern macroeconomics, namely new classical theory. Robert Lucas, Thomas Sargent and their associates have claimed to be reinstating an approach to economics whose pedigree runs back to the 18th century, and whose dominance in the subject was only temporarily interrupted by the 'Keynesian Revolution'. It is worth quoting Lucas and Sargent (1978) at some length on the approach to economics that Keynes was alleged to have subverted, and on the nature of the alternative he offered.

> Before the 1930s, economists did not recognise a need for a special branch of economics, with its own special postulates, designed to explain the business cycle. Keynes founded that subdiscipline, called 'macroeconomics,' because he thought explaining the characteristics of business cycles was impossible within the discipline imposed by its insistence on adherence to the two postulates (a) that markets clear and (b) that agents act in their own self-interest. The outstanding facts that seemed impossible to reconcile with these two postulates were the length and severity of business depressions and the large scale unemployment they entailed. A related observation was that measures of aggregate demand and prices were positively correlated with measures of real output and employment, in apparent contradiction to the classical result that changes in a purely nominal magnitude like the general price level were pure unit changes which should not alter real behaviour.
>
> After freeing himself of the straightjacket (or discipline) imposed by the classical postulates, Keynes described a model in which rules of thumb, such as the consumption function and liquidity preference schedule, took the place of decision functions that a classical economist would insist be derived from the theory of choice. And rather than require that wages and prices be determined by the postulates that markets clear – which for the labor market seemed patently contradicted by the severity of business depressions – Keynes took as an unexamined postulate that money wages are sticky, meaning that they are set at a level or by a process that could be taken as uninfluenced by the macroeconomic forces he proposed to analyse. (Lucas and Sargent, 1978, pp. 304–5)

As a description of the approach to cycle theory that Lucas and Sargent were trying to establish in 1978, and of its contrast to what, in the textbooks of the 1970s, was passing for 'Keynesian economics', and making due allowance for the polemical nature of the paper in which it appeared, this passage is fair enough. But it purports to be not a summary of a new research agenda but an account of the history of an important branch of economic thought. Judged as such, and to put it kindly, it leaves much to be desired: the business cycle, let alone the credit cycle, was a mainstay in the literature of economics from the early 1860s onwards; those who wrote about it took it for granted that markets didn't clear; some, who forged what Axel Leijonhufvud (1981) called 'the Wicksell Connection' located the problem in the capital market, and others, notably Marshall and Pigou, argued that wage stickiness, the reasons for which were extensively examined, both played a part in market failure, and underlay the fact that prices and output moved together; economists who insisted on decision functions derived from the theory of choice as a basis for cycle theory were few and far between before 1936; in the *General Theory,* which was not about the cycle, Keynes explicitly denied that his theoretical results depended upon wage stickiness; and so on.[2]

Nor is this passage an isolated example of the misrepresentation of the history of economics by modern monetary economists. Lucas himself (1996) returned to the discussion of the history of classical and neo-classical monetary economics in his Nobel Lecture along lines related to those which he and Sargent had followed in 1978. Blaug (2001) accurately tells us that he treats of David Hume and his successors (all the way down to Patinkin) as 'want(ing) to think in general equilibrium terms in which people are conceived as maximising over time' but 'resorting to loose equilibrium dynamics because the analytic equipment available to them offered no alternative' and comments as follows: 'It does not seem to occur to Lucas that this is *not* how the quantity theory of money was interpreted by Hume or anyone else in this golden age before the rational expectations revolution of the 1970s' (all quotations from Blaug, p. 155).

Another example of the rhetorical use of the History of Thought in modern macroeconomics is Sargent and Wallace's (1982) claim that, in proposing the 'overlapping generations' model as a potentially fruitful basis for a general monetary theory, they were also reviving and throwing new light on 18th and 19th century debates about the quantity theory and the real bills doctrine. They told their readers that the real bills doctrine 'asserts that unrestricted intermediation either by private banks or by a central bank has beneficial economic effects and should be promoted by public policy' (p. 1212), a proposition that their own theoretical results supported. They thereby appropriated a well-established label for the quite different hypothesis that *if bank money is always issued by way of discount of good quality short-term commercial paper issued to finance inventories and goods in process, variations in its quantity can impart neither inflationary nor deflationary impulses to the economy.* Since this latter hypothesis has been associated with the policies of the Reichsbank during the Weimar hyperinflation and the Federal Reserve system during the great contraction of 1929–33, among other episodes, the semantic confusion thus introduced has not been a minor matter for anyone trying to teach a little history to students who are simultaneously being 'well trained' in modern monetary theory.

Now none of this is intended as covert criticism of the *substance* of modern macroeconomics. Any body of ideas must stand or fall, not by the status of its intellectual antecedents, but by the conformity or lack thereof of its predictions to empirical evidence, and by its logical coherence. But the application of such tests, and the interpretation of their results, do not occur in an intellectual vacuum. Theories are not judged to be good or bad in isolation in economics, but better or worse in relation to other theories. If already existing literature is misrepresented by the exponents of a particular body of new ideas, and their readers accept their misrepresentations as accurate, then that body of ideas gets more than a head start in the race to become established. Thus, though (*pace* Arjo Klamer and Deidre McCloskey) modern economics is more than a series of 'good conversations' the effectiveness of the rhetoric that is deployed in support of particular points of view does affect the way in which questions of substance are settled.[3]

There is nothing new in macroeconomics about the self-conscious use of rhetorical devices to promote an intellectual cause. The *ad hominem* element in Harry Johnson's (1971) Ely Lecture on 'The Keynesian Revolution and the Monetarist Counter-Revolution' tended, at the time of its publication, to distract attention from its subtle and rather general discussion of the way in which debating tactics had helped to shape the development of macroeconomics in the previous thirty-five years or so. And though the deployment of ideas, purportedly drawn from the history of economic thought, to lend a little authority to the case for a contemporary piece of doctrine was by no means the only weapon in the rhetorical armoury that Johnson described there, he drew attention to the way in which competing and dubious versions of the history of ideas had been deployed in the debates he was discussing. As he noted:

> The Keynesian Revolution derived a large part of its intellectual appeal from the deliberate caricaturing and denigration of honest and humble scholars, whose only real crime was that they happened to exist and stand in the way of the success of the revolution. The counter-revolution had to endow these scholars, or at least their intellectual successors, with a wisdom vastly superior to what their opponents had credited them with. *Obiter dicta* and an oral tradition are at least a semi-legitimate scholarly means to this polemical end. (pp. 198–9)

With its final sentence removed, this passage could very well stand as a comment on the two paragraphs from Lucas and Sargent (1978) quoted above, but the counter-revolution to which Johnson referred was Friedman's monetarist counter-revolution, the *obiter dicta* were those of 'the great neo-classical quantity theorists' which had been 'combed . . . for any bits of evidence that showed recognition . . . of the fact that a decision to hold money involves a choice between holding money and holding wealth in other forms, and is conditioned by the rates of return on other assets' (p. 198), while the 'oral tradition' was one associated with the University of Chicago 'that was alleged to have preserved understanding of the fundamental truth among a band of the initiated through the dark years of the Keynesian despotism' (p. 198).[4]

It is nevertheless worth recalling that Johnson offered not just criticisms of Friedman's views on the history of thought in 1971, but of the substantive content of his monetarism too. In Johnson's view, Friedman had failed to come to grips with how the effects of monetary shocks divided themselves up between output (and/or employment) and prices, and had relied too much on the methodology of positive economics and too little on general equilibrium theory. Both of these points carried considerable weight, and it is surely no accident that they were directly met by the very features that distinguish new classical economics from monetarism: namely, its embedding of the rational expectations hypothesis in a Walrasian framework to produce a short-run aggregate supply curve, along which output, and therefore employment too, respond to surprise price level movements.[5] In highlighting these features, however, new classical economics rendered the Chicago quantity theory tradition of the 1930s, which lay in the mainstream of what Joseph Reeve (1943) termed 'fiscal inflationism' as a cure for the depression, irrelevant as an ancestry from which it could draw academic respectability. This perhaps explains why Lucas and Sargent laid claim to a very different and altogether broader set of intellectual antecedents for their ideas.

4. RATIONAL EXPECTATIONS AND TRUE MODELS

I did not single out Lucas, Sargent and Wallace for particular attention in the preceding section of this chapter without a constructive reason. It was they, above all, who showed the rest of us how fertile John Muth's idea of 'rational expectations' could be in simultaneously bringing extra rigour to the logic of macroeconomic theory and empirical novelty to its predictions.

As Sargent and Wallace (1973, p. 328) explained it, this hypothesis held that expectations about any variable's behaviour would 'depend, in a proper way, on the same things that economic theory says actually determine that variable'. Agents were assumed to have the same level of understanding of any model's behaviour as the economist constructing it. The 'money-supply surprise' class of models of cyclical fluctuations that was so popular in the 1970s, and in whose support Lucas and Sargent (1978) deployed the brief history of macroeconomic thought quoted earlier, postulated that agents all believed in the quantity theory of money, had information about the time series processes underlying the behaviour of the money supply, formed their expectations accordingly, and then acted on them when interpreting and responding to changes in the nominal prices ruling in the constantly clearing markets in which they were active.

When these models were tested empirically, they were found to be severely wanting.[6] The work that undermined them typically used post-Second World War data, usually drawn from the US. During the period over which those data were generated, however, to the extent that there was any dominant theory of price level behaviour within the economics profession, let alone among the public at large, it had nothing to do with the quantity theory of money. Rather it was an eclectic amalgam of 'cost-push inflation' ideas, overlaid from the early 1960s onwards with the idea of an inflation–unemployment trade-off that might be susceptible to 'demand-pull' forces; and among the latter forces monetary policy was but one of many. Thus, the economic ideas of the agents whose behaviour underlay the data that the exponents of money supply surprise models were trying to explain were anything but homogenous and bore no resemblance at all to the economic ideas attributed to them in those models.

The point here is quite general. Modern macroeconomics, like all of the sub-discipline's earlier incarnations, builds models which its exponents hope are 'true', or at least not proven to be false too quickly. Unlike earlier approaches, however, and this is its great advantage over them in the eyes of its exponents, it postulates that the agents who inhabit those models understand the economy in which they are operating as well as the economist who creates them, and condition their behaviour upon such knowledge. If we treat the History of Economic Thought with any degree of seriousness, however, three truths become apparent, and one conjecture becomes plausible: first, in the real world, it is economists, not agents in general, who specialise in creating models of the economy; second, at no time in the past have economists ever provided a single model with an undisputed claim to embody the truth; third, the models that they have provided have always evolved continuously in the face of logical and empirical criticism; and, finally, it seems unlikely that the future is going to differ from the past in any of these respects.

If economic agents do use economic theory to condition their behaviour, therefore, it is possible that, in the same economy at the same time, different agents will react differently to exactly the same information and incentives, and that, as time passes, those reactions are likely to change as the state of economic understanding changes. We should not, therefore, expect that what seems to be the 'true model' of the economy for any particular time and place should necessarily be able to explain the behaviour of the economy at any others. Nor, if a model that has been successful in the face of one set of data fails when confronted with a second, should we conclude that its first application was necessarily faulty. If we take the principles used to model the creation and use of expectations that underlie modern macro-economic theory seriously, that is to say we seem to be pushed hard in the direction of concluding that empirical economics needs to be informed by a heavy dose of narrative history dealing with ideas, events and their inter-action.

5. ECONOMIC IDEAS AND ECONOMIC POLICY

Now economic agents in general do show a capacity to learn from experi-ence, and to adapt their behaviour accordingly, but they do not act 'as if' they know as much about the economy as the specialists who model it.[7] However, there is one group for whom a literal version of the rational expectations hypothesis is more plausible: namely, policy-makers. They routinely have access to professional advice on specific issues, though the fact that there are usually differences of opinion among economists at any time implies that they have to choose which advice to take. But their actions can, nevertheless, often be clearly related to specific economic ideas.

The extent to which ideas in general and economic ideas in particular influence economic life and economic policy has long been contentious. On the one hand we have Keynes's well-known, and extremely comforting for economists (among others), testimonial:

> ... the ideas of economists and political philosophers, both when they are right and when they are wrong, are more powerful than is commonly understood. Indeed the world is ruled by little else. Practical men, who believe themselves to be quite exempt from any intellectual influences, are usually the slaves of some defunct economist. Madmen in authority, who hear voices in the air, are distill-ing their frenzy from some academic scribbler of a few years back. (1936, p. 383)

On the other hand, we have George Stigler's less flattering view that, in a world where policy, like everything else, is driven by the pursuit of self-interest, the support of intellectuals '. . . is available to the highest bidder, just as other resources in our society are allocated' (1982, p. 32), a view that he elaborated as follows:

> That intellectuals should believe that intellectuals are important in determining the course of history is not difficult to understand. The position is less easy for even an intellectual economist to understand, since it sets one class of labourers aside and attributes special motives to them. On the traditional economic theory

of occupational choice, intellectuals distribute themselves among occupations and among artistic, ethical, cultural, and political positions in such numbers as to maximise their incomes, where incomes include amenities such as prestige and apparent influence. (1982, p. 34)

The old Meade–Tinbergen approach to policy analysis enjoined the policy-maker to assign weights to various policy goals, and then deploy policy tools so as to maximise the resulting social utility function, subject to the constraints implied by a model of the economy, and it may be reformulated as a positive explanation of how policy-makers actually behave. In this guise, it points us to a middle ground between Keynes and Stigler. Economic ideas are used by policy-makers, even when they are self-interested, not just in defence of their policies, but in their design as well, and economics has the task of providing those ideas.

As the economic ideas available to policy-makers change, then, so perhaps will their conduct, and Keynes can be right about the importance of ideas, even if the services of those who generate them are, as Stigler suggests, for sale to the highest bidder. When there is a conflict between competing ideas about how the economy works, moreover, the conduct of policy will depend upon the choice of ideas made by those in charge of it. If economic policy is important to the way in which economies behave over time, then, anyone wishing to understand economic data must pay attention to the nature and evolution of the ideas that have underlain policy. In fact, economists often do just that, as I shall now illustrate with reference to work on the Great Contraction of the early 1930s and the Great Inflation of the 1970s.

6.   TWO ILLUSTRATIONS: THE GREAT CONTRACTION AND THE GREAT INFLATION

The Monetary History of the United States (Friedman and Schwartz, 1963), and particularly its chapters on the inter-war years, is arguably the most influential book written on a macroeconomic topic in the second half of the twentieth century. Anachronistic in approach and technique even at its time of publication, it nevertheless broke the influence of the so-called 'Keynesian consensus' about how market economies functioned in general, and had functioned in particular during the 1930s, and it reoriented economists' attention towards the power of monetary forces in a way that still marks the discipline.

It was not, however, Friedman and Schwartz's time series charts of the behaviour of the money supply and related variables that convinced their readers. Rather it was their detailed examination of the evolution of Federal Reserve policy in the 1920s and 1930s, of the way it was affected by the particular personalities of, and interactions among, those who were making it, and of the extent to which it reflected the climate of opinion in which they operated. It was narrative history, rather than state-of-the-art theory and econometrics, that so profoundly changed the views of economists in the 1960s and 1970s: strong testimony to the importance then attached to the analysis of the interaction of economic ideas with events as a means of bringing empirical evidence to bear on the assessment of economic theories.

In outlining the causes of the contraction, Friedman and Schwartz gave pride of place to '. . . a sequence of more or less accidental events and the running conflict for power within the [Federal Reserve] system'. In their view, the death of Benjamin Strong, Governor of the New York Bank, in 1928, and a partly consequent shift of power over open market operations in late 1929 from 'a 5-man committee dominated by the New York Bank' to a 'committee of the 12 Federal Reserve Bank governors' were of critical importance. This latter shift decisively reduced the influence of the New York Bank, where, '[d]espite the general climate of opinion, the technical personnel . . . were consistently in favor of the policies which seem to us in retrospect the ones that should have been followed' and 'stacked the cards heavily in favor of a policy of inaction and drift'. Crucially, Friedman and Schwartz concluded that the above-mentioned climate of opinion was 'certainly a necessary condition' for policy to evolve as it did (all quotations pp. 593–4), and they described it as one which

> . . . in the main regarded recessions and depressions as curative episodes, necessary in order to purge the body economic of the aftereffects of its earlier excesses. The prevailing opinion also confused money with credit; confused the elasticity of one component of the money stock with the elasticity of the total stock; regarded it as desirable that the stock of money should respond to the 'needs of trade', rising in expansions and falling in contractions; and attached much greater importance to the maintenance of the gold standard and the stability of the exchanges than to the maintenance of internal stability. Most of these attitudes characterized the public at large and not merely the financial community or the Reserve system in particular. (p. 692)

It is worth emphasising that Friedman and Schwartz did not claim that these erroneous economic ideas were universally held, nor that their existence was a sufficient condition for the depression to occur. But they did argue that their prevalence among those who had the upper hand in debates among policy-makers had a decisive influence on what was actually done and not done. Furthermore, the contrast that Friedman and Schwartz drew between those ideas, and their own explanation of events based upon a version of the quantity theory of money, was one of the key elements that made their claims about the importance of monetary factors in precipitating the contraction so convincing.[8]

The publication of the *Monetary History* coincided with the beginning of another great monetary upheaval: namely, the inflation that started with the Kennedy administration's pledge to 'get America moving' and slowly gathered speed in the later 1960s as the Vietnam War and President Johnson's War on Poverty were financed by money creation. This inflation finally came fully into view after the Nixon administration, encountering the constraints imposed upon even United States monetary policy by the Bretton Woods System, abandoned it, along with the last vestiges of the gold standard. This complicated episode has recently begun to attract the attention of macroeconomists. Bradford De Long (1997) and Thomas Mayer (1999) have recently analysed it along lines similar to those earlier followed by Friedman and Schwartz, and they also reach similar conclusions about the role of economic ideas: namely that the dominant climate of economic opinion did not cause the inflation, but did provide a necessary condition for it to begin and in due course accelerate. Mayer summed up this episode as follows:

> It would be nice if one could tell the story of the Great Inflation along the lines of a Victorian melodrama by identifying a single villain, preferably someone at whom the audience enjoys hissing. But such a story does not fit the facts. There were several villains, and the biggest one turns out to be then [*sic*] prevailing views of economists, and not malicious political interference with the central bank, or cartel imposed supply shocks. We have met the enemy and he is (or rather was) us. (Mayer, 1999, p. 117)

Patrick Minford (2000) has suggested that this conclusion is quite consonant with Thomas Sargent's (1999) recent econometric work on monetary policy during the Great Inflation. Sargent, however, states his view of the role of economic thought in the episode as follows:

> In 1960, Paul Samuelson and Robert Solow found a Phillips curve in the U.S. time series for inflation and unemployment. They taught that the Phillips curve was exploitable and urged raising inflation to reduce unemployment. Within a decade, Samuelson and Solow's recommendation was endorsed by many macroeconomists and implemented by policy makers. (Sargent, 1999, pp. 2–3)

The trouble with this story is that Samuelson and Solow (1960) did not urge raising inflation to reduce unemployment, and that policy-makers had begun to follow no such recommendation by 1970. As De Long and Mayer document in some detail, their views were altogether more complicated and confused than Sargent would have it.[9]

To begin with, as the then definitive Bronfenbrenner and Holtzman

(1963) survey of inflation theory demonstrates, the idea that inflation was largely a 'cost push' phenomenon on which monetary policy could exert little or no influence was widely held in the 1960s and early 1970s. De Long (p. 262) points out that among its adherents was Arthur Burns who succeeded William McChesney Martin as Chairman of the Board of Governors of the Federal Reserve System at the end of 1969. This view of inflation was complemented by the ideas that monetary policy's main influence was on output and employment, and that inflation was best tackled directly by way of wage-price 'guideposts', or even by outright controls. Its popularity meant that the attribution of rising inflation in the second half of the 1960s to monetary expansion associated with war (in Vietnam and on Poverty) finance was very much a minority viewpoint at the time. The same view underpinned the Nixon wage-price control programme of 1971–74, which was accompanied by a fiscal and monetary policy maybe 'looser . . . than otherwise would have been put in place', and which ended with inflation rising rapidly to double digits when controls were lifted.

De Long remarks, with respect to the 1971–74 episode, 'Perhaps the policies adopted truly were prudent and optimal given the consensus understanding of the structure of the economy held by both public- and private-sector decision makers. But this consensus understanding was flawed' (p. 267); and, as he might have remarked but didn't, those policies had absolutely nothing to do with deliberately inducing higher inflation in order to reduce the unemployment rate.[10]

Not that unemployment was unimportant in the policy calculus during the Great Inflation; on the contrary, De Long, and Mayer too, though the latter less forcefully, make a good case that the 1930s cast a long shadow over policy in the 1960s and 1970s. But, as De Long and Mayer also show, it was not until the Nixon wage-price control programme failed, and inflation reached double digits, that these concerns ceased to manifest themselves mainly in a search for policies that would 'shift the Phillips curve' to the left, and began to give rise to an explicitly expressed reluctance to use monetary policy to reduce inflation because of the perceived unemployment costs of doing so.[11]

This later development too has roots in the evolution of economic understanding. Samuelson and Solow did indeed present the Phillips curve as a policy menu in 1960, but that was only one ingredient to what Phelps (1972) would later call 'The Cost–Benefit Approach to Monetary Planning' that became influential for a while in the 1970s. The idea of maximising a social utility function in 'Okun gaps' and 'Harberger triangles' subject to a Phillips curve constraint had to be developed (Reuber, 1962, 1964), popularised (Johnson, 1968; Tobin, 1972) and dynamised (Phelps, 1967, 1972) before that could happen. And John Taylor's (1977) suggestion, made in the course of a commentary of De Long's paper, that the arrival shortly thereafter of the rational expectations idea was 'influential in changing views both about the costs of reducing inflation and the costs of inflation itself' (p. 279) towards the end of the decade is surely plausible.

Now the Great Depression and the Great Inflation are by no means the only episodes in monetary history that have been, or will be subject to, study along the lines described above. Historians of economic thought and economic historians have long been teaching their students about the first two great monetary debates of the 19th century – the Bullionist and Banking-School–Currency-School, controversies, and their treatment has usually dealt, not only with how versions of the quantity theory of money and the real bills doctrine were deployed in the intellectual arena, but also how those competing doctrines influenced and were influenced by the actual conduct of policy. The later controversy about Bimetallism is susceptible to similar treatment, with the declining influence among economists of the classical cost-of-production theory of value in the face of marginal utility and supply and demand analysis, forming a vital background to the evolution of the views of 'practical men' about metallic and managed currencies. And, in due course, as the creation of the euro passes into history, the economic debates that led up to and accompanied this event will also be studied as a necessary guide to understanding the evidence about the workings of the monetary system that it will generate.

7.   CONCLUDING COMMENTS

Historians of economic thought have routinely taken an approach to their work that is broadly consistent with what modern macroeconomic theory has to say about the role of ideas in conditioning economic behaviour. Perhaps they should take as much pleasure from the knowledge that this is so as did M. Jourdain from the discovery that he had been speaking prose all along, and find therein ample compensation for the discomfort that they feel when they see their subject being used, or misused, as a rhetorical device to justify the claims of particular economic ideas to professional attention. There is, after all, as we have seen, nothing new about this latter practice.

Even so, despite its continuing and widespread use for both persuasive and substantive purposes, there are grounds for disquiet about the current status of the history of thought in modern economics. The fact is that Lucas and Sargent's rhetorical deployment of historical arguments, discussed above, attracted far less attention and generated far less debate than did Friedman's earlier excursion into the area. This is not surprising, for Friedman's main critics were Don Patinkin (1969) and Johnson (1971), each of them a major figure in monetary theory in his own right, but each of them, by virtue of his training and understanding of the nature of the sub-discipline, well steeped in its history, and convinced of the importance of that history for understanding contemporary issues. Nowadays 'ancestor worship' is regarded by leading figures of the discipline as no more than an entertaining consumption good, so there is no professional gain to be had from critically examining any claims that might be made about the historical legitimacy of contemporary doctrines. Nor is there much point in graduate students taking courses in the area, and in departments offering them.

There is surely something amiss about the History of Economic Thought being used as a rhetorical weapon, in support of the intellectual credentials of their own work, by the same leading figures who denigrate the field's importance. The skills that would enable their intended audience to assess such arguments on their merits are, increasingly, not being taught. All this, when the substantive theoretical ideas that are defended by these means themselves imply that a knowledge of the economics of the past is critical to disciplining the empirical application and further development of those very ideas. In neglecting the History of Economic Thought, and discouraging its study, modern macroeconomic theorists are turning their backs on a tool of considerable potential, while simultaneously creating an intellectual monopoly for themselves in its rhetorical deployment. A quiet life may be the best of monopoly profits, but it will not be conducive to the longer term health of economics if they are allowed to enjoy such a life for much longer.

NOTES

* This paper has been prepared for a conference to be held at the Bank of England in November 2001 in honour of Charles Goodhart. I am grateful to Herb Emery and Rick Szostak for useful correspondence at an early stage of its preparation, to Milton Friedman, Peter Howitt, Tom Mayer, Roger Sandilands and members of the University of Toronto–York University History of Economic Thought Workshop for comments on earlier drafts, and to Otto Reich for assistance. Certain passages below in the section on *Economic Ideas and Economic Policy* draw on my contribution to a panel discussion on *The influence of politics on economics* which took place at the February 2001 meeting of the European Society for the History of Economic Thought, held at the Technical University of Darmstadt.

1. This may be the paper to which Romer refers in the preceding quotation. Certainly, it contains a discussion of Allyn A. Young's 1928 paper on 'Increasing returns and economic progress' which anticipates many of the themes of modern endogenous growth theory.

2. I have discussed all of these matters extensively in Laidler (1991, 1999), but in no case do I claim to have been the first commentator to have pointed out the often stark contradictions between the actual history of particular ideas and modern myths about them. Michael Woodford (1999) provides a balanced and carefully nuanced account of the evolution of macroeconomics in the 20th century, written from the viewpoint of a modern practitioner.

3. To avoid misunderstandings, let me explicitly note that I don't think Blaug (2001) would disagree about this.

4. Friedman's (1956, 1974) claims about the 'Chicago tradition' have been much debated over the years, and some of them, particularly those made in 1956 about the allegedly unique role played in that tradition by a stable demand for money function, have not withstood careful examination. But Friedman's (1974) argument, that the Chicago Department was home to a lively group of economists who discussed the Great Contraction in monetary terms and did advocate expansionary monetary and fiscal policies to combat it long before Keynes wrote the *General Theory*, was better grounded. Even though subsequent research has shown this version of the tradition to be neither as homogeneous, nor as uniquely associated with Chicago, as Friedman claimed, Johnson's characterisation of it as the product of 'scholarly chicanery' was at the very least uncharitable and overdone.

5. James Tobin (1981) referred to the money-supply surprise model at the core of early new classical economics as 'monetarism mark 2', and inasmuch as it represented a response to Johnson's challenge to Friedman, this classification is defensible. My own preference, however, has always been to regard its reliance on Walrasian general equilibrium analysis as setting it apart from any earlier macroeconomic doctrines.

6. Beyond doubt the main reason for the failure of money supply surprise models was their assumption that markets cleared instantaneously, with prices set 'as if' by a Walrasian auctioneer, which implied that, in aggregate data, the price level would move in response to money supply changes, and that the level of output would respond to the portion of the price level change which had not been anticipated. But it is, and, in the early 1970s, it already was, one of the best known stylised facts in the history of macroeconomics that quantity changes precede those in the price level. The first generation of money supply surprise models simply could not cope with this fact, and that is why those who work with their modern successors have contrived to bring various kinds of price stickiness assumptions back into the picture.

7. Boschen and Grossman's (1982) finding that money supply movements already apparent in published United States data seemed to have subsequent consequences for real economic variables, but that those which were hidden by initial measurement and reporting errors did not, is decisively inconsistent with this view; Jonung and Laidler (1986) found that inflation expectations as revealed by Swedish survey data, though unbiased relative to the true variable, could nevertheless have been systematically improved had agents made use of information, such as, for example, the lagged unemployment rate, that was already published and readily available to them.

8. I do not mean to imply that I regard Friedman and Schwartz as having had the last word on these matters. For example, Barry Eichengreen's (1992) work on the role of the gold standard in the international transmission of monetary disturbances in the inter-war years is an important addition to theirs, and shifts the emphasis away from purely domestic United States considerations in what is surely a helpful and constructive way. On the question of the economic thought of the period, it is now widely agreed that they paid insufficient attention to the views of such economists as Allyn Young and Lauchlin Currie. See Laidler and Sandilands (2002) on this, and Laidler (1993), which also gives extensive references to the earlier literature dealing with it.

9. Sargent defends his interpretation of Samuelson and Solow's views on the basis of 'reading p. 192 of their paper'. He acknowledges that qualifications to his interpretation appear on p. 193, but suggests that readers consult Chapter 10 of his book before 'thinking that I treat Samuelson and Solow unfairly' (p. 2, fn. 3). My own suggestion would be that readers also consult pp. 192–3 of Samuelson and Solow's paper, or Abba Lerner's

(1960) original discussion of it, which gently chides them for not recommending the purchase of less unemployment with more inflation.

10. See De Long (1997, pp. 266–7), and Mayer (1999, p. 119) on these matters. In this context it is worth noting that Sargent does not mention this crucial episode, even to wonder whether it might have distorted the behaviour of the data on which his econometrics were based.

11. A recent study by Orphanides (2001) estimates forward-looking Federal Reserve policy reaction functions for the 1970s and 1980s, and finds that a larger sensitivity to unemployment, rather than a smaller sensitivity to inflation forecasts, is the main factor distinguishing the earlier period.

REFERENCES

Blaug, M. (2001), 'No history of ideas please, we're economists', *Journal of Economic Perspectives*, 15 (Winter), 145–64.

Bronfenbrenner, M. and F. Holtzman (1963), 'Survey of inflation theory', *American Economic Review*, 53 (Sept.), 593–661.

Boschen, J. and H. Grossman (1982), 'Tests of equilibrium macroeconomics using contemporaneous data', *Journal of Monetary Economics*, 10, 309–33.

De Long, B. (1997), 'America's peacetime inflation: the 1970s', in C.D. Romer and D.H. Romer (eds), *Reducing Inflation: Motivation and Strategy*, Chicago; University of Chicago Press, pp. 247–76.

Eichengreen, B. (1992), *Golden Fetters: The Gold Standard and the Great Depression 1919–1939*, Oxford: Oxford University Press.

Friedman, M. (1956), 'The quantity theory of money: a restatement', in *Studies in the Quantity Theory of Money*, Chicago: University of Chicago Press, pp. 3–21.

Friedman, M. (1974), 'Comments on the critics', in R.J. Gordon (ed.), *Milton Friedman's Monetary Framework*, Chicago: University of Chicago Press, pp. 132–84.

Friedman, M. and A.J. Schwartz (1963), *A Monetary History of the United States, 1867–1960*, Princeton NJ: Princeton University Press, for the NBER.

Goodhart, C.A.E. (1969), *The New York Money Market and the Finance of Trade 1900–1913*, Cambridge, Mass.: Harvard University Press.

Goodhart, C.A.E. (2002), 'The endogeneity of money', in P. Arestis, M. Desai and S. Dow (eds), *Money, Macroeconomics and Keynes: Essays in Honour of Victoria Chick*, London: Routledge, pp. 14–24.

Johnson, H.G. (1968), 'Problems of efficiency in monetary management', *Journal of Political Economy*, 76 (Sept.–Oct.), 971–90.

Johnson, H.G. (1971), 'The Keynesian revolution and the monetarist counter-revolution', *American Economic Review*, as reprinted in E. Johnson and H.G. Johnson, *The Shadow of Keynes*, Chicago: University of Chicago Press (1978), pp. 183–202.

Jonung, L. and D. Laidler (1986), 'Are perceptions of inflation rational? Some evidence for Sweden', *American Economic Review*, 96 (Dec.), 1080–87.

Keynes, J.M. (1936), *The General Theory of Employment Interest and Money*, London: Macmillan.

Laidler, D. (1991), *The Golden Age of the Quantity Theory*, Hemel Hempstead: Harvester Wheatsheaf.

Laidler, D. (1993), 'Hawtrey Harvard and the origins of the Chicago tradition', *Journal of Political Economy*, 101 (Dec.), 1068–103.

Laidler, D. (1999), *Fabricating the Keynesian Revolution*, Cambridge and New York: Cambridge University Press.

Laidler, D. and R.J. Sandilands (2002), 'An early Harvard memorandum on anti-depression policies', with an introduction, *History of Political Economy*, 34 (2) (Fall), 515–32.

Leijonhufvud, A. (1981), 'The Wicksell connection: variations on a theme', in *Information and Co-ordination*, Oxford: Oxford University Press, pp. 131–202.

Lerner, A.P. (1960), 'Comment', *American Economic Review*, 50 (May Papers and Proceedings), 215–18.

Lucas, R.E. Jr. (1996), 'Nobel lecture: monetary neutrality', *Journal of Political Economy*, 104 (Aug.), 661–82.

Lucas, R.E. Jr. and T.J. Sargent (1978), 'After Keynesian macroeconomics', as reprinted in R.E. Lucas Jr. and T.J. Sargent (eds), *Rational Expectations and Econometric Practice*, London: George Allen and Unwin (1984), pp. 295–319.

Mayer, T. (1999), *Monetary Policy and the Great Inflation in the United States: The Federal Reserve and the Failure of Monetary Policy 1965–79*, Cheltenham: Edward Elgar.

Minford, P. (2000), 'Review' [of T. Mayer (1999) and T.J. Sargent (1999)], *Economic Journal*, 110 (June), 474–5.

Orphanides, A. (2001), 'Monetary policy rules, macroeconomic stability and inflation: a view from the trenches', Washington: Board of Governors of the Federal Reserve System.

Patinkin, D. (1969), 'The Chicago tradition, the quantity theory and Friedman', *Journal of Money, Credit and Banking*, 1 (Feb.), 470.

Phelps, E.S. (1967), 'Phillips curves, expectations of inflation and optimal unemployment over time', *Economica*, NS 34, 254–81.

Phelps, E.S. (1972), *Inflation Policy and Unemployment Theory: The Cost–Benefit Approach to Monetary Planning*, New York: W.W. Norton.

Reeve, J. (1943), *Monetary Reform Movements: a Survey of Recent Plans and Panaceas*, Washington, DC: American Council of Public Affairs.

Reuber, G.L. (1962), 'The objectives of monetary policy', working paper prepared for the Royal Commission on Banking and Finance (the Porter Commission), Ottawa.

Reuber, G.L. (1964), 'The objectives of Canadian monetary policy, 1949–1961: empirical trade-offs and the reaction function of the authorities', *Journal of Political Economy*, 72, 109–32.

Romer, P. (1991), 'Increasing returns and new developments in the theory of growth', in W.A. Barnett, B. Cornet, C. d'Aspremont, J. Gabszewicz and A. Mas-Coleil (eds), *Equilibrium Theory and Applications: Proceedings of the Sixth International Symposium in Economic Theory and Econometrics*, Cambridge: Cambridge University Press, pp. 83–110.

Samuelson, P.A. and R. Solow (1960), 'Analytic aspects of anti-inflation policy', *American Economic Review*, 50 (May, Papers and Proceedings), 177–94.

Sargent, T.J. (1999), *The Conquest of American Inflation*, Princeton, NJ: Princeton University Press.

Sargent, T.J. and N. Wallace (1973), 'Rational expectations and the dynamics of hyperinflation', *International Economic Review*, 14 (April), 169–83.

Sargent, T.J. and N. Wallace (1982), 'The real bills doctrine and the quantity theory: a reconsideration', *Journal of Political Economy*, 90 (Dec.), 1212–36.

Smith, A. (1776), *An Enquiry into the Nature and Causes of the Wealth of Nations*, London.

Snowdon, B. and H.R. Vane (1999), 'Paul M. Romer', in *Conversations with Leading Economists: Interpreting Modern Macroeconomics*, Cheltenham: Edward Elgar, pp. 292–313.

Stigler, G. (1982), *The Economist as Preacher and Other Essays*, Chicago: University of Chicago Press.

Taylor, J.B. (1977), 'Comment' [on De Long], in C.D. Romer and D.H. Romer (eds), *Reducing Inflation: Motivation and Strategy*, Chicago: University of Chicago Press.

Tobin, J. (1972), 'Inflation and unemployment', *American Economic Review*, 82 (March), 1–18.

Tobin, J. (1981), 'The monetarist counter-revolution today; an appraisal', *Economic Journal*, 81 (March), 29–42.

Woodford, M. (1999), 'Revolution and evolution in twentieth century macroeconomics', working paper, Princeton University (June).

Young, A.A. (1928), 'Increasing returns and economic progress', *Economic Journal*, 38 (Dec.), 527–42.

Discussion of 'The role of the history of economic thought in modern macroeconomics'

Jacques Melitz

David Laidler argues for the importance of the history of thought in the study of macroeconomics. First, he shows that our judgements about ideas in macroeconomics are affected by real or alleged connections to previous thought. In this connection, he cites efforts to promote new ideas in macroeconomics by associating them with earlier writers. Second, David stresses the effect of social currents of thought on policy-makers' actions, and therefore economic performance. For both reasons, he deplores the diminished attention to the history of thought in the training of young economists. It is interesting to read the chapter in conjunction with a recent essay by Blaug, 'No history of ideas, please, we're economists,' to which David refers favorably, and which also deplores the decline of the history of thought in the graduate curriculum.

I agree with David on both points: knowledge of the history of thought may provide ammunition in economic policy debate; and the history of thought is important in understanding the past. But I think we can say more to recommend including the subject in the professional education of young economists.

Let me begin with a question Blaug poses but David doesn't: why has the history of economic thought declined in importance in the teaching of economics? When I was a graduate student, the subject attracted some of the best minds in the profession: Viner, Schumpeter, Hayek, Stigler. Moreover, top economists generally did not hold a dismissive attitude toward the field.

The answer to the question lies in an observation I remember from Viner as a graduate student: the clarity of the distinction between a discipline and its history is a direct function of its state of development. The distinction is plain in the advanced sciences, such as mathematics and physics. But it is muddy in the less developed ones. Viner used politics as an example of a discipline where the general principles were difficult to divorce from the history of the subject. Economics, he thought, was in an intermediate stage.

Blaug essentially takes the same view, but limits his entire response to two wonderful quotes that I cannot help repeating: 'The more perfect the science, the shorter its history' (Jean Baptiste Say); and much more arresting, 'A science which hesitates to forget its founders is lost' (Alfred North Whitehead). However, Blaug doesn't draw the implication, at least explicitly: namely, the decline of interest in the history of thought in economics is a manifestation of progress in the field. Some teachers of economics, I believe, even avoid history for this very reason. They are saying: this is a hard subject; it can be taught independently of its history. Contrary to Marxists and a host of critics, economics is not just a history of economic doctrines.

But has economics progressed to the point where the distinction between the state of the subject and its history is clear in all fields: in macroeconomics as well as in microeconomics or econometrics? To this question, I think a negative answer must be given. Granted, we do not need to know the history of microeconomics to be a price theorist, or the history of econometrics to be an econometrician. But the same is far from evident in the case of macroeconomics. The subject has not supplanted its own past over the last couple of centuries, despite notable progress over the last thirty years. The doctrinal divisions in the field attest to this state of affairs. What separates the *Journal of Monetary Economics* from the *Quarterly Journal of Economics* is not strictly a matter of scientific debate. The controversy over the real theory of business cycles still divides us into camps, with some people on both sides who do not even care to discuss with one another.

Essentially, I read David's paper as documenting our inability to distinguish between the analysis of macroeconomic events and past doctrine. He repeatedly illustrates the importance of assertions about earlier thought in supporting current empirical positions. Take the example of Friedman and Schwartz's *Monetary History of the United States*. To quote David: 'It was not ... Friedman and Schwartz's time series charts of the behaviour of the money supply and related variables that convinced their readers [about the monetary causes of the Great Depression]. Rather it was their detailed examination of the evolution of Federal Reserve policy in the 1920s and 1930s, of the way it was affected by the particular personalities of, and interactions among, those who were making it, and the extent to which it was conditioned by the climate of opinion in which they operated.' But if David is right, doesn't this mean that, based on Friedman and Schwartz's work, readers could not distinguish between the monetary causes of the Great Depression and the causes of monetary policy during the depression? And – however unintentional – isn't this condemnatory? Consider an analogy: following a murder, there is an inquest about what killed the victim, who killed the victim and why. We are told that the diagnosis of the causes of the death gained currency because of the associated analysis of who killed him and why. Surely this can only mean that the explanation of the death is a bit shaky.

Thus, the fundamental case for the study of the history of thought in macroeconomics goes beyond arming students for persuasion in economic debate and understanding what lies in the minds of policy-makers. The quality of the students' research is at stake. If we have not superseded the past in macroeconomics, then the usefulness of studying the history of thought lies in mastering the subject as such, widening our perspectives, retaining a broader range of hypotheses, discouraging adherence to fad or fashion, and – yes, even – avoiding indoctrination. When we read nineteenth-century and early twentieth-century discussions of macro-economics and macroeconomic policy, whether the discussions concern default on the national debt, colonialism, bimetallism, devaluation, crises or inflation, we distinctly do not have the impression that we could reformulate the content in contemporary terms without losing anything. The analyses often remain enlightening not only for what they tell us about history, but in connection with the same substantive issues today.[1] David not only attests to this in these pages, but far more, where he had more room, in his impor-tant works, *The Golden Age of the Quantity Theory* and *Fabricating the Keynesian Revolution*.

With the advance of macroeconomics, can we expect the progressive divorce of the subject from the history of thought? On this question, I find Max Weber to be particularly worthy of attention. Weber remains compel-ling for his combination of insistence on the possibility of an objective, value-free social science, together with the view that in the social sciences, a distinct methodology was required. General laws were not of interest. I quote: 'In the cultural sciences, the knowledge of the universal or general is never valuable in itself' (p. 80). The distinct methodology Weber thought necessary in the social sciences rested on 'ideal types'. But without going into 'ideal types,' let me focus on his larger point: in the social sciences, we are always interested in some unique, non-recurrent aspects of the phenom-ena at hand. That is why we need a special method. For him, this was a con-dition that would never change. He also put a certain glow on the situation. 'There are sciences', he said, 'to which eternal youth is granted' (p. 104). In rereading his *Methodology of the Social Sciences*, I had the strong sense that he would have modified his position today. What he failed to foresee is not so much the enlarged place of mathematics in the social sciences, but the role that statistical inference has come to play. Nevertheless, however, he might have stuck to his guns with respect to macroeconomics. For in macroeconomics – and for many of the reasons Weber had in mind – we may simply be tied to small samples. One intrinsic difference between issues of macro, as opposed to micro, is precisely a reduction in the number of observations. Much of the most imaginative work in macroeconomics consists of enlarging relevant sample sizes. Yet, with respect to many of the questions that interest us – the exceptional length of the recent economic expansion in the US, monetary union, and so forth – as few as 100 observations will possibly always remain a lot. If so, the history of thought might perpetually retain an important place in the study of macroeconomics, and thus, in the economics curriculum as a whole. Macroeconomics then may be a subject to which 'eternal youth is granted'.

NOTE

1. Just to make my stand clearer, let me state that I do not believe the same to be true of nineteenth-century discussion of many other topics, including the labor theory of value, marginal productivity, or the measure of inflation. On these matters, a modern restatement would indeed deprive us of nothing of substance.

REFERENCES

Blaug, Mark (2001), 'No history of ideas, please, we're economists', *Journal of Economic Perspectives*, Winter, 145–64.

Laidler, David (1991), *The Golden Age of the Quantity Theory*, Princeton, NJ: Princeton University Press.

Laidler, David (1999), *Fabricating the Keynesian Revolution*, Cambridge: Cambridge University Press.

Weber, Max (1949), *The Methodology of the Social Sciences*, translated and edited by Edward A. Shils and Henry A. Finch, New York: The Free Press. (The original essays date 1903–17.)

2. Charles Goodhart's contributions to the history of monetary institutions

Michael D. Bordo and Anna J. Schwartz

1. INTRODUCTION

The focal point of Charles Goodhart's research studies has undoubtedly been the evolution of central banks. He has offered reasons for the rise of the central bank institution and analysed its operation from the 19th century on, particularly during the gold standard era. Subjects that he has investigated include not only how central bank conduct of monetary policy has changed over the decades but also their relation to the financial systems that they headed. He has paid particular attention to their role as lenders of last resort, and another paper at this conference will deal with Charles's studies of central bank monetary policies. Our chapter examines his work on the history of monetary institutions: central bank operations under the gold standard, their behaviour in relation to the financial system in which they functioned, including their responses to banking crises, and their performance as lenders of last resort.

Charles has compared the origins and structure of at least eight European central banks as well as of the Bank of Japan at the end of the 19th century with corresponding features of the Bank of England. He has also summarised the objectives and functions of 32 central banks, listed in chronological order of their founding, beginning with the Sveriges Riksbank the forerunner of which was founded in 1668, and ending with the Central Bank of Uruguay founded in 1967. It is, however, the Bank of England that he has been most intimate with, so it is not surprising that his main contributions to the study of monetary institutions revolve about the Bank's operations.

As important as central banking has been to Charles's research interests, it does not exhaust them. He has studied monetary regimes with no central bank, such as regimes with currency boards. In fact, he has had more than an academic relation to the Hong Kong experience; he has also been an adviser to its government. In addition, he has examined with an open mind the claims for free banking that would deny the need for a central bank.

We begin with a review of the work that Charles published as a fledgling PhD (Section 2). His subject was the gold standard, the rules of the game for the Bank of England, the role of commercial banks, financial crises, and the need for a lender of last resort. We then go on to discuss the highlights of his research as a mature scholar. The main subject is the evolution of central banks from government banks to bankers' banks to independent central banks (Section 3). We report Charles's analysis of what he regards as the central bank function to safeguard the condition of individual members of the banking system and to serve as the banking club manager. In Section 4 we turn to Charles's discussion of the development of the central bank as the domestic lender of last resort, and in Section 5 to his discussion of the need for an international lender of last resort. Some of the conclusions that he believes his studies of monetary institutions support understandably reflect a British perspective. An American perspective may differ, and in several cases we point out the differences. Section 6 concludes.

2. THEMES OF HIS EARLY RESEARCH

In his glance backward on his professional career, Charles reports that since his 1962 PhD thesis successfully 'reinterpreted US (1900–1914) monetary history, using a high frequency data base, the obvious continuation was to try the same trick for the UK. Monthly banking data were also available (though heavily window-dressed in some respects) in the form of the monthly reports of the London Joint Stock Banks, which Chancellor of the Exchequer Goschen had required to be collected and published following the first Barings crisis in 1890. The problem was that no one had previously systematically collected, checked, and analysed these. So the better part of two years (1963/64) was then taken up with primary historical research, collecting, checking, and assembling as much monthly banking and macro-economic data as existed into usable time series format' (Goodhart, 1997, pp. 395–6).

We thus learn that from his initial research undertakings Charles was prepared to invest the requisite time and effort to construct the data base for empirical investigations, a practice he has maintained throughout his career. Having collected the data, what were the issues that Charles chose to examine?

2.1 The US Pre-Federal Reserve Gold Standard

As indicated, the main focus of this chapter is Charles's contributions to the history of monetary institutions, and his first study dealing with a pre-Federal Reserve episode when the US was on the gold standard, fits in well with his broader interest. Some of the themes of Charles's later studies are already encountered in this early work. These include the role of commercial banks under the gold standard, financial crises, and the need for a lender of last resort.

For Charles, received wisdom is not to be believed before checking that it agrees with the data. He was led to revise accepted hypotheses of US economists of the period 1900–1913 (E.W. Kemmerer, A.P. Andrew, and O.M.W. Sprague) about the functioning of the financial system because their interpretation of seasonal variations in interest rates 'does not obtain any confirmation from the available quantitative data' (Goodhart, 1969, p. 126). Specifically, their claim that interior banks withdrew their balances from New York in the fall was belied by the stability of interest rates in the interior. In addition, when other methods by which interior banks could transfer funds to and from New York were included, it turned out that interior banks actually sent money to New York during the fall rather than withdrew it. Charles concluded that the interior's favourable balance of trade during the fall improved liquidity there enough to offset increased demand for money, hence avoiding seasonal interest rate variations.[1] In New York, however, reduced liquidity due to payment for crops raised interest rates, which attracted a capital inflow from the interior that restored equilibrium. At the same time New York had a relatively favourable balance of trade with foreign countries in the fall and a relatively unfavourable balance in the summer.

Why did not trade with foreign countries offset trade with the interior? Charles's answer is that, under gold standard conditions, exchange rate variations (within the gold points) were important in the international market while in the national market they were relatively small. In international trade the autumnal export surplus raised the exchange value of the dollar towards the gold export point. This was an incentive to sell dollars or to avoid buying dollars spot and instead to buy dollars future when they would be cheaper. There was thus an offsetting short-term capital outflow, cutting down gold imports. New York did not receive cash for exports abroad but paid cash for imports from the interior. Therefore New York interest rates, especially in the call loan market, rose in the autumn relative to interest rates in the interior and in Europe. This checked the cash flow to the interior and started a gold inflow from Europe. The major disadvantage of the system was, since there was no lender of last resort, that rising interest rates could lead to a financial collapse rather than an opportunity for increased profits.

2.2 The Pre-World War I Gold Standard in Britain

Charles's next study was a full-fledged examination of the adjustment mechanism by which balance of payments equilibrium was achieved under the gold standard in Britain from 1891 to 1913 (Goodhart, 1972). The traditional story was that the Bank of England altered Bank rate whenever its gold reserves were threatened. A rise would induce a short-term capital inflow and would check domestic economic activity, the domestic price level, and the price of imports (Cunliffe, 1918). Charles proceeded to set out a series of connected hypotheses about causal relationships implied by the classical analysis of the equilibrating mechanism of the gold standard and to subject them to statistical testing.

Testing some of the hypotheses required only Bank of England statistics; others required use of the banking data he had collected. The tests confirmed that Bank rate rises induced short-term capital inflows. The tests failed to confirm that the domestic channel behaved in accordance with the classical analysis. The money supply process was to some extent endogenous. In response to changes in the Bank of England's gold reserve, domestic money supply changed little, and domestic economic activity changed little in response to changes in the interest rate. There was no close, positive association between commercial bank reserves, measured by bankers' balances at the Bank of England, and the Bank's gold reserves or its proportion, but they were related to the level of domestic activity.

According to Charles, the direction of causation was the reverse of that proposed by the classical analysis. Increased economic activity led to increased commercial bank lending and deposits. He reports a regression of the balance of trade surplus on a domestic activity variable for the 1890s and early 1900s that yields a significant negative coefficient. By reducing other assets the Bank of England then supplied the required increase in commercial bank reserves to maintain stable reserve ratios at commercial banks. The effect was a lower gold-reserve ratio at the Bank of England – the proportion in the banking department of the Bank – and a higher Bank rate, which produced a gold inflow and restored the Bank's proportion. It was short-term capital inflows that permitted autonomous domestic expansion uninterrupted by monetary balance of payments disturbances.

Thus Charles's study discussed two issues that have since been at the heart of scholarly work on the operation of the gold standard: Were the external channel of adjustment by capital inflows and outflows and the domestic channel by varying domestic expenditure equally effective in restoring balance of payments equilibrium? And did central banks follow the rules of the game? According to Charles the external channel was highly effective, but he found the domestic channel ineffective, since the money supply was not responsive to changes in the Bank's gold reserves. In the literature on the rules of the game, different authors have variously defined them. One definition was that a central bank should reinforce the effects of payments imbalances, varying domestic credit with international reserves (Bloomfield, 1959). In Dutton's view (1984), obeying the rules also meant avoiding the use of countercyclical monetary policy. He estimated the Bank of England's Bank rate reaction to several measures of its gold reserves and several measures of domestic economic conditions. To avoid the problem of two-way causality between policy tools and policy targets, he generated forecasts of the policy targets. His key finding was that Bank rate responded strongly and negatively to the Bank's reserve position, but it also responded positively to domestic economic conditions and negatively to unemployment. Countercyclical action by the Bank was a violation of the rules, a finding in accord with Goodhart's finding that the Bank varied its holdings of domestic assets independent of the level of gold reserves.

Pippenger (1984) reinterpreted Goodhart's results.[2] He examined both the long-run and short-run operations of the Bank. In the short run the Bank may have accommodated domestic activity, but in the long run it complied with rules. Its primary concern was preserving convertibility of sterling.[3]

So the themes that were to engage Charles in the decades after his thesis and post-doc research emerged early on. The grand theme was not only how the Bank of England's role in the financial system changed over time but also how the role of other central banks changed. It is useful to trace the development of his views on this matter and related subjects in the course of his employment by the Bank and his later academic experience.

3.   THE EVOLUTION OF CENTRAL BANKS

Charles's exposure to the literature on free banking that questioned the need for and functions of central banks motivated him to examine the theoretical and historical bases for their existence (Goodhart, 1985). The question he sought to investigate was whether the introduction of an agency to regulate and control the banking system was an undesirable intervention into what otherwise was a satisfactory free market banking industry.

Charles traced the historical basis for the creation of central banks to the financial advantage governments obtained from them, their unification of a chaotic system of note issue, their management and protection of the country's metallic reserve, and their improvement of the payments system. Once established, a central bank gained political power as the government's bank. Only later in the 19th century did it become the bankers' bank, when commercial banks deposited their own cash reserves as balances at the central bank. Central banks, moreover, had the ability to inject liquidity by rediscounting, according to Charles, and to provide even more when the banks experienced difficulties.

Charles holds that the functions of central banks developed naturally from their relationships with the government and the banks. The functions were twofold: a macro function relating to monetary conditions of the economy, and a micro function relating to the condition of the individual members of the banking system. When central banks competed for customers with other banks, the macro function was secondary to the micro function, in Charles's view. Since no commercial competitor to a central bank could provide reserves and liquidity to other banks and regulate them, historic central banks founded before the 19th century that began as a competitive, profit-maximising institution alongside many others had to change to a non-competitive non-profit-maximising one if they were to exercise their micro function. Central banks founded at later dates that began as non-competitive, non-profit-maximising institutions have been readier to leave the micro function of supervision to separate government bodies (Goodhart and Schoenmaker, 1995). In his survey of the objectives and functions of 32 central banks, arranged chronologically by date of founding, he distinguishes the evolution from the original objectives and functions and traces the changes in the degree of their independence (Capie, Goodhart et al., 1994)

The development of historic central banks in Charles's account occurred in three stages. They began as government banks. They then also had commercial profit-maximising banking interests. They remained the governments' bankers throughout, and governments may have dominated their objectives and policy actions. At a second stage historic central banks relinquished their commercial interests and became bankers' banks, devoting themselves to the welfare and safety of their former rivals, individual commercial banks, and to the financial system in general. A question that Charles considers is whether this purpose requires the central bank to undertake regulation and supervision of the financial system or whether a separate financial supervisory authority should shoulder the job. The commercial banks initially form a club that the central banks manage, but as dividing lines between different kinds of financial intermediaries become blurred, the club feature declines.

Historically, the institutions founded in the 19th century that gradually transformed themselves into central banks enjoyed relative independence from government but were constrained in their potential for conducting independent policy by the commitment to convertibility. That independence ended with the advent of the First World War, according to Charles and his co-authors (Capie, Goodhart et al., 1994, p. 49).[4] We note that some central banks retained their independence until the Great Depression undermined it. Only recently has the trend begun to be reversed. So there is now a third stage in the development of central banks as they gain independence from governments, which may retain the right to define the objectives but delegate to central banks the choice of instruments to achieve them.

We summarise further each stage of central bank development that Charles describes.

3.1   The Central Bank as Government Bank

Central banks, established by government charter, have invariably been designated as the governments' bankers. Governments naturally seek cheap finance from their banker, especially during wars or similar types of crisis. In those circumstances central banks have had to subordinate whatever objectives they might otherwise have sought to pursue – convertibility, price stability, economic growth – to their government's wishes. Extricating themselves from subservience to the government has usually entailed a political struggle over an extended period. Charles and his co-authors (Capie et al., 1994, pp. 48–63) discuss three determinants of the relationship between central banks and governments: peace or war, the dominant political philosophy – laissez faire in trade and monetary matters, or state economic management – and the exchange-rate regimes – the gold standard, for example, viewed as a single central bank objective that diminished the state's role. The influence on the relationship of the government and the central bank of exchange-rate regimes other than the gold standard is not discussed by the authors.

3.2   The Central Bank as Bankers' Bank

For Charles, a core function of central banks is concern for the well-being of the banking system inclusive of the payments system. This priority becomes possible when two developments occur: the central bank does not compete with commercial banks for customers and profit and commercial banks deposit their reserves at the central bank. Because of this concern, central banks or a surrogate exercise supervisory and regulatory responsibilities.

The concern arises because Charles (1991) regards commercial banks as inherently unstable. They are imprudent lenders and investors, in need of outside direction and protection. Banks exist to make loans to small- and medium-size borrowers with no access to capital markets. Financial markets for them are incomplete, so bank loans are substitutes for non-existing markets. The reason a financial market does not exist is that information is unavailable on the prospects of the projects for which borrowers seek loans. Indeed, there is information asymmetry in the banker–customer relationship, since the borrower knows more about the likely outcome of his project than does the commercial bank. According to Charles, bankers also exhibit herd-type behaviour that leads to periods of overexpansion culminating in financial crises followed by periods of retrenchment and recession.

Central banks may not be wiser than commercial banks, Charles acknowledges, but should be able to check and limit contagious crises that arise. Moreover, central bank regulation can prevent imprudent bank behaviour that leads to banking crises.

Questions may be raised concerning Charles's views on bank instability and on the contagious effects of an illiquid or insolvent bank on other liquid or solvent banks. It is arguable that instability does not inhere in banks since they can hold prudent reserves and adequate capital. Instead, unstable monetary policy and bad regulatory actions produce unstable banks. Moreover, only under exceptional bank panic conditions, does evidence support the belief that distress and failure of individual financial firms is a threat to the system as a whole. Contagion is rare, not endemic (Benston and Kaufman, 1995).

In addition, Charles's view that a central bank exists to provide special assistance to individual banks by discount window lending has been challenged (Goodfriend and King, 1988). Open market operations that provide liquidity to the market are sufficient to take care of the needs of solvent institutions with liquidity problems. A central bank can shut down the discount window in the knowledge that its open market operations can accommodate the system and the market will allocate the reserves it creates to individual banks that require an infusion.

Charles emphasises two other aspects of the central bank–commercial bank symbiosis: commercial banks need a central bank to serve as their lender of last resort (discussed in Section 4), and commercial banks under central bank leadership operate like a club, in order to control the conduct of their members; the aim of control he believes to be guaranteeing quality of service to depositor-customers. However, commercial banks operate like a club even in the absence of a central bank, for example Canada before 1935.

Free banking proponents on the other hand advocate self-regulation by the club members. In Charles's view, that course is incompatible with conflicts of interest among banks, so he rules out a voluntary club with an independent arbiter. What emerges instead is an official body – the central bank, or alternatively, according to Charles, a private clearing house – to run the system with a legally imposed set of rules. As the supervisory agency the central bank or clearing house sets the terms of entry into the club and rules of behaviour. Terms of entry, of course, may be set by a clearing house, but terms of entry into the banking system are not determined by the central bank but by a chartering agency. In the US the agency may be state or federal. In addition, a clearing house in the US had no legal power. It was a private organisation with no official standing.

Associated with the club, before there was a central bank, there was a private clearing house to provide support to member banks that needed help. Although Charles recognises the need for a club manager, he asks whether a body less powerful than current central banks could not do the job.

3.3   Central Bank Independence

We indicated above that we do not agree with Charles's view that central bank independence ended with the First World War. Some central banks in fact retained independence until the Great Depression. He, nevertheless, holds that it was inconceivable in the decades following the war. The monetary authorities after all were both the central bank and treasury. Charles asks: What changed the climate of opinion thereafter? His answer is that the campaign for independent central banks in recent decades has been supported by theoretical arguments and empirical evidence. The working definition of independence that Charles and his co-authors adopt is 'the right to change the key operational instrument without consultation or challenge from the government' (Capie et al., 1994, p. 50). The government, however, chooses the objective the central bank is mandated to fulfil. They regard the recent debate on central bank independence as having settled on the use of the central bank's single main instrument in the light of its own discretion for the generally agreed objective – medium-term price stability. Other questions have become subsidiary – accountability and management structure – to which independent central banks give different answers. They caution that independence may be oversold as the solution to monetary ills.

4.   THE CENTRAL BANK AS DOMESTIC LENDER OF LAST RESORT

A traditional monetarist view is that the role of a lender of last resort is to prevent or check banking panics by injecting funds into the banking system. Charles disagrees. He argues that convertibility of deposits into currency is not the key feature of banking panics that a central bank exists to prevent. It is rather the fact that any major shift of deposits within the banking system (from banks perceived to be weak to banks perceived to be strong) will be destabilising. The reason is that the transfer of deposits is much easier than the transfer of bank loans. 'It is the collapse of the borrowing relationships, as failing banks call in loans, leaving borrowers without the ability to replace the money at all easily or reasonably quickly, that is at least as responsible, as the loss of the depositors' wealth, for the resulting dislocation' (Goodhart, n.d.).[5]

From an American viewpoint, two questionable assumptions underlie Charles's argument. One is the loss of depositors' wealth that is contrasted with the loss of borrowers' bank relationship. In fact, the real contrast that he should have drawn is between bank failures that destroy the money stock and bank failures that destroy the bank–customer relationship. We note that destruction of the money stock affects every market in which money is used. And it is not at all inevitable that bank failures destroy the relationship, for reorganised banks may operate with the same management. Charles's second assumption about a special relationship between the bank and the borrower is that what inhibits establishing a new relationship with another bank is the cost to a bank to obtain information known privately only to the borrower.[6] Many borrowers in the US, however, have relationships not just with one source of funds – banks, insurance companies, factors – but with several of each. More importantly, banks to which deposits have been transferred are surely eager to invest the funds. Why would borrowers of good standing not find a responsive lender in the circumstances?

Charles (1999) regards Bagehot's prescription for a lender of last resort to lend freely at a penalty rate on good collateral to be hopelessly out of date. What Bagehot also stressed was that a central bank should leave no uncertainty about its intention to provide assistance. Charles believes that central banks nowadays do not conform to Bagehot's rules. He regards the ability of central banks to distinguish cases of illiquidity from those of insolvency as a myth. The reason is that a central bank faces difficulties in valuing the assets of a bank seeking assistance, so cannot know whether it is insolvent rather than illiquid. Advising a central bank to lend only to illiquid banks, in Charles's view, is facile and unworkable. It is not clear what the circumstances are that Charles has in mind. Is this a problem for a central bank when it is approached for a discount window loan by single banks? (On the frosted window at the Bank of England that obscures the identity of the borrower, see Capie, 2002). Or does the problem arise under panic conditions when many banks seek assistance?

As Geoffrey Wood (2000) has noted, Hawtrey (1932) long ago disposed of Charles's view that it was impossible for a central bank to distinguish between illiquidity and insolvency. Hawtrey explained that it was a bank's ability to furnish collateral more than sufficient to cover a central bank loan that made it unnecessary to judge the bank's solvency.

In the US, where regulators grade banks on their performance according to a scale of 1 to 5, the grades based on 5 measures known by the acronym of CAMEL (Capital adequacy, Asset quality, Management, Earnings, Liquidity), the Fed has no difficulty in distinguishing between an illiquid and an insolvent bank (see Schwartz, 1992).

With respect to penalty-rate lending and collateral requirements in accordance with Bagehot's prescriptions, one commentator suggests that they are observed as far as ordinary last-resort operations are concerned but not in the case of 'truly extraordinary' operations (Giannini, 1999, p. 14). He does not, however, define the latter.

Charles also accepts another buzz phrase associated with the new view of the way a lender of last resort operates – *creative ambiguity*. Far from assuring the market that it will with complete certainty provide assistance, the new view of a lender of last resort is that it should leave the market in doubt about its intentions. The defence of this approach is that it lessens moral hazard that would otherwise increase the likelihood of crises and financial instability (Giannini, 2002). Yet the incidence of panics and crises declined while Bagehot's teachings prevailed. What successes can the new view claim? Does the failure to observe Bagehot's rules validate central bank waywardness? Charles passes judgement neither on central bank nor regulators' behaviour. Whatever they do is deemed to be right conduct.

Charles refers to 'relief operations during crises' (Goodhart, 1985, p. 51). During crises, he asserts, a central bank does not have sufficient resources to be able to manage them out of its own funds. This may have been the case under the gold standard, when the Bank of England's gold reserves were scanty, but that cannot be the case under a fiat money regime.

The assistance by a consortium that the Bank of England organised to rescue Barings in 1890, one should remember, was to save an illiquid but a solvent bank. The fear that actuated support of the bank was that its failure might have prompted an external gold drain. No single bank had the resources to overcome Barings' shortage. Hence the grounds for the need for concerted action in this case differ from the circumstances that Charles alludes to to justify concerted action generally.

It is odd to describe a central bank in today's regime as short of sufficient resources. What distinguishes a central bank from other authorities is its ability to create unlimited amounts of the monetary base and subsequently to withdraw them. So currently insufficient resources cannot be the ground for a central bank to encourage other commercial banks to participate in rescues. An exception may be an emerging market country that lacks credibility and has a huge proportion of bank deposits in foreign currency so that open market operations in domestic currency will be insufficient and may lead to capital outflow.

Nevertheless, Giannini (1999) cites two reasons that resource availability may be a problem. First, the central bank may lend to a bank that in the end becomes insolvent and is unable to repay its borrowings. Second, emergency lending may conflict with monetary policy. These are not compelling reasons in a fiat money regime, but Giannini believes that they account for concerted lending – rescue operations conducted by a small group of banks including the central bank. Concerted lending, he says, involves a redistribution of existing reserves instead of the creation of additional amounts, exemplified, according to Giannini, by the 19th century US clearing house system. But he is mistaken in claiming that clearing house rescues merely redistributed existing reserves. Clearing houses created additional amounts on the basis of collateral supplied by member banks. Concerted lending has less to do with resource limitations than with the new view that it is a virtue for the authorities to involve the institutions that comprise the financial system in crises situations.

Concerted lending has been the rule in 104 bank crises in the 1980s and 1990s (Goodhart and Schoenmaker, 1995). In only two cases did a central bank undertake a rescue on its own. The Fed, however, has not sought assistance from the domestic financial community in the past decade in resolving crises (Giannini, 1999, p. 7). Its intervention in dragooning concerted lending by LTCM's financial backers in the 1998 Russian default crisis did not involve a monetary contribution by the Fed.

In any event, we question the case that Charles makes that rescuing an insolvent institution should be a central bank responsibility. An insolvent bank requires recapitalization or termination. A central bank has no responsibility to provide capital for financial institutions. If fiscal authorities believe that the financial system would be impaired by the failure of a large insolvent institution, they rather than the monetary authority should do the bailout.

5. AN INTERNATIONAL LENDER OF LAST RESORT?

If the rationale for a domestic lender of last resort is that one is needed to prevent or offset a shift of deposits within the banking system, then by analogy Charles argues that an international lender of last resort is needed when there is a major shift of funds from one country to others. He advocates restoring the funds to the country from which they have fled. Should one advocate such a move whether or not policy reform has been implemented if misguided policies of the country in question occasioned the capital flight?

Goodhart and Huang (2000) build an open economy model with several economies in the Diamond–Dybvig genre. They analyse conditions under which international financial contagion emerges that provides a useful role for an international lender of last resort. In the model the central bank in each economy uses foreign reserves to maintain a pegged exchange rate. Each economy has a banking system with domestic and international depositors, both with domestic currency deposits, but international depositors convert withdrawals into foreign currency. A central bank can prevent a domestic liquidity crisis but, in the absence of an international lender of last resort, a foreign currency liquidity crisis can trigger both a domestic liquidity crisis and a domestic banking crisis. If the economies are linked by an international interbank market, it may be able to provide needed liquidity. However, if liquidity in the interbank market were not adequate to save all illiquid banks, some banks would face a currency run which could trigger a domestic banking crisis. The failure of one bank informs all depositors in every bank and economy that the international interbank system has exhausted its available liquidity. An international currency crisis ensues that triggers an international banking crisis. The conclusion is that an international lender of last resort can provide international liquidity and reduce international contagion.

We ask Goodhart and Huang to explain how there can be an international lender of last resort when there is no single central bank acting as the global world's monetary authority. An existing international financial institution cannot create high-powered money in any national currency, so it cannot create international reserves. Goodhart and Huang, moreover, do not define the attributes of an international lender of last resort that they have in mind. As for their assumption of international financial contagion, actual examples of multi-country financial disturbances during the 1990s illustrate not contagion but capital flight from countries with similar unsustainable policies.

Discussion of an international last-resort lender inevitably applies to the IMF. It is acknowledged that extension of its role to the international domain encounters severe problems (Giannini, 1999, p. 39). Limited resource availability, however, is said not to be a key problem. The latest IMF quota increase, the increases in GAB-NAB, and the possibility of activating bilateral contributions, the argument goes, indicate that the IMF can mobilise resources in case of need. The real problems are said to be more fundamental.

One fundamental problem the international last-resort lender will encounter is the risk of politicisation of its rescues so that they serve the interest of stronger countries rather than the collective interest.[7] Another problem is that the international lender has limited enforcement powers. Finally, international creditors are not subject to the control of international organisations whereas national authorities have some control over domestic creditors. Therefore a universal lender of last resort is likely to suffer from important weaknesses. And the suggestion to transform the IMF into a Bagehotian lender of last resort would risk creating an unacceptable degree of moral hazard (Meltzer Commission, 2000).

Given these obstacles facing a would-be international lender of last resort as described by someone sympathetic to such a function, we question that there is a need for IMF lending (Fischer, 1999). The widening and deepening of capital markets in recent decades have established them as willing providers of loans to creditworthy countries. The internal problems of emerging market countries that have gotten them into trouble in the 1990s can be solved not by the IMF but only by the countries themselves and the actions of their national central banks.

6. CONCLUSIONS

In assessing Charles's contributions to the history of monetary institutions, it is noteworthy that the views he has espoused are widely recognised as uniquely his. Many economists believe that banks are fragile but only Charles has defined that fragility in terms of the asset side of their balance sheets. Also associated with Charles is the description of banks as operating like a club. His emphasis on the micro rather than macro function of central banks is again special to Charles. Most students of central banking would assign a more important role to the monetary policy function than he does. That regulation and supervision are central to Charles's concerns reflect his belief in the fragility of banks.

Despite the special nature of Charles's approach to the foregoing matters, he has been a mainstream economist who finds evidence that markets fail more readily than that policy-makers and regulators fail. He has applied this philosophy to the history of central banks and other institutions.

One of the interesting features of Charles's work as a mature student of monetary institutions is the dialogue he has conducted throughout with the free bank proponents. A mainstream economist, he more than anyone else has given their views a hearing. What is even more interesting is to juxtapose his and their views. They are opposites. Free bank proponents believe private banks are stable institutions that have a self-interest to be conservative lenders who scrupulously honour their promises to redeem their monetary liabilities at par, in the past redeemed their monetary liabilities in gold or foreign exchange without devaluation, were self-regulated, and that central banks were not only not needed but also were unreliable in fulfilling their commitments to redeem domestic currency at par.

Charles's views are diametrically different. Banks are unstable, periodically either overissuers or underissuers, unless constrained by regulators and central banks, which are essential even if not exemplary performers. Charles's views emerge from a rich familiarity with the nuances of financial markets in the past as well as their very latest manifestations. In this regard, free bank proponents appear to be dependent on selective elements of past financial history and not at all well grounded in contemporary financial developments. In this contest Charles is clearly the winner. Yet Charles may well have been influenced by the free bank literature to the extent that he has acknowledged the shortcomings of central bank performance. At the same time he has been an ardent advocate of the indispensable role of central banks as regulators and supervisors of the financial system and as providers of lender of last resort funds. Although we do not see eye to eye with Charles on issues he has addressed, we are happy to participate in the tributes to his labours in the vineyard of monetary institutions.

NOTES

1. See Miron (1986) on seasonal movements in nominal interest rates before 1914 and their elimination after 1914 by seasonal open market operations by the Fed.
2. Subsequent research employs newer techniques to deal with the Bank of England pre-World War I gold standard rules of the game – Giovannini (1986), Jeanne (1995), Bordo and MacDonald (1997) – but also with the interwar gold standard – Davatyan and Parke (1995), Eichengreen, Watson, and Grossman (1985) – and with the pre-World War I Reichsbank – Eschweiler and Bordo (1994).
3. As the discussant of the papers by Dutton and Pippenger on Bank of England behaviour under the pre-World War I gold standard, Goodhart defended his own views. He argued (1984) that what is at issue is not the actual way that the Bank operated but the interpretation of the reasons for its behavior. He regards the fundamental objective of the Bank in unusual circumstances was 'the maintenance of the basic fabric and structure of the banking and financial system'. Under normal circumstances the most important function of the Bank was to protect convertibility. He offers two possible interpretations of its behaviour. One is that there was a trade-off in objectives: for a given loss of reserves, the Bank would raise Bank rate by more if domestic activity was higher than if it was lower. Another interpretation is that the state of domestic activity served as an indicator of risk of future gold drains, either internal or external, from its reserves. Goodhart cites statements by both Pippenger and Dutton in support of his finding that the Bank provided some accommodation of monetary changes to domestic activity. He notes three differing views to explain the Bank's behaviour. Dutton attributes it to inertia during periods when interest rates are fixed. Pippenger attributes it to concerns to maintain profits. Goodhart attributes it to concern with market share and profit when the Bank's size fell progressively

relative to the size of the joint stock banks. He doubts that the Bank was consciously trying to support the needs of trade.

4. The text reads: 'A considerable degree of independence therefore obtained [before the First World War], particularly in so far as it related to the central bank assisting in the smooth working of the gold standard. The period from the First World War to the 1970s has in contrast been the age of the state, of economic management, of socialism. It was in this period that there was a move to greater government control, and of more dependent central banks.'

In discussing our paper at the Conference, Forrest Capie claimed that the text did not support our statement that, according to the authors, the loss of central bank independence dated from 1914. He cited a paragraph on p. 53, which does refer to 'the pursuit of independence' in the years to the Great Depression. The ambiguity is unresolved.

5. The same point appears in Goodhart (1987) but not the quoted sentence.

6. Goodhart's view is related to but not the same as that of Bernanke (1983) that widespread bank failures raise the cost of financial intermediation.

7. The record of recent IMF rescues suggests that such efforts have not always led to prompt recovery (Bordo and Schwartz, 2000).

REFERENCES

Benston, George J. and George G. Kaufman (1995), 'Is the Banking and Payments System Fragile?', *Journal of Financial Services Research*, 9 (3/4) (December), 209–40.

Bernanke, B.S. (1993), 'Credit in the Macro-economy', *Quarterly Review*, Federal Reserve Bank of New York, 18 (1) (Spring), 50–70.

Bloomfield, Arthur I. (1959), *Monetary Policy Under the International Gold Standard*, New York: Federal Reserve Bank of New York.

Bordo, Michael D. and Ronald MacDonald (1997), 'Violations of the "Rules of the Game" and Credibility of the Classical Gold Standard, 1880–1914', NBER Working Paper 6115 (July).

Bordo, Michael D. and Anna J. Schwartz (2000), 'Measuring Real Economic Effects of Bailouts: Historical Perspectives on How Countries Fared With and Without Bailouts', *Carnegie Rochester Series on Public Policy*, 53 (December), 81–167.

Calomiris, Charles W. (1998), 'The IMF's Imprudent Role as Lender of Last Resort', *Cato Journal*, 17 (3), 275–95.

Capie, Forrest (2002), 'The Emergence of the Bank of England as a Mature Central Bank', in Donald Winchard and Patrick O'Brien (eds), *The Political Economy of British Historical Experience, 1688–1914*, Cambridge: Cambridge University Press.

Capie, Forrest, Charles Goodhart, Stanley Fischer, and Norbert Schnadt (1994), *The Future of Central Banking: The Tercentenary Symposium of the Bank of England*, Cambridge: Cambridge University Press.

Cunliffe (1918), *First Interim Report of the Committee on Currency and Foreign Exchanges After the War*, UK Parliament, Cmnd. 9182.

Davatyan, Nathan and William R. Parke (1995), 'The Operations of the Bank of England, 1890–1908: A Dynamic Probit Approach', *Journal of Money, Credit, and Banking*, 27 (4) (November, Part 1), 1099–112.

Dutton, John (1984), 'The Bank of England and the Rules of the Game under the International Gold Standard: New Evidence', in M.D. Bordo and A.J. Schwartz (eds), *A Retrospective on the Classical Gold Standard 1821–1931*, Chicago: University of Chicago Press, pp. 173–202.

Eichengreen Barry, Mark W. Watson, and Richard S. Grossman (1985), 'Bank Rate Policy Under the Interwar Gold Standard: A Dynamic Probit Analysis', *Economic Journal*, 95 (September), 725–46.

Eschweiler, Bernard and Michael D. Bordo (1994), 'Rules, Discretion, and Central Bank Independence: The German Experience, 1880–1989', in Pierre Siklos (ed.), *Varieties of Monetary Reforms: Lessons and Experience on the Road to Monetary Union*, Boston: Kluwer Academic Publishers.

Fischer, Stanley (1999), 'On the Need for an International Lender of Last Resort', *Journal of Economic Perspectives*, 13 (4) (Fall), 85–104.

Giannini, Curzio (1999), 'Enemy of None But a Common Friend of All? An International Perspective on the Lender of Last Resort Function', *Essays in International Finance*, no. 214 (June), Princeton: Princeton University.

Giannini, Curzio (2002), 'Pitfalls in International Crisis Lending', in Charles Goodhart and Gerhard Illing (eds), *Financial Crises, Contagion, and the Lender of Last Resort: a Book of Readings*, Oxford: Oxford University Press.

Giovannini, Alberto (1986), 'Rules of the Game During the International Gold Standard: England and Germany', *Journal of International Money and Finance*, 5 (December), 467–83.

Goodfriend, Marvin and Robert G. King (1988), 'Financial Deregulation, Monetary Policy and Central Banking', in W.S. Haraf and R.M. Kushmeider (eds), *Restructuring Banking and Financial Services in America*, Washington, DC: American Enterprise Institute.

Goodhart, Charles A.E. (1969), *The New York Money Market and Finance of Trade, 1900–1913*, Harvard Economic Studies, vol. 132, Cambridge, Mass.: Harvard University Press.

Goodhart, Charles A.E. (1972), *The Business of Banking 1891–1914*, London School of Economics and Political Science.

Goodhart, Charles A.E. (1984), 'Comment', in M.D. Bordo and A.J. Schwartz (eds), *A Retrospective on the Classical Gold Standard 1821–1931*, Chicago: Chicago University Press, p. 227.

Goodhart, Charles A.E. (1985), *The Evolution of Central Banks*, London School of Economics and Political Science.

Goodhart, Charles A.E. (1987), 'Why do Banks Need a Central Bank', *Oxford Economic Papers*, 39, 75–89.

Goodhart, Charles A.E. (1991), 'Are Central Banks Necessary?', in Forrest Capie and Geoffrey E. Wood (eds), *Unregulated Banking: Chaos or Order?*, London: Macmillan.

Goodhart, Charles A.E. (1993), 'Institutional Separation between Supervisory and Monetary Agencies', in F. Bruni (ed.), *Prudential Regulation, Supervision and Monetary Policy*, Universita Commerciale Luigi Bocconi, pp. 353–439.

Goodhart, Charles A.E. (1997), 'Whither Now?', *Banca Nazionale del Lavoro Quarterly Review*, 50 (December), 385–430.

Goodhart, Charles A.E. (1999), 'Some Myths About the Lender of Last Resort', *International Finance*, 2–3 (November), 339–60.

Goodhart, Charles A.E. (n.d.), 'Why Do We Need a Central Bank?', Processed.

Goodhart, Charles A.E. and Haizhou Huang (2000), 'A Simple Model of an International Lender of Last Resort', IMF Working Paper, WP/00/75.

Goodhart, Charles A.E. and Dirk Schoenmaker (1995), 'Should the Functions of

Monetary Policy and Bank Supervision Be Separated?', *Oxford Economic Papers*, 47, October.

Hawtrey, Ralph G. (1932), *The Art of Central Banking*, London: Longmans, Green & Co.

Jeanne, Olivier (1995), 'Monetary Policy in England 1893–1914: A Structural VAR Analysis', *Explorations in Economic History*, 32, 302–26.

Meltzer, Allan H. et al. (2000), *Report*, Washington, DC: International Financial Institution Advisory Commission of the US Government.

Miron, Jeffrey A. (1986), 'Financial Panics, the Seasonality of the Nominal Interest Rate, and the Founding of the Fed', *American Economic Review*, 76 (March), 125–49.

Pippenger, John. (1984), 'Bank of England Operations, 1893–1913', in M.D. Bordo and A.J. Schwartz (eds), *A Retrospective on the Classical Gold Standard 1821–1931*, Chicago University Press: Chicago, pp. 203–21.

Schwartz, Anna J. (1992), 'The Misuse of the Fed's Discount Window', *Federal Reserve Bank of St. Louis, Review*, 74 (5) (September–October), 58–60.

Wood, Geoffrey E. (2000), 'The Lender of Last Resort Reconsidered', *Journal of Financial Services Research*, 18 (2/3) (December), 203–27.

3. Crises now and then: what lessons from the last era of financial globalization?[1]

Barry Eichengreen and Michael D. Bordo

1. INTRODUCTION

For more than a third of a century, Charles Goodhart has sought to employ financial history to shed light on current developments in the world economy. *The New York Money Market and the Finance of Trade* (1969) was an effort to link the development of financial markets to the growth of trade, a topic of clear relevance to those contemplating the connections between the euro and the Single Market. *The Business of Banking* (1972) sketched the links between banking and economic performance, a subject that is again timely as banking worldwide experiences a wave of consolidation. *The Evolution of Central Banks* (1988) developed an interpretation of the emergence of the lender of last resort that is directly relevant to the controversy over the role of the International Monetary Fund in a world of globalized finance.

If a single paper can be said to epitomize this approach, it is, for us, Goodhart's 1999 comparison of the Asian financial crisis with late-19th- and early-20th-century banking and currency crises.[2] The Asian crisis, he argues, was not the singular event portrayed in recent accounts. Rather, it bore a striking resemblance to financial crises a century before because it erupted in circumstances that, in important respects, recreated the economic and financial environment of that earlier era. The capital flows of the 1990s, like those of the 1890s, were directed toward the private sector, Goodhart argues, in contrast to the period centered on the 1970s, when the public sector was on the borrowing end. Hence, late-19th-century crises, like their late-20th-century counterparts, were not typically preceded by chronic government budget deficits. Rather, problems originated in the private sector, generally in poorly-managed, poorly-regulated banking systems and in the boom- and bust-prone real estate and property markets. Fuel was poured on the fire by foreign lending encouraged by open capital markets and buoyant export growth. When something – typically a shock to capital markets or a shock to exports – disrupted these processes, the entire financial house of cards could come tumbling down. The subsequent crises were strikingly similar in the overseas regions of recent European settlement at the end of the 19th century and in East Asia at the end of the 20th.

Progress in the study of history occurs by quibbling over details. In this paper we quibble over aspects of Goodhart's characterization of late-19th-century financial crises.[3] In a sense we attempt to do both more and less than our predecessor. We present a quantitative analysis for a larger number of pre-1914 banking and currency crises, 32 in all, and some comparisons with the interwar and post-World War II periods.[4] At the same time, we limit our qualitative discussion to one crisis: the Argentina–Baring crisis of 1890–91, an episode that has some particularly revealing parallels with the 1990s.[5]

2. THE EARLIER PERIOD OF GLOBALIZATION

Goodhart dates the first age of globalization to the laying of the transatlantic telegraph cable, which by providing a real-time communications link between England and North America transformed the information environment. Financial markets are markets in information; by speeding transatlantic communication, the advent of the cable in the 1860s thus transformed their operation.[6] While there was a lag before the consequences were felt owing to the US Civil War, which disrupted the country's export trade and access to foreign finance, by the late 1860s the process of large-scale capital transfer had resumed, reaching levels never seen before. The first age of globalization spanned the next 40 years until World War I brought it to a close.

This, however, is only part of the story. However appealing to modern readers may be the notion that changes in information and communications technologies drove the expansion of global financial markets, there were other, perhaps equally important, factors at work. One was the growth of trade, stimulated by the Cobden–Chevalier Treaty of 1860 which was generalized to other countries through the operation of most-favored-nation clauses. In the four decades leading up to World War I, as transport costs fell and governments adopted trade-friendlier commercial policies, there was nearly a doubling of the share of exports in GDP in Angus Maddison's sample of countries.[7] Certainly the enthusiasm of British investors for Argentine railway bonds would have been less in the absence not just of cable traffic and refrigerated steamships but also of an open

British market for chilled beef. Without access to foreign goods markets, debtors could not have earned the foreign exchange needed to service and repay their loans, and in the absence of expanding export markets their incentive to stay on good terms with their creditors, who were also their customers, would have been less. For all these reasons, the connections between trade liberalization and the expansion of lending were prominent prior to World War I, just as in the 1990s.[8]

The monetary regime was another important factor in the expansion of global capital markets in the late 19th century. The international gold standard was a post-1870 affair. Adherence to the gold standard signalled a government's commitment to sound and stable policies. Credibly subordinating other goals of policy to the maintenance of a fixed domestic gold price and limiting exchange-rate movements against the currencies of the creditor countries (which meant, above all, against Britain and the pound sterling) made it easier to accumulate and service foreign-currency-denominated debts. For countries borrowing in foreign exchange (which meant most countries, in practice), this limited balance-sheet problems caused by sharp exchange-rate changes. Limiting balance-sheet risk *ex post* in turn enhanced the ability of overseas regions to borrow in foreign exchange *ex ante*.[9]

The destinations of British capital tended to be abundant in natural and human resources. This is clear from the fact that more than 10 per cent of British overseas lending in the first age of globalization was for enterprises engaged in natural-resource extraction, while much of the rest was for resource-based or resource-intensive industries, as in the case of the railways providing transport services to the wheat farmers of Canada, Argentina and the United States.[10] (See Table 3.1.) Harnessing this resource base in an export-relevant way entailed the immigration of European workers who brought with them knowledge of the industrial and agricultural techniques of the 'first industrial revolution,' not to mention labour power.[11] Like high levels of trade, these high levels of immigration would not have been possible in the absence of technological advances in ocean- and land-going transportation (O'Rourke and Williamson, 1999).

The point is that the first age of financial globalization resulted from technological, institutional and policy changes extending well beyond the realm of information and communication. It presupposed a technological revolution that vastly increased the productivity of resource-based traded-goods industries.[12] It depended on tariff reductions and a transport revolution to facilitate the growth of trade. And it would not have thrived without a technological and political environment that encouraged cross-border labour flows.

Table 3.1 Industrial composition of British capital exports to the ten major recipients, 1865–1914 (percentage of capital called in each country)

Broad Industrial group	United States	Canada	Argentina	Australia	India	South Africa[1]	Brazil	Russia[2]	New Zealand	Mexico	All countries
Government	5.8	33.9	22.4	65.8	45.8	50.9	45.9	50.3	64.3	19.7	36.3
Railways	61.6	40.3	57.5	0.0	40.5	1.9	31.6	24.8	2.0	36.6	31.7
Public Utilities	9.5	5.6	8.9	3.5	3.1	2.4	10.2	3.0	5.1	12.1	6.4
Financial	6.3	6.2	5.4	11.6	1.5	6.4	2.1	5.9	17.8	9.0	7.3
Raw Materials	5.5	3.7	0.5	13.4	5.9	33.7	2.9	12.0	6.4	15.5	10.0
Mines	4.6	3.5	0.5	12.9	3.2	33.5	1.3	3.9	6.1	8.9	7.6
Industrial & Misc.	10.8	10.1	4.6	3.5	2.0	4.1	6.5	3.9	2.7	5.8	7.2
Mfg.	5.7	3.1	1.5	0.6	0.7	0.6	1.3	2.3	0.6	2.2	2.9
Shipping	0.5	0.2	0.8	1.2	1.1	0.4	0.9	0.2	1.6	1.2	1.3
Total Private[3]	94.2	66.1	77.6	34.2	54.2	49.1	54.1	49.7	35.7	80.3	63.7

Notes:
[1] Includes South Africa, Cape of Good Hope, Natal, Orange River Colony, Transvaal, and Orange Free State.
[2] Includes European and Asian Russia.
[3] All broad industrial groups with exception of Government.

Source: Stone (1999).

3.   INFORMATION, INSTITUTIONS AND MARKETS

The bulk of the overseas finance in question went to economies whose financial markets and institutions were well developed by the standards of the time.[13] (See Table 3.2.) It went to countries with bank branch networks capable of gathering information on local market conditions and with well-developed interbank and commercial paper markets capable of redeploying liquidity. It went to countries that welcomed the independent subsidiaries of European investment banks.[14] It went to countries where the issuers of listed securities disclosed information on their financial affairs. It went to countries where contracts were enforced and insolvency procedures operated reliably.

Table 3.2   Income per capita in creditor and debtor countries, selected years (US dollars)

	1913	1929	1980	1997
Major creditors[a]	4,779	6,025	10,976	28,474
Top 10 borrowers[b]	1,698	2,200	2,485	3,756
Low-income borrowers[c]			492	808
Memo item				
Share of low-income borrowers in total private flows to emerging markets			14	29

Notes:
[a] For 1913 and 1929, France, Germany, United Kingdom, and United States; for 1980 and 1997, the same countries plus Japan; average reflects GDP weights.
[b] Top 10 recipients of net long-term private flows. Average weighted by GDP in 1913 and 1929, and by net long-term flows in 1980 and 1997.
[c] Top 10 low-income recipients of long-term private flows. Average weighted by net long-term flows.

Source: World Bank (2000).

In our enthusiasm for the sophistication of late-19th-century international capital markets, we should not lose sight of the other side of this coin, namely, the persistence of information problems rooted in the still-early development of financial institutions and markets. Foreign capital flowed into US securities despite the chronic failure of the New York Stock Exchange to require the disclosure of financial information by companies listing shares.[15] It flowed to the US despite the absence of uniform auditing and accounting standards prior to the establishment of the Interstate Commerce Commission in 1887 and its imposition in the 1890s of a uniform accounting standard on the railways for which it set rates. Foreign capital financed Argentina's provincial banks despite their well-known tendency to issue false balance sheets and report nonexistent dividends.[16]

These examples remind us that, the advent of the transoceanic cable and radio-telephone notwithstanding, the information environment was highly imperfect by today's standards. There was no worldwide web on which to gather information on stocks, bonds and debentures; *The Investor's Monthly Manual, Burdett's Stock Exchange Official Intelligence, Poor's Manual of Railroads,* and *Herapath's Railway Journal,* while serviceable, were imperfect substitutes. There was no IMF Data Dissemination System to provide information on public finances, although the annual reports of the Corporation of Foreign Bondholders aspired to some of the same functions. There were no sovereign rating agencies or credit departments prior to the establishment of such functions within the *Credit Lyonnais* at the end of the 19th century.[17] Even the geographical correlation of capital and labour flows reminds us of the limits of the information environment: many investors relied on the information about foreign market conditions sent back to their native country by recent immigrants.[18]

From the imperfect nature of the information environment flow the distinctive aspects of late 19th century lending that differentiate it from international lending today. First, the vast majority of overseas and foreign investment in the half century before 1914 was in debt securities and interbank deposits; only a small fraction took the form of equity. Debt has priority; those who hold it sacrifice a share of extraordinary profits in return for the security that seniority provides. There is an incentive to do so when the information environment is impacted and serious principal–agent problems result from the separation of ownership from control. Thus, we regularly see firms graduate from bank finance to equity finance as information about their economic and financial prospects becomes standardized and assimilated.[19] We similarly observe economies graduating from debt to equity finance as the information environment improves.[20] In the late 19th century, however, this graduation ceremony for the most part remained a distant prospect, and debt securities dominated international financial flows.

Second, the operation of decentralized financial markets was importantly supplemented by the operation of financial institutions. Financial intermediaries – banks in particular – are in the business of information. They develop monitoring technologies in order to assemble and process information at lower cost than is possible for individuals. That overseas investors appreciated the efficiency of these monitoring technologies is evident in the willingness of Scottish savers to make deposits with British branches of Australian banks, and in the willingness of British investors, institutional and individual, to place deposits with Argentine banks. It is evident in the underwriting role of the great investment banks, which staked their reputations on the success of overseas bond flotations.[21] Unfortunately, we know little about the volume of foreign lending directly carried out by banks; quantitative analysis has focused on bond flotations since this segment of the international capital market is amply documented.[22]

A third reflection of the prevalence of information asymmetries is the sectors into which foreign finance flowed. The data on bond flotations suggest (subject to the preceding caveats) that some 40 per cent of British overseas investments in quoted securities was in railways, while 30 per cent was in the issues of national, state and municipal governments, 10 per cent was in resource-extracting industries (mainly mining), and 5 per cent was in public utilities. Commercial, industrial and financial activities that are so prominent today are notably absent from this list. That the Feldstein–Horioka puzzle (the high correlation of national savings and investment rates) was less evident before 1913 has been widely touted as proof of the exceptional integration of late-19th-century capital markets.[23] But while 19th-century current account deficits reached high levels and the emerging markets of the day financed substantial shares of their investment from foreign sources, what is striking is that wide swathes of their economies remained virtually untouched by foreign finance.

Asymmetric information can explain this sectoral composition of investment portfolios.[24] Consider the dominance of railway bonds. Investors could verify how much track had been laid, where it had been laid, and how much traffic it carried more easily than they could evaluate the investment decisions of the managers of manufacturing, financial and service-sector concerns, many of whose assets were intangible. These considerations explain the preference of British investors for 'coal roads', that is, railways whose traffic was disproportionately comprised of coal haulage, for which it was relatively straightforward to forecast operating revenues. The information environment similarly helps to explain the disproportionate importance of investment in resource extraction and public utilities. Mining companies had tangible assets; it was relatively straightforward to monitor the number of mines dug or tons of coal raised to the surface. Utility companies laid gas lines, strung electrical cables, and built power plants. Notwithstanding scandals like the Buenos Aires Water Supply and Drainage Loan of 1888, such investments were relatively straightforward to monitor. A similar argument can be made about governments and their ability to tax. It is thus not surprising that six out of every seven pounds sterling of portfolio investment were in securities of debtors with tangible, transparent assets (the ability to tax in the case of governments, track and rolling stock with a well-defined revenue-raising capacity in the case of railways, mineral reserves in the case of mining companies).[25] Information asymmetries can also explain the limited role of foreign direct investment in this earlier age of financial globalization. A considerable majority of foreign investment prior to 1914 was portfolio investment, whereas today direct investment is the more important component. Direct investment was discouraged by the difficulty of controlling branch plants and foreign subsidiaries and of preventing management from pursuing private agendas in an age when information and communications technologies were more rudimentary. When European producers established operations in the New World, they created them as freestanding companies. Freestanding companies were those incorporated in Britain, France, Belgium and other European countries for the sole purpose of investing and doing business in an overseas market. Their partners made special investments in information about foreign markets, and by bundling management and control they limited agency problems.[26]

The dominance of infrastructure investment, which flowed in part from the nature of the information environment, had implications for the transfer problem. It meant that much of the relevant infrastructure network had to be put in place before the returns began to accrue; this created an incentive to invest when other investment was taking place so that returns were not unduly delayed.[27] Foreign investment tended to cluster in time, in other words. But the nature of this investment made debt service difficult because of the long gestation period. In the case of a railroad, the funds had to be raised, the track had to be laid, and only then might settlement, cultivation and finally traffic respond to the availability of transportation services. Receipts to service the loan could be few initially, making it hard to keep current in the absence of additional debt finance.

This brings us finally to the crisis problem. It can be argued incomplete information created an environment conducive to herding and volatility (Kindleberger, 1978). Investors had an incentive to mimic other investors on the chance that the latter were better informed. Working in the other direction was the fact that foreign investment was more geographically concentrated in the late 19th century than today. It was heavily directed toward the United States in the 1870s, Australia and Argentina in the 1880s, and Canada and Brazil in the first decade of the 20th century.[28] (See Table 3.3.) By implication, the phenomenon pointed to by Calvo and Mendoza (2000) – that the more diversified are portfolios, the less is the incentive for investors to engage in the costly acquisition and processing of information about each market in which they invest, and hence the greater is the tendency toward herding – may have been less prevalent a century ago.[29]

Delargy and Goodhart suggest that pre-1914 crises resembled the Asian

Table 3.3　Major recipients of British capital exports, 1865–1914

Rank		Percentage of total capital called	Cumulative percentage	Amount (£000)
1	United States	20.5		836,371
2	Canada	10.1		412,283
3	Argentina	8.6		349,243
4	Australia	8.3		339,001
5	India	7.8	55.3	317,174
6	South Africa	6.4		262,233
7	Brazil	4.2		172,742
8	Russia	3.4		139,348
9	New Zealand	2.1		84,495
10	Mexico	2.0	73.4	81,532
11	Japan	1.9		78,285
12	China	1.8		73,747
13	Egypt	1.6		66,193
14	Chile	1.5		61,818
15	France	1.4	81.7	57,920
16	Rhodesia	1.1		46,232
17	Turkey	1.0		42,268
18	Italy	1.0		41,427
19	Austria-Hungary	1.0		39,954
20	Peru	0.9	86.8	37,173
21	Spain	0.8		33,912
22	Uruguay	0.8		30,678
23	Cuba	0.6		26,314
24	Germany	0.6		24,493
25	Greece	0.5	90.1	19,300
	Total Capital Called	100.0		4,079,254

Source:　Stone (1999).

crisis in that they originated in the private sector. Nineteenth century capital transfer, they argue, was private-to-private lending: funds flowed from private investors to private-sector recipients. It follows that the typical 19th-century crisis was not preceded by ballooning public-sector deficits leading to unsustainable current account balances. Rather, it occurred when private investment went awry – when, owing to misjudgment, malfeasance or unexpected shocks, a project did not pay.

This characterization is too simple, in our view. Some 40 per cent of the overseas investment intermediated by the bond market in the period 1865–1913 went into government and government-guaranteed loans (Table

Table 3.4   Share of private-source debt flows, by recipient sector (per cent)

Sector	1865–1913[b]	1921–1931		1980	1997
		London	New York		
Public sector[a]	40	62	80	80	33
Private sector	60	38	20	20	67

Notes:
[a] Includes government-guaranteed borrowing where data are available.
[b] Refers to British overseas investments only.

Source: World Bank (2000).

3.4). Authors like Feis (1930) and Fishlow (1986) emphasize the problematic nature of much of this lending. Governments borrowed for military adventures, pork-barrel projects, and public consumption.[30] These 'revenue borrowers' had chronic fiscal problems, almost by definition. As *The Bankers' Magazine* wrote on the eve of the Baring Crisis, 'The Government . . . has recklessly squandered the public funds. State grants have been made to every kind of undertaking; and although all the latter cannot be said to be useful, a good many were not required at present. Concessions have been lavishly given for new railways with heavy State subsidies, all of which are to be paid in gold, often where lines already exist, or where there is no demand for them. Grants have been furnished to canals, the utility of which may be greatly questioned and gold shot into ports which will not be required for a long time to come'.[31]

The problem, in other words, was not limited to the private sector. Debt-servicing difficulties were prevalent (and default rates were high) where borrowing took the form of 'revenue finance' (to supplement normal sources of public-sector revenue) rather than 'development finance' (to finance economic development and the development of export capacity, in particular). These observations suggest that focusing on the private-sector sources of crises loses sight of important aspects of the problem.[32]

4.   NINETEENTH-CENTURY FINANCIAL CRISES: HOW DO THEY COMPARE TO TODAY'S?

Pegged exchange rates, high capital mobility, asymmetric information, and weak institutions clearly comprised a fertile environment for crises. In these respects if not others, the crises of the pre-1914 era bear no little resemblance to the Asian crisis of 1997–98 and other recent crises. But how extensive are the parallels? To answer this question, we have attempted to apply a consistent set of criteria to date and measure crises. We follow 21 countries, classified as industrial or emerging (although changes in their economic development lead us to reclassify several emerging markets as industrial economies as we move between periods). Since the number of candidate countries has increased considerably since the independence movements of the 1960s, we also conduct the same exercise for a larger sample of 56 countries starting in 1973. We distinguish banking crises, currency crises and twin crises.[33] For an episode to qualify as a currency crisis, we must observe a forced change in parity, abandonment of a pegged exchange rate, or an international rescue.[34] For an episode to qualify as a banking crisis, we must observe either bank runs, widespread bank failures and the suspension of convertibility of deposits into currency such that the latter circulates at a premium relative to deposits (a banking panic), or significant banking sector problems (including but not limited to bank failures) resulting in the erosion of most or all of banking system collateral that are resolved by a fiscally-underwritten bank restructuring.[35] For an episode to classify as a twin crisis, we must observe both a currency crisis and a banking crisis in the same or immediately adjacent years. In tabulating the results, we distinguish the pre-1914 period, the interwar years, the Bretton Woods period (from the close of World War II through 1971), and the post Bretton Wood era (1973–98). Here we concentrate on the comparison between the two eras of globalization, 1880–1913 and 1973–98.[36]

The number of crises is shown in Table 3.5, the corresponding frequencies in Table 3.6. Evidently, a randomly-selected country had a 5 per cent probability of experiencing a crisis in a randomly-selected pre-1914 year. Since 1973, in contrast, the corresponding probability has been twice as high (10 per cent for the same sample of countries, 12 per cent for the expanded sample, the latter reflecting the even greater incidence of crises in low-income developing countries). While the frequency of banking crises was roughly the same before 1914 and after 1972, currency crises were much

Table 3.5   Crisis frequency

Year	Banking crises	Currency crises	Twin crises	All crises
1880–1913	2.30	1.23	1.38	4.90
1919–1939	4.84	4.30	4.03	13.17
1945–1971	0.00	6.85	0.19	7.04
1973–1997 (21 countries)	2.03	5.18	2.48	9.68
1973–1997 (56 countries)	2.29	7.48	2.38	12.15

Source: See text.

Table 3.6   Number of crises – distribution by market

Market	Year	Banking crises	Currency crises	Twin crises	All crises
Industrial countries	1880–1913	4	2	1	7
	1919–1939	11	13	12	36
	1945–1971	0	21	0	21
	1973–1997	9	29	6	44
Emerging markets	1880–1913	11	6	8	25
	1919–1939	7	3	3	13
	1945–1971	0	16	1	17
	1973–1997	17	57	21	95

Source: See text.

more frequent in the final quarter of the 20th century (and, as a result, there was a growing frequency of twin crises).[37] Evidently, the credibility of the commitment to peg the exchange rate under the gold standard was part of the explanation for the stability of the pre-1914 financial environment.[38] Note also that the distinction between gold-standard core and periphery, which features prominently in the historical literature, is evident in the disproportionate concentration of prewar currency crises in late-19th-century emerging markets.

Delargy and Goodhart argue that these 19th century crises were preceded by credit booms that fueled unsustainable rates of growth.[39] Foreign capital flooded into emerging markets via the banking system and the bond market and was deployed to domestic uses, some productive, some less so. The construction and real-estate sectors boomed. The current account deficit widened, reflecting rising spending on imported consumption and investment goods. In Argentina, a classic instance of a foreign-capital-led consumption boom, the level of domestic savings fell by some 20 per cent in the decade of the 1880s.[40] The problem was poor governance of domestic financial institutions together with the naivety of foreign investors. The result, all too often, was a sharp shock which curtailed capital inflows and required a shift in the current account from deficit to surplus, something that could only be accomplished through a significant compression of domestic spending.

To this picture must be added several additional aspects of the financial setting without which analysis of the prewar crisis problem is incomplete. First, in the late 19th century, as in the late 20th, crises were more likely when loose credit conditions in the lending countries first pushed investors, searching for yield, toward emerging markets, and when those loose credit conditions were then suddenly tightened.[41] For much of the decade preceding the Argentina–Baring crisis, for example, interest rates were low in the money centers, reflecting the weak state of international demand. London and Edinburgh were soon 'honeycombed with agencies' collecting money for banks in South America and the Antipodes.[42] Goschen's 1888 debt conversion, which locked in lower interest rates for the British government, ignited a rise in the price of French 3 per cent *rentes* and allowed the Prussian government to issue 3 per cent consols. As Max Wirth described the situation, 'German investors, at this time, preferred to purchase foreign securities with high rates of interest; and were so imprudent as to be caught by the radiant descriptions of rising wealth in Argentina, and to buy stocks and bonds from this ill-governed republic'.[43]

This process had within it an equilibrating mechanism but not one that operated smoothly. As lending boomed and bank reserves declined, private financial institutions borrowed from central banks. The latter, following what later came to be called the rules of the game, raised interest rates. The Bank of England, for example, raised its discount rate from 4 to 6 per cent in the second half of 1889. It is no coincidence that the Argentina–Baring crisis erupted in the wake of this policy action.

The speculative boom that developed along with the influx of foreign capital typically reflected more than the inadequate internal controls of local banks. Repeatedly, governments distorted the incentives of bankers so as to become implicated in their actions. In Australia, problem banks secured government accounts through 'backstairs influence'; those which succeeded in doing so entered into an agreement to support one another in the event of distress.[44] In Argentina, the provincial banks that aggressively chased foreign funding in the 1880s were little more than the borrowing arms of provincial governments; they were 'banks in name only' (Williams, 1920, p. 58). Some made advances not just to provincial governments but to the politicians personally.[45] 'Persons with influence in "high quarters" were favoured by the banks,' *The Bankers' Magazine* complained, 'often in preference to old well-known firms'.[46] National and provincial mortgage banks extended loans to large landowners on the security of their real estate. Many of these loans reflected 'encroaching nepotism' (to again quote Max Wirth). 'Loans were allowed less by reason of gold security than as a matter of personal favor.'[47] 'It has long been notorious that the [National] Bank was grievously mismanaged', *The Statist* observed (with benefit of hindsight in 1890), 'and it is almost universally believed that the mismanagement has been accompanied by gross corruption . . . People in the Republic believe, in short, that the Bank has been made a convenience of by those in high places . . .'.[48] The influence of these politicians and of large landowners (frequently one and the same) gave grounds for thinking that the banks financing them would not be allowed to fail. Thus, as early as 1889 the Argentine Government surreptitiously authorized the issue of additional paper money by the National Bank and the Provincial Bank of Buenos Aires to deal with mounting banking-sector problems. It is not surprising, given this backdrop of implicit guarantees, that European investors were inadequately critical of the value of the banks' mortgage-backed securities.[49]

When capital flows reversed direction, the result was a downturn in 'both economies and national industries often exceeding 10% or 20%', as Goodhart and Delargy put it. The authors base this estimate on statistics of industrial production, railroad freight haulage and imports for their nine crisis episodes. Historical time series on GDP for the present sample of 21 countries yield smaller estimates, because GDP is less volatile than imports and industrial production and because many of Delargy and Goodhart's nine cases are exceptionally severe crises.[50] Table 3.7 reports estimates of output losses analogous to those in the modern literature on financial crises.[51] The output loss from crises appears to have been slightly larger before 1913 than after 1973 (some 10 percentage points of cumulative growth lost versus 8).[52] Output losses were larger then than now for both currency crises and banking crises. Both then and now, output losses were larger in emerging markets than industrial countries. The notable exception is twin crises. These, clearly, have grown more severe. Recall from the preceding that they have also grown more prevalent. This points to what is new and disturbing about the final quarter of the 20th century.

These findings are robust to limiting consideration to only those crises with output losses, as in Table 3.8. And it does not appear that the unusual severity of recessions accompanied by crises simply reflects causality running from the recession to the crisis. The additional severity of downturns that occur in the wake of crises is robust to the inclusion of other explanatory variables that help to account for the unusual amplitude of some business cycles and for instrumentation of the crisis indicator.[53]

The lending-boom interpretation of these episodes is supported by the behavior of the current account. Typically, the current account deficit widened by an additional 2 per cent of GDP in the run-up to a crisis.[54] But sharp shifts from deficit to surplus in the wake of the event are not uniformly evident: on average, all that occurs is the elimination of the preceding 2-per-cent-of-GDP widening of the deficit, while larger movements which shift the current account into substantial surplus are only evident in the wake of twin crises. Delargy and Goodhart also note that sharp current-account reversals are not uniformly evident; they did not occur in US in 1907 or in Italy in 1893 and 1907 (a third of the authors' nine cases).[55]

Table 3.7   Output loss

	1880–1913 21 countries	1919–1939 21 countries	1945–1971 21 countries	1973–1997 21 countries	1973–1997 56 countries
Currency crises					
All countries	8.31	14.21	5.25	3.81	5.91
	(8.35)	(19.05)	(7.96)	(6.34)	(7.53)
Industrial	3.73	11.36	2.36	2.86	3.66
countries	(4.10)	(17.85)	(3.56)	(4.23)	(5.60)
Emerging	9.84	26.53	9.03	8.54	7.00
markets	(9.12)	(22.98)	(10.40)	(12.38)	(8.23)
Banking crises					
All countries	8.35	10.49	–	7.04	6.21
	(6.29)	(10.52)		(7.94)	(7.36)
Industrial	11.58	11.51	–	7.92	7.04
countries	(6.01)	(11.20)		(7.94)	(7.89)
Emerging	7.18	8.89	–	0.00	5.78
markets	(6.23)	(9.99)		–	(7.27)
Twin crises					
All countries	14.50	15.84	1.65	15.67	18.61
	(21.54)	(14.66)		(10.05)	(12.53)
Industrial	0.00	13.79	–	17.54	15.64
countries	–	(14.08)		(14.38)	(13.68)
Emerging	16.31	24.03	1.65	14.10	19.46
markets	(22.29)	(16.96)		(5.48)	(12.41)
All crises					
All countries	9.76	13.42	5.24	7.77	8.29
	(12.79)	(14.99)	(7.96)	(9.06)	(10.10)
Industrial	7.68	12.29	2.39	6.69	6.25
countries	(6.78)	(14.65)	(3.65)	(8.97)	(8.49)
Emerging	10.37	16.46	8.60	10.80	9.21
markets	(14.13)	(16.09)	(10.23)	(9.01)	(10.65)

Note: Standard deviation in parentheses.

Source: See text.

Table 3.8   Output loss, for crises with output losses only

	1880–1913 21 countries	1919–1939 21 countries	1945–1971 21 countries	1973–1997 21 countries	1973–1997 56 countries
Currency crises					
All countries	11.09	25.26	7.19	5.08	7.56
	(7.80)	(19.14)	(8.56)	(6.78)	(7.90)
Industrial	3.73	21.10	4.13	3.57	4.61
countries	(4.10)	(19.94)	(3.89)	(4.39)	(5.87)
Emerging	14.77	39.79	9.63	17.08	8.84
markets	(5.43)	(0.19)	(10.48)	(12.97)	(8.47)
Banking crises					
All countries	9.63	15.61	–	10.56	8.50
	(5.72)	(9.66)		(7.41)	(7.39)
Industrial	11.58	15.82	–	10.56	10.56
countries	(6.01)	(10.05)		(7.41)	(7.41)
Emerging	8.77	12.45	–	–	7.55
markets	(5.73)	(9.71)			(7.48)
Twin crises					
All countries	18.64	16.59	1.65	15.67	18.61
	(22.99)	(14.23)		(10.05)	(12.53)
Industrial	–	16.54	–	17.54	15.64
countries		(13.84)		(14.38)	(13.68)
Emerging	18.64	24.03	1.65	14.10	19.46
markets	(22.99)	(16.96)		(5.48)	(12.41)
All crises					
All countries	12.11	18.95	7.19	9.60	10.64
	(13.23)	(14.57)	(8.56)	(9.16)	(10.29)
Industrial	8.96	17.93	4.35	7.98	7.72
countries	(6.44)	(14.55)	(4.00)	(9.27)	(8.82)
Emerging	13.10	21.39	9.14	14.85	12.02
markets	(14.74)	(15.09)	(10.32)	(6.88)	(10.70)

Note: Standard deviation in parentheses.

Source: See text.

In our larger sample, sharp current account reversals are observed on average only in response to twin crises – events that produce particularly dramatic falls in domestic absorption.

Monetary variables (the money stock and interest rates) display the same striking behavior in our larger sample as in the Delargy–Goodhart cases. While interest rates shoot up with the outbreak of a crisis, they fall back rapidly. By the second post-crisis year, the real interest rate is back at pre-crisis levels; the same is not true in the post-1972 period, when interest rates remain persistently higher for a period of years.[56] While the rate of growth of the money stock accelerates sharply following the typical post-1972 emerging-market crisis, the same is not true of the pre-1914 years, when there is little movement in the rate of growth of the money stock.[57]

5.   THE ROLE OF THE MONETARY REGIME

The relatively rapid stabilization of money supplies and interest rates following these pre-1914 crises plausibly reflects what economists refer to as the resumption rule.[58] If a crisis forced a government to allow the currency to depreciate, the argument goes, such depreciation was expected to be temporary. If the depletion of its reserves left the authorities no alternative but to suspend the convertibility of the currency into gold, they were expected to restore convertibility at the pre-crisis gold price once they had put their immediate difficulties behind them. Aware that the authorities were committed to the early elimination of the gold premium, investors had no grounds to fear a loss of monetary and fiscal control. They had no reason to continue to flee domestic financial assets and markets. To the contrary, to the extent that the authorities were expected to reverse the previous depreciation (as had England in the paper-pound period that ended in 1821, and again following other crises like those of 1825, 1847 and 1857), capital losses today increased the likelihood of capital gains subsequently. Capital flows might not just stabilize but gradually reverse direction.

From the rapid stabilization of interest rates and money supplies and the behavior of industrial production and imports in their selection of cases, Delargy and Goodhart conclude that recovery from financial crises was relatively rapid before 1914 because of the credibility of this resumption rule. McKinnon (1997) makes a similar argument; in his variant, currency crises were less acute before 1914 because of the operation of what he calls 'the restoration rule'.[59] 'What gave the pre-1914 gold standard its long-run resilience,' he asks? 'After any short-run crisis that forced the partial or complete suspension of gold parities, the unwritten "restoration" rule . . . was that the country in question return to its traditional gold parity as soon as practicable. Even during a liquidity squeeze or other short-run trauma, longer-term exchange rate expectations remained regressive with respect to these traditional parities.'

Compared to these pre-1914 cases, Asian countries in the 1990s fared less well because of the absence of an analogous rule.[60] There, as Delargy and Goodhart put it, 'the combination of a downwardly flexible exchange rate (raising the domestic burden of dollar debt) combined with efforts to keep the Asian countries from imposing moratoria on outward debt payments, plus high (often sky-high) interest rates has led to a cocktail of external/internal financial conditions far less conducive to rapid recovery than pre-1914'.[61]

Our quantitative analysis suggests that these arguments need to be carefully nuanced. Our estimates do not suggest, contra McKinnon, that currency crises were shorter before 1914 – the opposite, if anything, was true. Table 3.9 documents this fact. Recovery time is calculated there as the number of years before the rate of GDP growth returns to its pre-crisis average (where that average is defined in terms of the five years preceding the event).[62] Clearly, these calculations do not support the notion that recovery from currency crises, so measured, was faster before 1913.[63] For the emerging markets in our 21 country sample, it took on average 2½ years for growth to resume before 1914 but only 2 years after 1972. For the industrial countries it took 3 years before 1914 but only 2 years after 1972.

For banking and twin crises, there *is* some evidence that recovery was faster before 1914. The contrast is most notable for twin crises: before 1914, it took two years following the occurrence of one of these events before growth resumed, while the same took nearly four years in the post-1972 period. But this result is heavily driven by the single industrial country case in the pre-1914 sample, France in 1888–89, which was a relatively mild episode. The background to this event was a scheme to corner the copper market in 1888.[64] The Comptoir d'Escompte discounted copper warrants in conjunction with this scheme. When copper prices suddenly fell, the Comptoir suffered heavy losses, and its director committed suicide, prompting a run. Its assets not being sufficiently liquid to satisfy the demands of depositors, the Comptoir then appealed to the Bank of France for assistance, the latter advanced it some 200 million francs on the guarantee of several Paris banks, and the currency came under pressure as a result. But while the banking system came under pressure, widespread bank failures did not occur, and while there was speculation against the franc, it was successfully resisted. This relatively mild crisis drives the contrast in Table 3.9. Putting it aside, the same conclusion follows for twin crises as for currency crises: there is no evidence of faster recovery before 1914.

Why was the resumption of growth following currency crises, in particular, no faster before 1914? The answer is not hard to find: it lies in the fact

Table 3.9   Recovery time

	1880–1913 21 countries	1919–1939 21 countries	1945–1971 21 countries	1973–1997 21 countries	1973–1997 56 countries
Currency crises					
All countries	2.63	1.94	1.84	1.87	2.07
	(1.85)	(1.65)	(1.17)	(1.29)	(1.63)
Industrial	3.00	1.92	1.67	1.84	2.04
countries	(1.41)	(1.80)	(1.20)	(1.30)	(1.91)
Emerging	2.50	2.00	2.06	2.00	2.09
markets	(2.07)	(1.00)	(1.12)	(1.41)	(1.49)
Banking crises					
All countries	2.27	2.39	–	3.11	2.62
	(1.03)	(1.46)		(2.45)	(1.86)
Industrial	3.00	2.55	–	3.38	3.11
countries	(1.15)	(1.75)		(2.45)	(2.42)
Emerging	2.00	2.14	–	1.00	2.35
markets	(0.89)	(0.90)		–	(1.50)
Twin crises					
All countries	2.22	2.73	1.00	3.73	3.78
	(2.22)	(1.87)		(2.83)	(2.93)
Industrial	1.00	2.33	–	5.40	5.00
countries	–	(1.37)		(3.51)	(3.29)
Emerging	2.38	4.33	1.00	2.33	3.43
markets	(2.33)	(3.06)		(1.03)	(2.80)
All crises					
All countries	2.35	2.35	1.78	2.64	2.53
	(1.62)	(1.67)	(1.16)	(2.15)	(2.09)
Industrial	2.71	2.26	1.60	2.84	2.71
countries	(1.25)	(1.65)	(1.19)	(2.40)	(2.43)
Emerging	2.25	2.62	2.00	2.09	2.45
markets	(1.73)	(1.76)	(1.12)	(1.14)	(1.92)

Note: Standard deviation in parentheses.

Source: See text.

that rapid resumption at the old parity was actually the exception, not the rule. Argentina after the Baring crisis took nine years to restore convertibility, hardly a case of quick resumption. Even then the paper pesos that had been circulating since 1885 at a large discount to gold were frozen at 2.3 per gold peso, which represented a large effective devaluation. Brazil took 17 years to resume following its 1889 suspension. Greece suspended in 1885 and only resumed in 1910. Italy suspended in 1894 (in this case silver rather than gold had been the circulating medium) and only resumed in 1927. Portugal suspended in 1891 and only resumed in 1931. It is no surprise that rapid resumption did little to shorten the length of currency crises in the emerging markets of the period, since rapid resumption was not the practice.[65]

The major difference between then and now, we would argue, lay not in currency crises *per se* but in banking crises and their tendency to spill over to the currency market. Banking crises, although as frequent then as now, were less prone to undermine confidence in the currency in the countries that were at the core of the gold-standard system. Today, the outbreak of a banking crisis typically leads investors to anticipate that the authorities will engage in large-scale credit creation to bail out the banks. Banking crises undermine currency stability, creating the notorious twin crisis problem (Kaminsky and Reinhart, 1998). This was not the case a century ago at the centre of the gold standard system. Then, banks suspended the convertibility of deposits into currency, currency went to a premium (relative to deposits), and foreign capital – undeterred by exchange risk – flowed in to arbitrage the difference, so long as countries remained on gold (Gorton, 1987). Perhaps the currency went to a discount relative to foreign exchange or the gold parity, but if it did it was expected to recover subsequently; more arbitrage capital flowed in, in anticipation. Banking crises were still a problem – indeed, Table 3.7 suggests that the associated output losses were even larger before 1914 than today – but the frequency of twin crises was less. When twin crises nonetheless occurred as a result of banking-sector distress spilling over to the currency market (mainly in emerging markets, where the credibility of the commitment to gold convertibility was least – namely Argentina), the time to recovery was roughly the same then as now. It was almost exactly the same for the emerging markets in our 21 country sample; the difference in the 21 country averages between the two periods is entirely accounted for by the relatively minor twin crisis in France, as discussed above.

What mattered in the high-gold-standard period, then, was not so much the readiness of the core countries to resume, since they never had an opportunity to display that readiness. With few noteworthy exceptions, they remained on the gold standard throughout. There are a few industrial-country currency crises in the first column of Table 3.9, but these were episodes like 1893 and 1907 where currencies came under pressure but that pressure was successfully resisted.[66] For them, it was the hardness of the peg, not their readiness to suspend and resume, that made the difference, and it made that difference most dramatically when other parts of the financial sector (the banking system in particular) were at risk.[67] Where suspensions did take place and the resumption rule could have been practiced – at the periphery – it was not. It is not surprising, then, that the image of short currency crises under the gold standard is more fable than reality.

6. CONCLUSIONS

This chapter extends a line of research prompted by a question posed to one of the authors by then Deputy Treasury Secretary Lawrence Summers at the height of the Asian crisis. 'You study history. Can you tell us, then, whether the crisis problem is growing more severe?'

The answer, so far as we can determine, is that crises are growing more frequent but not more severe. Relative to the pre-1914 era of financial globalization, crises are twice as prevalent today. This increase in frequency can be traced to the growing incidence of currency crises, which in turn points to the role of the monetary regime. A theme of recent research has been the fragility of soft currency pegs in a world of high capital mobility and democratic politics.[68] Central banks should evacuate this unstable middle ground, it follows, in favor of hard pegs (dollar- or euro-ization) or more flexible rates. It will not surprise readers familiar with our earlier writings that we have considerable sympathy for this view. Nor does it surprise us that the frequency of currency crises is greater today than under the gold standard of a century ago.

But there is less evidence that the output losses from crises are growing or that the time required for recovery is lengthening. The output losses associated with crises, as we measure them, were roughly the same before 1914 as today. And taking all crises together, there is little evidence of an increase between then and now in the time to recovery.

This last finding is troubling in light of the predictions that flow from the resumption rule. Those who emphasize the tendency for central banks and governments, when forced to suspend gold convertibility, to restore it subsequently at the pre-crisis level predict a rapid end to capital flight, the early initiation of stabilizing capital flows, and early economic recovery. There is little evidence of this in the data on the duration of currency crises. Recovery from such crises was not faster before 1914. The explanation is straightforward. In emerging markets, where suspensions were not uncommon, the resumption rule was not practised. And in the industrial world, countries clung tight to the gold standard rather than suspending and resuming subsequently. They only suspended in a national emergency such as a major war. Establishing their commitment to the peg in times of financial difficulty had non-negligible costs, which showed up as recessions. But that commitment at least prevented financial-sector problems from spilling over to the currency market and producing twin crises.

Thus, where 'the pre-1914 system appears to have worked better' (quoting Delargy and Goodhart, 1999, p. 11) was in limiting the tendency for banking problems to destabilize the currency market. Twin crises being a particularly virulent strain, the importance of this achievement should not be underestimated. A very hard currency peg, like that practiced in the countries at the core of the European gold standard in the late 19th century, could thus prevent financial problems arising elsewhere in the economy from also undermining the currency and then feeding back to the rest of the economy in destabilizing ways. Of course, even a very firm commitment to the peg was no guarantee against other financial problems, serious banking-sector problems in particular. This is an important lesson of history for emerging markets today.

NOTES

1. Prepared for the conference in honour of Charles Goodhart, held at the Bank of England, 15–16 November. We thank Forrest Capie for helpful comments and the National Science Foundation for financial support.
2. See Goodhart and Delargy (1998). We also draw on the longer version of this paper (Delargy and Goodhart, 1999) for documentation and citations below.
3. This chapter draws heavily on our previous work on this subject, some of which was done in collaboration with Douglas Irwin, Daniela Klingebiel and Soledad Maria Martinez-Peria.
4. In contrast, Delargy and Goodhart analyze nine pre-1914 crises: Austria and the United States in 1873, Argentina and the US in 1890–91, Australia, Italy and the US in 1893, and Italy and the US in 1907.
5. In particular, there are parallels with the Mexican crisis of 1994–95 as well as with the Asian crisis of 1997–98, as one of us has emphasized previously (Eichengreen, 1999). In contrast, Delargy and Goodhart provide qualitative accounts (in the Appendix to their paper) of each of their nine crisis cases.
6. Garbade and Silber (1978) report that the time required to transmit information between London and New York, which had previously been as long as three weeks, dropped to one day with the inauguration of the cable; by 1914 the time required for cable transmission had fallen to less than a minute. Comparing data on the prices of US bonds in New York and London four months before and after the cable, the authors find a significant decline in the mean absolute difference. There is good reason to think that there were comparable changes when the cable reached Buenos Aires in 1878 and Tokyo in 1900.
7. Maddison (1995), Table 2–4.
8. While this is not a chapter on the 1920s and 1930s, this is the obvious period to point to in order to highlight the difficulties that arise for cultivating and sustaining a high level of international financial transactions when trade is depressed by tariffs, quantitative

restrictions, and macroeconomic problems. A recent treatment of these themes is James (2001).

9. This is the argument for dollarization made today by, *inter alia*, Hausmann et al. (1999), namely, that only by adopting the currency of a creditor country can emerging markets eliminate the currency mismatches that allow exchange-rate changes to become a transmission belt for financial fragility and thus limit access to international capital markets. Evidence that adherence to the gold standard enhanced terms of financial market access can be found in Bordo and Rockoff (1996).

10. See Stone (1999). The role of natural resources as a magnet for British investment is a theme of Clemens and Williamson (2000).

11. Which was equally essential given the decimation of native populations by the immigrants' guns and germs. European immigration was importantly supplemented, of course, by involuntary immigration from Africa, especially to tropical areas where climate was inhospitable and work in plantation agriculture was unattractive to European labour.

12. Industry, in this context, should be understood to include late-19th-century agriculture, which was increasingly mechanized and utilized the hybrid seeds churned out by manufacturing concerns and government agencies. On the natural-resource basis of American industry in this period, see Wright (1990) and Irwin (2000).

13. Clemens and Williamson (2000) refer to this tendency for capital to flow to relatively advanced high-income countries as 'the Lucas Paradox'. Twomey (2000) similarly shows that, after controlling for other determinants of its volume and direction, per capita income in 1913 has a positive, large and statistically-significant effect on the level of capital inflows. This is a different pattern than today, when large amounts of foreign investment go to relatively low-income countries.

14. Each of the seven leading London merchant banking houses established a North American counterpart – Davis and Gallman (2000) refer to them as 'junior partners' – to gather market intelligence and arrange local transactions. The senior partners provided short-term credit to the underwriters and marketed the securities to British investors.

15. See Sylla and Smith (1995).

16. Williams (1920), p. 58.

17. See Flandreau (1998).

18. Clemens and Williamson (2000) refer to this as the 'venerable capital-chased-after-labour explanation'. The extent to which it reflected the derived demand for population-sensitive investment or the reverse flow of information, both of which could have attracted foreign capital, is a topic for future research.

19. This is the so-called 'pecking order' theory of finance, as applied to history by Baskin and Miranti (1997).

20. Rajan and Zingales (1999) describe the pattern but also a number of instances where it was overridden by government intervention.

21. It is even evident within countries, as in the case of the US commercial paper market, which was limited to those parts of the United States where the banking system was sufficiently developed to provide an adequate supply of reputable one-name paper (Davis, 1965).

22. Then as now, a substantial fraction of these flows were short term, which compounds the difficulty of estimating the volume of short-term capital flows and comparing it with today. Bloomfield's (1968) discussion suggests that short-term flows were significantly smaller than long-term flows, in contrast to today: Bank for International Settlements data on turnover in foreign exchange markets suggest that gross flows are in the range of $1.25 trillion a day, or more than $250 trillion a year, much larger than corresponding figures for long-term capital flows.

23. Including by Delargy and Goodhart themselves.

24. So too can other factors, although this takes us away from our story. America's transcontinental railways were built only once, in this period. Private as well as social returns on railway investment were attractive. The dominance of infrastructure investment and railway investment in particular in the capital flows of this period cannot be overstated.

Twomey (2000) finds that 'railroadization' (kilometres of railroads in operation divided by GDP) was a significant determinant of both total and portfolio capital inflows in this period and even stimulated complementary FDI.

25. Davis and Gallman (2000), focusing on the '19th-century emerging markets' (Argentina, Australia, Canada and U.S.), find that nine of every ten pounds of British investment in between 1865 and 1890 went into railroads and government bonds. According to their estimates, the fraction ranges from 86 per cent in Australia to 92 per cent in Canada. Davis and Huttenback (1986) provide comparisons with domestic investment in quoted securities. Their Chart 2.8 confirms the picture of a pattern of overseas portfolio investment concentrated in agricultural and extractive activities (especially in the Empire), in transportation, and in public utilities. Domestic portfolio investment, in contrast, was disproportionately concentrated in manufacturing and in the commercial and financial sectors.

26. Freestanding companies, in the words of Wilkins (1998, p. 13), 'were structured to solve the problem posed earlier; business abroad was risky; it was hard to obtain adequate and reliable information about firms in distant lands; returns were unpredictable; but there were clearly opportunities abroad; a company organized within the source-of-capital country, with a responsible board of directors, under source-of-capital country law, to mobilize capital (and other assets) and to conduct the business in foreign countries could take advantage of the opportunities, while reducing the transaction costs by providing a familiar conduit.'

27. While there were incentives not to build ahead of demand, it was also important not to allow potential competitors to preempt the market. Thus, railroads attempted to collude, holding off from building in advance of settlement and cultivation, but to jump in and preempt the most attractive markets as soon as there were signs of the collusive agreement breaking down. Hence, railroad construction tended to cluster in time, as did the external finance needed to underwrite it.

28. Argentina again became important in the period 1901–13, investment there having been forestalled by the financial crisis that set in after 1889.

29. This suggests that contagion due to herding may have been less of a problem a century ago. Historical evidence on this question is scant. The two studies of which we are aware, Bordo and Murshid (2001) and Mauro, Sussman and Yafeh (2000), reach opposing conclusions. Bordo and Murshid observe that the correlation of asset returns across markets (both advanced and emerging) rises in turbulent periods and ask whether this tendency has been growing stronger in recent years (compared to the earlier period 1880–1914). They find scant evidence of this; to the contrary, their findings point in the other direction, to a declining tendency for cross-market correlations to rise in turbulent periods. Mauro, Sussman and Yafeh study the co-movement of emerging market spreads in the two periods of financial globalization, 1870–1913 and the 1990s. They find that country-specific events played a larger role in the determination of spreads in the earlier period, while global conditions play a larger role today. This is suggestive of a growing role for common shocks, common policies, or contagion.

30. Fishlow cites Munhall's reference to the large equalizing sum on the Egyptian public accounts for 'ballet dancers, etc.'

31. *The Bankers' Magazine* (May 1890), p. 776.

32. Two partial correctives are Flandreau (2000) and Bordo and Flandreau (2001).

33. See Appendix 3A.1 for our chronology of crises and business cycle turning points, based on a bandpass filter of real GDP as described in Bordo et al. (2001).

34. In addition, we construct an index of exchange market pressure, calculated as a weighted average of the percentage change in the exchange rate, the change in the short-term interest rate, and the percentage change in reserves, all relative to the same variables in the centre country. A crisis is said to occur when this index exceeds one and a half standard deviations above its mean. We count an episode as a currency crisis when it shows up according to either or both of these indicators.

35. This allows us to distinguish between pre-1914 crises in which lender of last resort intervention was either absent or unsuccessful, and subsequent crises in which a lender

of last resort or deposit insurance was in place, and the main problem was bank insolvency as opposed to illiquidity. This generalization is not to deny that a number of banking crises occurring in Europe in earlier years did not involve panics and in this respect were not dissimilar from episodes occurring more recently.

36. The complete comparison is in our earlier article (Bordo et al., 2001).
37. While the frequency of banking crises was strikingly similar in 1880–1913 and 1973–98, the interwar and Bretton Woods periods are strikingly different, the former for the absence of banking crises (there was in fact one episode of banking instability in the sample, in Brazil in 1964, which is recorded as a twin crisis), the latter for the exceptional frequency of banking-sector problems (primarily in the Great Depression of the 1930s).
38. Others (for example McKinnon, 1997) would also point to the absence of large swings in the bilateral exchange rates of the creditor countries, analogous to today's dollar–euro and dollar–yen swings, as an aspect of this international financial system that was conducive to currency stability in the developing world.
39. 'Growth in our pre-1914 crisis countries was generally high on average in the five years preceding the crises, and it fell fairly sharply in the five years following the crises' (Delargy and Goodhart, 1999, p. 16).
40. Eichengreen (1999), p. 261. Saving is calculated as the current account balance minus investment. The comparison is between 1884–86 and 1887–89.
41. The stage was set for the debt crisis of the 1980s, for example, by lax monetary policies in the industrial core followed by the sharp interest-rate increases of the 'Volcker shock'. Calvo, Leiderman and Reinhart (1993) similarly showed that the resumption of capital flows to emerging markets in the early 1990s was stimulated by the decline in interest rates in Japan, Europe and the United States, and famously predicted that financial difficulties would develop when this trend was reversed. Eichengreen and Rose (2000) show that rising interest rates and declining growth rates in the industrial core were, in this same period, significant predictors of the probability of banking crises.
42. Bailey (1959), p. 252.
43. Wirth (1893), p. 227. The tendency for low interest rates to inflate a financial bubble is also clear in this episode. In the words of *The Economist* (2 August 1890, p. 984), 'Reckless borrowing and lavish expenditure have been the order of the day both within the Governments and with the people, and the readiness with which European investors have responded to the never-ending appeals for new loans has done little to credit their intelligence. But the speculative bubble has now been pricked . . .'.
44. *Bankers' Magazine* (1893), cited in Delargy and Goodhart (1999), pp. 2–3.
45. *The Economist* (9 August 1890, p. 1018) writes of lending under the presidency of Dr Juarez Celman that 'Dr Celman had been President all through the great boom in Argentine finance, and was credited generally in Buenos Ayres with having played into his own hands and those of his friends after the most bare-faced fashion. Indeed, he was openly classed amongst the "robbers" of his country'.
46. *Bankers' Magazine* (May 1890), p. 777.
47. Wirth (1893), p. 219.
48. *The Statist* 26 (5 July 1890), pp. 15–16.
49. Here, clearly, is an important parallel with the Asian crisis that cannot be overemphasized.
50. The present sample of 32, we believe, is more representative. By these measures, the fall in output in the recent Asian crises was especially steep: Korea's growth rate declined 7 percentage points below its pre-crisis five-year-average growth rate, 8 percentage points below its three year pre-crisis average and 7 percentage points from the year preceding the crisis. Indonesia's performance was similar, while Thailand's was the worst (at minus 13, 13, 11 percentage points respectively). The severity of these countries' crises in 1997–87 is well known; the point here is that their recessions were dramatic relative to the typical crisis in emerging markets prior to 1914. Turning from typical to exceptional, how does recent Asian experience compare with the worst of the pre-1914 era? The two most infamous pre-World War I crises in emerging markets, the US in 1893 and Argentina in 1890, were even worse than Asia in recent years. For the US, growth during

the crisis years declined by 9 percentage points relative to its previous five-year trend, 12 percentage points below its three-year pre-crisis trend, and 14 percentage points from the pre-crisis year. For Argentina the numbers are even more dramatic if the conventional statistics are to be believed: minus 17 per cent, 20 per cent, 24 per cent, with recovery in growth not complete after 5 years. The exceptional severity of these episodes should serve as a warning that generalizations about the pre-1914 period must be drawn cautiously, since that period appears to have featured a small number of extraordinarily severe crises along with numerous milder episodes.

51. The output loss is calculated as the sum of the differences between actual GDP growth and the five year average preceding the crisis until growth returns to trend. Obviously, there is no single or, for that matter, best way of measuring output losses. In previous work (for example Bordo and Eichengreen, 1999; Bordo, Eichengreen, and Irwin, 1999), we have used somewhat different measures, obtaining rather different results. While this underscores our point about the sensitivity of these calculations to method, we would also argue that the estimates presented here are more reliable than those we have published previously, for many of the reasons argued in IMF (1998). (That successive revisions produce changes is disconcerting, but this is how progress occurs in the social sciences.) Mulder and Rocha (2000) argue that the approach used here will overstate the output loss because pre-crisis growth tends to be unsustainably high, rendering it an inappropriate basis for comparison. They also observe that truncating the calculation at the point where the growth rate returns to trend will understate the loss because the level of output, as distinct from the growth rate, remains depressed for several subsequent years. Using a Hodrick–Prescott filter to estimate the trend, they obtain output losses for the 1973–98 period that are a multiple of ours. However, some of their other estimates yield smaller losses for emerging markets than those reported here. It will be evident that these alternatives are no less problematic than the present method. Adjustments to the pre-crisis growth rate are arbitrary. And truncating the calculation at, say, the point where growth returns to the level extrapolated from some pre-crisis trend rather than at the point where the growth rate recovers to its pre-crisis rate implies the equally arbitrary assumption that the level of output is invariant with respect to the crisis, even over short periods. Fortunately, there is no reason to think that these biases are more severe in one period than another. Since we are primarily concerned with intertemporal comparisons, in other words, such biases are likely to be of less moment here than in other applications. Note that sample averages are accompanied by their standard deviations. These again underscore the difficulty of making valid generalizations about the severity of crises. Previous authors have emphasized the heterogeneity of business cycles. The same, evidently, is true of crises.

52. In addition to the large standard deviations surrounding these estimates, it is worth recalling the problem of spurious volatility that may infect retrospective estimates of GDP for earlier historical periods (Romer, 1989). Insofar as estimates for these earlier periods are spuriously volatile and the most volatile cycles are those accompanied by crises, there may be a tendency to exaggerate prewar output losses.

53. See Bordo et al. (2001), Table 1.

54. Bordo and Eichengreen (1999), Figure 1.

55. Interestingly, we would classify two of these three cases (Italy in 1893 and 1907) as twin crises.

56. The contrast between pre- and post-crisis interest rates is particularly evident in the case of currency crises.

57. The data are for M2. The pattern for all crises is, of course, a weighted average of that foreign banking and currency crises. There is some evidence of an acceleration in M2 growth following currency crises, as if countries freed of the constraints of the gold standard followed less stringent monetary policies, while M2 growth decelerates following banking crises, presumably reflecting a shift out of deposits.

58. See for example Bordo and Kydland (1995).

59. McKinnon (1997), pp. 518–19.

60. Or so it is argued. This notion is implicit in the advice of authors like Hanke that crisis

countries suffering currency depreciation like Indonesia in 1998 should push their currencies back up to pre-crisis levels. See, *inter alia*, Hanke (1998).
61. Delargy and Goodhart (1999), pp. 8–9.
62. It may be that this conclusion is sensitive to how recovery time is measured. For example, if the credit booms that preceded currency crises were more pronounced in the pre-1914 period, so too could have been the unsustainable acceleration of pre-crisis economic growth, making the re-achievement of that pre-crisis rate of growth a more demanding standard. In fact, however, the estimates in Table 3.9 differ from those of other studies (namely IMF, 1998) by calculating the pre-crisis trend over a longer period (five years versus three years in the IMF study), which will tend to moderate the impact of any transitory pre-crisis domestic boom. On the other hand, it could be that the depressing effect on the macroeconomy of the persistent deflation needed to push the currency back up to pre-crisis levels could have swamped any beneficial effects of the early stabilization and reversal of capital flight. This would likely be the interpretation favored by the critics of Britain's post-World War I return to gold.
63. Note that all of our pre-1913 currency crises were in countries on the gold standard, so the statistic in Table 3.9 is the relevant one. Not only was recovery in fact slower to commence than after 1972, but it was also slower to commence than in the two other periods considered in Table 3.9 (1919–39 and 1945–71).
64. See Bordo and Eichengreen (1999).
65. Bordo and Schwartz (1996) provide more detail on these cases.
66. Resisting these pressures was not costless; post-currency-crisis recessions in the industrial countries prior to 1914 were large, although here there may be special reason to worry that what we are picking up is the tendency for recessions to cause crises rather than for crises to cause recessions. We discuss (and attempt to correct) for this simultaneity problem in Bordo et al. (2001).
67. It is not surprising that countries grew increasingly reluctant, as the century progressed, to suspend and resume when their currencies came under pressure. Willingness to suspend implied the existence of an exchange-rate escape clause. But when the authorities' priorities are uncertain (it is not clear when and whether they will suspend), the existence of an escape clause becomes potentially destabilizing (Obstfeld, 1997). Hence, their gold standard commitment grew increasingly rigid, rendering temporary suspensions rare to nonexistent in the industrial world.
68. See *inter alia* Eichengreen (1996).

REFERENCES

Bailey, J.D. (1959), 'Australian Borrowing in Scotland in the Nineteenth Century', *Economic History Review*, 12, 268–79.
Baskin, Jonathan and Paul Miranti, Jr. (1997), *A History of Corporate Finance*, Cambridge: Cambridge University Press.
Bloomfield, Arthur I. (1968), *Patterns of Fluctuation in International Finance Before 1914*, Princeton Studies in International Finance no. 21, International Finance Section, Department of Economics, Princeton University.
Bordo, Michael and Barry Eichengreen (1999), 'Is Our Current International Economic Environment Unusually Crisis Prone?', in David Gruen and Luke Gower (eds), *Capital Flows and the International Financial System*, Sydney: Reserve Bank of Australia, pp. 18–75.
Bordo, Michael and Marc Flandreau (2001), 'Core, Periphery, Exchange Rate Regimes and Globalization', NBER Working Paper no. 8584.
Bordo, Michael and Finn Kydland (1995), 'The Gold Standard as a Contingent Rule', *Explorations in Economic History*, 32, 423–64.

Bordo, Michael and Antu Murshid (2001), 'Are Financial Crises Becoming More Contagious: What is the Historical Evidence on Contagion?', in Stijn Claessens and Kristin J. Forbes (eds), *International Financial Contagion*, Boston: Kluwer, pp. 367–403.

Bordo, Michael and Hugh Rockoff (1996), 'The Gold Standard as a Good-Housekeeping Seal of Approval', *Journal of Economic History*, 56, 389–428.

Bordo, Michael and Anna Schwartz (1996), 'The Operation of the Specie Standard: Evidence for Core and Peripheral Countries', in Jorge Braga de Macedo, Barry Eichengreen and Jaime Reis (eds), *Currency Convertibility: The Gold Standard and Beyond*, London: Routledge, pp. 11–86.

Bordo, Michael, Barry Eichengreen and Douglas Irwin (1999), 'Is Globalization Today Really Different from Globalization a Hundred Years Ago?', *Brookings Trade Policy Forum 1999*, 1–73.

Bordo, Michael, Barry Eichengreen, Daniela Klingebiel and Soledad Maria Martinez Peria (2001), 'Is the Crisis Problem Growing More Severe?', *Economic Policy*, 24, 51–82.

Calvo, Guillermo and Enrique Mendoza (2000), 'Rational Herding and the Globalization of Financial Markets', *Journal of International Economics*, 51, 79–114.

Calvo, Guillermo, Leo Leiderman and Carmen Reinhart (1993), 'Capital Inflows and Real Exchange Rate Appreciation in Latin America', *Staff Papers*, 30, 108–31.

Clemens, Michael and Jeffrey Williamson (2000), 'Where Did British Foreign Capital Go? Fundamentals, Failures and the Lucas Paradox, 1870–1913', NBER Working Paper no. 8028 (December).

Davis, Lance (1965), 'The Investment Market, 1870–1914: The Evolution of a National Market', *Journal of Economic History*, 25, 355–93.

Davis, Lance and Robert Gallman (2000), *Waves, Tides and Sandcastles: the Impact of Capital Flows on Evolving Financial Markets in the New World, 1865–1914*, Cambridge: Cambridge University Press.

Davis, Lance and Robert Huttenback (1986), *Mammon and the Pursuit of Empire: The Political Economy of British Imperialism, 1860–1912*, Cambridge: Cambridge University Press, pp. 1–29.

Delargy, P.J.R. and Charles Goodhart (1999), 'Financial Crises: Plus ca change, plus c'est la meme chose', Special Paper no. 108, LSE Financial Markets Group (January).

Eichengreen, Barry (1992), *Golden Fetters: The Gold Standard and the Great Depression, 1919–1939*, New York: Oxford University Press.

Eichengreen, Barry (1996), *Globalizing Capital: A History of the International Monetary System*, Princeton: Princeton University Press.

Eichengreen, Barry (1999), 'The Baring Crisis in a Mexican Mirror', *International Political Science Review*, 20, 249–70.

Eichengreen, Barry and Andrew Rose (2000), 'Staying Afloat When the Wind Shifts: External Factors and Emerging-Market Banking Crises', in Guillermo Calvo, Rudiger Dornbusch and Maurice Obstfeld (eds), *Money, Capital Mobility and Trade: Essays in Honor of Robert Mundell*, Cambridge, Mass.: MIT Press, pp. 171–206.

Feis, Herbert (1930), *Europe, the World's Banker*, New Haven: Yale University Press.

Fishlow, Albert (1986), 'Lessons from the Past: Capital Markets During the 19th

Century and the Interwar Period', in Miles Kahler (ed.), *The Politics of International Debt*, Ithaca: Cornell University Press, pp. 37–94.

Flandreau, Marc (1998), 'Caveat Emptor: Coping with Sovereign Risk, 1870–1914', CEPR Discussion Paper no. 2004.

Flandreau, Marc (2000), 'Crime and Punishment: Moral Hazard and the Pre-1914 International Financial Architecture', unpublished manuscript, OFCE.

Garbade, Kenneth D. and William L. Silber (1978), 'Technology, Communication, and the Performance of Financial Markets, 1840–1975', *Journal of Finance*, 33, 819–32.

Goodhart, Charles (1969), *The New York Money Market and the Finance of Trade 1900–1913*, Cambridge, Mass.: Harvard University Press.

Goodhart, Charles (1972), *The Business of Banking, 1891–1914*, London: Weidenfeld and Nicolson.

Goodhart, Charles (1988), *The Evolution of Central Banks*, Cambridge, Mass.: MIT Press.

Goodhart, Charles and P.J.R. Delargy (1998), 'Financial Crises: Plus ca change, plus c'est la meme chose', *International Finance*, 1, 261–87.

Gorton, Gary (1987), 'Bank Suspension of Convertibility', *Journal of Monetary Economics*, 15, 177–93.

Hanke, Steve (1998), 'How to Establish Monetary Stability in Asia', *Cato Journal*, 17, 295–301.

Hausmann, Ricardo, M. Gavin, C. Pages-Serra and E. Stein (1999), 'Financial Turmoil and the Choice of Exchange Rate Regime', unpublished manuscript, Inter-American Development Bank.

International Monetary Fund (1998), *World Economic Outlook*, Washington, DC: IMF (May).

Irwin, Douglas (2000), 'How Did the United States Become a Net Exporter of Manufactured Goods?', NBER Working Paper no. 7638 (April).

James, Harold (2001), *The End of Globalization*, Cambridge, Mass.: Harvard University Press.

Kaminsky, Graciela and Carmen Reinhart (1998), 'The Twin Crises: The Causes of Banking and Balance-of-Payments Problems', *American Economic Review*, 89, 473–500.

Kindleberger, Charles P. (1978), *Manias, Panics and Crashes: A History of Financial Crises*, New York: Basic Books.

Maddison, Angus (1995), *Monitoring the World Economy 1820–1992*, Paris: OECD.

Mauro, Paolo, Nathan Sussman and Yishay Yafeh (2000), 'Emerging Market Spreads: Then Versus Now,' IMF Working Paper WP/00/190 (November).

McKinnon, Ronald (1997), *The Rules of the Game*, Cambridge, Mass.: MIT Press.

Mercer, Lloyd (1974), 'Building Ahead of Demand: Some Evidence for the Land Grant Railroads', *Journal of Economic History*, 34, 492–500.

Mulder, Christian and Manuel Rocha (2000), 'The Soundness of Estimates of Output Losses in Currency Crises', unpublished manuscript, IMF.

Obstfeld, Maurice (1977), 'Destabilizing Effects of Exchange Rate Escape Clauses', *Journal of International Economics*, 43, 61–77.

O'Rourke, Kevin and Jeffrey Williamson (1999), *Globalization and History*, Cambridge, Mass.: MIT Press.

Rajan, Raghuram and Luigi Zingales (1999), 'The Great Reversals: The Politics of Financial Development in the 20th Century', unpublished manuscript, University of Chicago.

Romer, Christina (1989), 'Prewar Business Cycles Reconsidered: New Estimates of Gross National Product 1869–1918', *Journal of Political Economy*, 97, 1–37.

Stone, Irving (1999), *The Global Export of Capital from Great Britain, 1865–1914*, London: Macmillan.

Sylla, Richard and George David Smith (1995), 'Information and Capital Market Regulation in Anglo-American Finance', in Michael Bordo and Richard Sylla (eds), *Anglo-American Financial Systems*, New York: Irwin, pp. 170–206.

Twomey, Michael J. (2000), *A Century of Foreign Investment in the Third World*, London: Routledge.

Wilkins, Mira (1998), 'Conduits for Long-Term Investment in the Gold Standard Era', unpublished manuscript, Florida International University.

Williams, John H. (1920), *Argentine International Trade Under Inconvertible Paper Money, 1880–1900*, Cambridge, Mass.: Harvard University Press.

Wirth, Max (1893), 'The Crisis of 1890', *Journal of Political Economy*, 1, 214–35.

World Bank (2000), *Global Development Finance 2000*, Washington, DC: The World Bank.

Wright, Gavin (1990), 'The Origins of American Industrial Success, 1879–1940', *American Economic Review*, 80, 651–68.

APPENDIX 3A.1   CRISES DATES AND BUSINESS CYCLE TURNING POINTS

A: 1880–1913

Date	Argentina	Belgium	Brazil	Canada	Chile	Denmark	Finland	France	Germany	Greece	Italy	Japan	Netherlands	Norway	Portugal	Spain	Sweden	Switzerland	UK	USA
1883													T							
1884		T																		
1885	CC					BC		P												BC
1886							T			CC				T				P	P	T
1887	T			T	CC	T		T	P				P		T	P	P	P		
1888		P			T		CC	P			T				P		T		T	
1889	P	BC, CC		P				P,BC	T			T		P		T				
1890	BC, CC	BC		P							BC			P	BC, CC		P	P	BC	CC
1891	BC			CC	P								T		T					P,CC
1892	T								P		P	P								
1893	T,BC			CC		T	T	T	BC		BC	P				P	T	T	P	P,BC
1894	P								CC		CC			T		T				CC
1895													P			P				T

Notes: BC represents banking crises, CC represents currency crises, P represents business cycle peaks, T represents business cycle troughs. No entries are shown for Belgium and Greece because of missing data.

B: 1919–1939

Date	Argentina	Australia	Belgium	Brazil	Canada	Chile	Denmark	Finland	France	Germany	Greece	Italy	Japan	Netherlands	Norway	Portugal	Spain	Sweden	Switzerland	UK	USA
1913																					
1914																					
1915					T		T		T									T	T		T
1916				T	T			P				P	P	P	P	P	P	P	P	P	P
1917		T											T	T	T				P		
1918	T		P	P	P	P		T				T				P		P			P
1919		T			T				T			T	T			T					T
1920	P	T			CC		T,BC	P,BC, CC				BC	P,CC	P,BC	P,BC	T,BC	BC	P	T	T	T
1921	T			T	CC	BC	CC							CC	BC						
1922		T					CC		T					CC	T,BC						
1923	P	P,CC	BC	P	P	P	P	T	CC			P		BC	BC	BC	P	T	T		P
1924		BC	P	P	T	BC	P	P	P			P		T	P	P	BC			P	
1925	T	BC	BC	T	BC		T	T				T				T	T,BC				
1926		T	T	P	T	P	T	T	CC	T		P	T,BC	T	T	T				T	T
1927	P								T	T		P	T,BC			T,BC					
1928										P		P									
1929	P,CC		P	CC	P,CC	P	P	P	P	P		BC	P	P	P	P	P	P	P	P	P
1930	CC			CC	P,CC	P	P	BC	BC	P		BC		P	P			P	P	P	BC

84

1931	BC, CC	T	BC	CC	CC	CC	BC, CC, CC	BC, CC	T,BC, CC	BC, T,BC, CC	BC, CC	T,BC, BC	CC	BC, CC	BC, CC, T	BC, CC, T	BC, CC, BC, CC	BC, CC	BC	CC	BC	BC
1932	T,CC	CC	T	T	T	T,BC	T,BC	CC	T	CC	T	T		BC	T	BC, CC	T	T	T	T	BC
1933	CC		T		T,BC	BC	CC	T		T			T				T	T,BC, CC	
1934	BC	T,BC, CC		P	CC	CC											
1935	P	CC	P	P	P	P	BC, CC	T,CC	T,CC	CC	P	P	P	
1936		P	P	P	T	T,CC	T			P	T	T,CC	P	P
1937	P	CC	P	CC	P	CC	P		P	T	T	P	T	
1938	T	CC	P	P		T			P	P, CC	BC, CC	T	
1939	T	BC	T	BC			P	PC	T	P, CC	T	P,CC	T

Notes: BC represents banking crises, CC represents currency crises, P represents business cycle peaks, T represents business cycle troughs. Missing entries for business cycle turning points during and after World War I reflect the absence of GDP data.

85

C: 1940–1971

Date	Argentina	Australia	Belgium	Brazil	Canada	Chile	Denmark	Finland	France	Germany	Greece	Italy	Japan	Netherlands	Norway	Portugal	Spain	Sweden	Switzerland	UK	USA
1940	P		T					T						P		P	P				
1941		P		T	T	T	T						T	P		P	T	T	P	P	
1942	T				P	P		P					P	T		T	P	T	T		P
1943																					
1944	T	T	T	P	T	P	P	T,CC	P	CC	T	P	T	P	T	P	P	P	P	T	T
1945				T		T		CC	P	CC	P		P,T	CC	CC	P	T	CC	P	CC	
1946										P	CC	T		T					T	CC	
1947											T	P	T	T	P,CC		T		P	P	T
1948	P	P,CC	P	CC	T	T	P	T	T	T	P	T	P		T	T	T	T	T		P
1949	CC	T,CC	P	P	CC			CC		P			P	CC		P	P	CC	P	CC	
1950						P,CC											T,P		T	P	
1951	T		T	T	P	T		P	T	T		T	T	T	T	T	P	T	P	T	P
1952		T																			
1953		P	P	T	T	T	P	P	T	P	T	P	P	P	P	P	T	T	P	T	T
1954			P	P			T	P	P	P	P				P	P	P	P		T	P
1955			P			P								P		T	P	P	P	P	P
1956	P					P	P	P	CC												
1957								T									CC				
1958										T		T					T	T	T	T	

86

1959	CC		T	CC					T	T	T		T
1960		T						P			P		P,CC
1961	CC		T		P		T		T	P	T	T	
1962	CC	T,CC	CC	P,CC		P	T	P	P	P	P	P	T
1963	T	BC, CC			T	T		T	T				
1964				T							CC	CC	CC
1965	P	P,CC			P	CC	P		P	T	P	P,CC	P,CC
1966	P		P							P		CC	CC
1967	CC	T	T	P	T		T	T	T	T,CC	P,CC	T,CC	T,CC
1968	T		CC	P	T					T			P
1969	CC		T									P	
1970												T	T
1971	T,CC	CC	T	CC	CC	CC	P	CC	CC	T,CC	CC	CC	CC

Notes: BC represents banking crises, CC represents currency crises, P represents business cycle peaks, T represents business cycle troughs. Missing entries for business cycle turning points during and after World War II reflect the absence of GDP data.

87

D: 1972–1998

Date	Argentina	Australia	Austria	Bangladesh	Belgium	Brazil	Canada	Chile	Columbia	Costa Rica	Denmark	Ecuador	Egypt	Finland	France	Germany	Greece	Hong Kong	Iceland	India	Indonesia	Ireland	Israel	Italy	Jamaica
1972	P				P			P							P	P	P						P	P	
1973		P									T				P	P									
1974	CC		P				P	CC			P		CC	P					CC		CC				
1975			P, CC	CC		P	P	CC	T	T	T, CC	CC					CC	T	CC		CC				
1976	T, CC		T				T	T, BC	T	T	T				T	T	T	T	T		T	T, CC		CC	CC
1977	T	T	T			T	CC	CC	T	T	T, CC	P	P		T	BC	T	T	CC		T	CC	BC, CC	T	CC
1978			P					P	P	P		CC			P	P	P		CC	P	CC		T	CC	
1979	P		CC	CC		P	P	P, CC	P	P			CC		P	P	P	P	P	P	CC	P	P	CC	CC
1980	BC		T, CC	T, CC	P	P	CC BC	P, BC				BC	T, CC		P	P	P	P	P	T, P	P	P	P	P	T, CC
1981					CC		CC BC	CC		CC		BC	BC					CC	CC			CC			
1982	CC						CC		BC	T	T	CC						BC	P	P	CC				CC
1983	T, CC					T	T	T	T	T	T		T	P	T	T	T, CC	BC, CC					T, P	T	T
1984	CC		P				P	T, CC			P, CC						CC	T, CC					T		T
1985	BC	CC	P T								T, CC														T

1986

1987 P, CC   T BC   P, CC   CC   P   P   T, BC P   P   P   T   CC CC   P, CC

1988   T   BC BC   P   P   T, CC   T, CC   P   T P   T T   P

1989 BC, CC T   T   P   CC   T   T   P   P   P   P T   P T   P T   CC CC

1990 T   P BC, CC   T   BC CC   P   T, CC P, CC BC   P, CC BC   P   P   T   P, BC CC

1991 CC   P   T   CC   P T T P   T, CC   BC, CC CC   P   T   CC CC   CC

1992   T   CC T T   T, CC   BC, CC   P   P   BC CC CC   T

1993 P   T   T, CC P   T, CC   T, BC   T   T T   P

1994   BC   P   P   T   P   T P T   CC   P

1995 BC, CC CC   T P   T P   P   T   P   T P   P P   P, BC BC, CC CC BC, CC

1996

1997 T T   P   T   P   T   P   T   P   P P, CC   T T

1998 P   P   CC   T   P   CC   T   P   P   T   CC   T

D: 1972–1998 (continued)

Date	Japan	Korea	Malaysia	Mexico	Netherlands	New Zealand	Nigeria	Norway	Pakistan	Paraguay	Peru	Philippines	Portugal	Singapore	South Africa	Spain	Sri Lanka	Sweden	Switzerland	Taiwan	Thailand	Turkey	UK	Uruguay	US	Venezuela	Zimbabwe
1972						P								P					P						P		
1973									P														P		P		
1974																											
1975		CC	CC	CC		P, CC	P	P	T	P	P, CC				P, CC	P		P			T			CC			CC
1976	T	T	CC	T								T	T, CC	T						T			T, CC	CC	T		
1977									T		CC	T, CC	CC		BC		BC, CC		T, CC			P, CC					
1978	P			T		CC					T	CC	CC		T, CC					T						P	T
1979	CC					P		P	P	CC					T, CC		CC	P		P	P	CC	P	CC	P		
1980	P	CC				T, CC	P, CC		P						P, CC				P		P			P		BC	
1981		T	P, BC						P	P	P			BC	P, CC						T	T		BC	P		P, BC
1982			CC									P, CC		BC	CC				T	T, BC	CC	BC	BC				BC
1983	P	CC	T					T			BC, CC	CC, CC	CC	P	CC, CC			T	T	BC		T, CC	T, CC	CC	CC	BC	CC

90

1984			CC					CC	T				T		CC			CC								CC
1985	T	BC	CC	P	T	CC	T	CC	T	T			BC			P	T	P	CC	T	BC	CC	T		
1986				P	CC			CC	T, CC			CC	P		P		T	P	CC	CC	T, CC				
1987		T	T	BC		P				T					T		P		P						
1988			T	CC	CC				P, CC			P	CC	P		P			P	P	T, CC				
1989	P									T, BC						P		T			P, CC				
1990	P	P	CC	P		T	CC		CC	CC	P				P		T		T						
1991					BC, CC		T				BC		P		BC, CC										
1992	BC		P	CC	T				CC	CC	CC	T			P	T, CC		T	P	T	P	CC			
1993		T	T			CC				T	T				P					P		BC	T		
1994		BC, CC, CC	T		CC					T	P		BC, CC		BC, CC						CC	T			
1995				P		CC	BC	P		T	P	CC	CC		BC	P	T, CC				CC				
1996		P	P	T					P					P							CC		T		
1997		BC, CC, CC	T		CC			T	P		CC		P	T	BC, CC	P		P	T	P	T				
1998		BC, BC, CC, CC	P	P	T		P	T	BC	CC			T		BC, CC		P	P	P						

Notes: BC represents banking crises, CC represents currency crises, P represents business cycle peaks, T represents business cycle troughs.

Discussion of 'Charles Goodhart's contributions to the history of monetary institutions' and 'Crises now and then'

Forrest Capie

I am delighted to be part of this tribute. I must begin by saying that Charles on occasions describes himself as a monetary historian, and this can be a bit dispiriting for the rest of us monetary historians, since he knows more about money, monetary theory, monetary policy, and monetary practice. We can only thank David Ricardo for comparative advantage that allows us to carry on doing something moderately useful.

Bordo and Schwartz have demonstrated the huge contribution to the subject Charles has made by focusing on just one strand in his portfolio of interests, the history of monetary institutions, with a heavy concentration on the Bank of England's role in the financial system over time. In this field as in others his early interests have proved lasting and are almost invariably the big issues of today. In the football commentator's cliché Bordo and Schwartz have produced a chapter of two halves. The first surveys Charles's earlier writing, and the second raises some large areas of serious disagreement with his more recent work. There are many interesting questions in the early research some of which remain unresolved and are still provoking research, but it is their criticisms of his views on the role of the central bank in relation to the banking system that are of chief interest. These views derive in part from his earlier work.

They argue that Charles holds distinctive views. He sees commercial banks as inherently unstable and imprudent lenders and investors, and believes that regulation can prevent imprudent behaviour and avoid banking crises. Further, banks exhibit herd-type behaviour that leads to financial crises. The authors are diametrically opposed to this, arguing instead that it is unstable monetary policy and bad regulatory action that produces unstable banks. They also reject Charles's view of the lender of last resort and what it entails for the insolvency/illiquidity, too-big-to-fail, and related issues. On these points they seem to me to be convincing. When Bagehot's teachings prevailed there was great stability; when ignored there was much less stability. They say that Charles accepts the new buzz phrase 'creative ambiguity' – I think he might even have invented it – and yet pre-commitment to the market as a whole did seem to work well. All this culminates in their conclusion that, 'Charles passes judgement neither on central banks nor regulator behaviour. Whatever they do is deemed to be right conduct' (p. 18).

Bordo and Schwartz suggest that they bring to this an American perspective. But there is something slightly puzzling in this. On an occasion such as this it does not seem out of place to try to understand better the subject of the Festschrift. Charles spent a very formative part of his early life in the US and returned there to do his first major research – on American institutions, and has other connections there. I wonder quite what his perspective is. But if it is British then more interestingly, why, given what seems to me to be overwhelming evidence from British experience does he hold these views to the extent that he does? That evidence is that English banks, after a long learning process found their own way to extremely prudent behaviour (before regulators were invented – though admittedly with considerable guidance from the Scots). The story can be told in terms of ever less regulation going with ever greater stability. In fact a principal criticism of British banks that has been running from the late nineteenth century is that from an early date they were overly cautious. Further, there was the fact that the Bank of England had developed over the same period as a lender of last resort in the Thornton/Joplin/Bagehot sense. Together, prudent banks and a lender of last resort, produced remarkable stability and long before there was any sign of a cartel that could claim any credit.

To what extent though are Bordo and Schwartz exaggerating Charles's views for the sake of sharpening the focus? There were points at which I wondered if he did hold the views they claimed. For example, that central bank independence ended in 1914 rather than in the great depression. I thought he happily inclined to the latter as he and I once jointly wrote. Independence did disappear in World War I but was desired and restored after that (Capie et al., 1994, p. 53). But more importantly, in his most recent paper there is some evidence of doubt on regulation. To paraphrase, he says there is the danger of banking regulation worsening matters, making the system more prone to crisis, and asks, 'what then is the point of this huge regulatory edifice, with its ever increasing complexity and use of resources?' (Goodhart, 2001, p. 13). Might it be that when there is too much agreement and a sign of a bandwagon appearing Charles develops reservations?

Eichengreen and Bordo set out to do something quite different, in order to answer the question: are crises worse now than they were then? This picks up on the Delargy and Goodhart paper, a principal finding of which was that recovery from crises was faster in the period before 1914 than in recent crises; something they attributed to the nature of the gold standard and the commitment to it. Eichengreen and Bordo examine a large number of countries in four periods: 1880–1913; interwar; Bretton Woods; and post-Bretton Woods; with the main comparison being between the first and last. Their conclusions differ from Delargy and Goodhart; they find that crises are now more frequent, but not more severe, and that recovery from currency crises was not faster under the gold standard. Now Eichengreen says quibbling over detail is how progress is made in history so we are about to make some progress.

A first problem is definition and the two parties disagree over this with Eichengreen and Bordo reclassifying some of Delargy and Goodhart's currency crises as twin crises. This makes for serious difficulty. Some of the difference also lies in the choice of countries. In measuring severity different measures of output are used. The extent of the difficulties in the exercise can be appreciated when a comparison is made between the paper in this volume and an earlier paper by the same authors, Eichengreen and Bordo (2000), which it updates. With the benefit of additional research Bordo and Eichengreen are now convinced that the average output loss in present crises is less than a century ago and not the reverse. Whatever the reason for these differences, questions about data do need to be raised: are there really reliable output data (GDP as used here) for 21 countries for the nineteenth century, or for the interwar years when there was so much turmoil? Even for the UK where data are generally thought to be good, the margin of error surrounding GDP estimates for the nineteenth century is around 25 per cent. What they are like for emerging market economies in the nineteenth century can only be guessed at. Since Eichengreen and Bordo are measuring differences between years, rather than considering trends, this matters. Are there really data on more than a handful of countries – are there 21 interesting countries before 1914? Further, in measuring severity Eichengreen and Bordo use the length and depth of the cycle. They determine peaks and troughs that do not always coincide with the accepted dating.

On banking crises their definition is: one where most or all of banking capital is eroded. They show a crisis in Britain in 1890 when the system as a whole was almost completely undisturbed when judged by this criterion. What of other countries? (And why ignore Anna Schwartz's definition of crises that has proved operationally useful and would certainly reject 1890 on other grounds as well.) Their definition of a currency crisis is: 'a forced change of parity or an international rescue'. Based on that were there really four crises in Britain in the years 1964, 1965, 1966, and 1967 or just one – it obviously matters for frequency? They show a currency crisis in Britain in 1931 but might it not be reasoned on the same basis that this was present each year from 1925 onwards? Perhaps more importantly, if the question of frequency is to be answered we need to know the universe. There are more data for more countries for the recent past than there are for the nineteenth century.

Finally, there is a heavy obligation on the historian to establish the facts first. Eichengreen and Bordo explain the Argentine crisis of 1890 in part by low interest rates in Britain pushing investors abroad. They say the Bank of England's discount rate 'never rose above 3 per cent between 1884 and 1888 encouraging British investors to search for yields abroad' (p. 18). In fact the annual average was always above 3 per cent, and in 37 of the 60 months it was above 3 per cent, frequently being at 4 and 5 per cent.

Perhaps when each of these points is adjusted for the results would not change greatly. But these are illustrative and there may be other parts of the series susceptible to the same need for adjustment.

Hegel said that the only lesson of history was that we do not learn from it. Sadly, there seems to confirmation of that here for in spite of there being lessons to be learned things seem to be getting worse – or are they? I could not help feeling that throughout these chapters there was some evidence of the tension common between the economist and the historian. The economist is continually looking for patterns and generalities and the historian always cautioning over the uniqueness of events. But tension is no bad thing and both these chapters in their different ways illustrate how our understanding of the issues can be advanced and they certainly show how influential Charles has been in this particular field.

REFERENCES

Bordo, M. and B. Eichengreen (2000), 'Is the crisis problem growing more severe?', mimeo, May.

Capie, F. and C.A.E. Goodhart, S. Fischer, and N. Schnadt (1994), *The Future of Central Banking*, Cambridge: Cambridge Universtiy Press.

Goodhart, C.A.E. (2001), 'The inter-temporal nature of risk', *Lecture Brussels*, October.

Goodhart C.A.E. and P.J.R. Delargy (1998), 'Financial crises; plus ca change plus c'est la meme chose', *International Finance*, vol. 1, no. 2, 261–87.

Schwartz, A.J.S. (1986), 'Real and pseudo crises', in F.H.Capie and G.E. Wood, *Financial Crises and the World Banking System*, London: Macmillan.

4. Exchange rate regimes in theory and practice

Andrew Crockett

The choice of exchange rate regime is a subject that attracts strong opinions, often based on weak theory. At various times during the twentieth century, there has been an academic or policy consensus for pretty much the full range of possible regimes: fixed rates (the gold standard); floating rates; *neither* fixed *nor* floating rates (the Bretton Woods adjustable peg); agnosticism ('anything goes'); and *either* fixed *or* floating rates (the 'bipolar view'). This last, based on the presumed instability of intermediate exchange rate systems, seems close to becoming the new conventional wisdom.

Given this shifting policy perception, it seems worthwhile to reexamine the issue. Has the evolution of thinking been the result of increased wisdom – a better understanding of the basic model? Does it reflect shifts in economic structures and responses – changing model structures? Or is it a matter of different preferences for economic outcomes – shifts in policy-makers' objective functions?

To some extent, all three factors have played a role. Theoretical and empirical insights have brought increased awareness of the characteristics of different regimes. Concepts such as the 'impossible trinity', optimum currency areas, exchange rate overshooting, and multiple equilibria, together with real-life experience of currency and banking crises have sharpened our awareness of the physiology of exchange rate regimes and their pathology under stress.

Changes in economic structures may have also been a factor in how exchange regimes work. From a theoretical standpoint, the case for one regime against another depends on some imperfection in the way markets operate. If prices and wages adjusted smoothly to supply and demand shifts, it would not matter much which regime was adopted. But in the real world we know prices and expectations are sticky. Moreover, factors of production can be immobile. Just *how* sticky and *how* immobile can change over time, affecting the choice of exchange regime.

Finally, economic preferences play an important role. The 'impossible trinity' teaches that countries cannot simultaneously have free capital mobility, an independent monetary policy and a fixed exchange rate. They have to choose two out of the three, or at least pick a feasible combination that involves giving up part of each of the objectives. Preferences in this regard have undoubtedly shifted over time.

I will use this chapter to examine several questions that are of practical relevance to countries considering which exchange rate regime is suitable for them. These questions are: (i) is there a 'disappearing middle' (that is are countries increasingly forced to choose between the polar solutions of fully fixed or fully flexible exchange rates)?; (ii) to the extent that countries do have to move away from intermediate solutions, toward which pole should they move?; (iii) if a country wishes to change a pegging regime, how can it best 'exit' from its existing peg?; and (iv) what are the choices for the monetary regime that go with the choice of exchange rate regime? Finally, I will offer some more speculative thoughts on the subject of how global exchange rate arrangements might evolve over time.

This is a demanding set of questions, and in the interest of preventing the chapter from growing to unmanageable length, I will try not to delay in addressing them. Still, it is useful to begin with a bit of history, and a qualification. The history, to which I come in a moment, is a recapitulation of the reasons why previous exchange rate regimes were thought to be appropriate at the time they were in operation, and what were the causes of their eventual demise. The qualification is that an exchange rate regime cannot be analysed in the abstract. In virtually all circumstances, it carries important implications for monetary policy. Moreover, it determines the ways in which the authorities can respond to the build up of financial imbalances or to the outbreak of a financial crisis.

SOME HISTORY

The classical gold standard may not be the beginning of exchange rate history, but it is a convenient starting point for considering the evolution of conventional wisdom on the subject. For several decades around the end of the 19th century, the gold standard functioned with apparent success. Equilibrium in the system was maintained by the 'price-specie-flow' mechanism elegantly described (albeit in simplified form and more than a century earlier) by Hume (1752). Rising prices in one country relative to others caused a payments deficit and a loss of reserves. Reserve losses in turn led to a contraction of money and credit, reining in price increases and restoring equilibrium. In this sense, the gold standard merely translated to the global level the disciplines that applied within a domestic economy using gold as the base of a fractional reserve banking system. By doing so, it enabled the benefits of free trade and capital market integration to be extended to the world level.

However, the gold standard that apparently worked so well in the pre-First World War period did not prevent chaos and depression in the 1920s and 1930s. Why the change? In part, of course, the smoothness with which the system had worked in the late nineteenth century was an illusion. It had not prevented periodic banking crises, nor had it avoided cycles of economic expansion and recession. But nothing quite prepared observers for the Great Depression. Eichengreen (1994) makes a persuasive case that the difference can be explained largely through the erosion of credibility and international cooperation. Credibility and cooperation were strong in the classical gold standard, but had largely disappeared by the 1930s. Credibility meant that market participants based their expectations on the belief that the necessary actions would be taken to preserve the system, and that they would be successful. 'Going off' gold was unthinkable except as a wartime exigency. If a country's external position deteriorated and its exchange rate weakened toward the 'gold points', domestic interest rates would be allowed to rise to restrain demand and attract capital from abroad. And if support was needed for the process, the 'rules of the game' required central banks to extend each other almost unlimited support.

Neither of these conditions applied in the 1930s. By then, it was clear that currencies could, if conditions were serious enough, be taken off gold. And it was equally clear that there could be no assurance of international support. There had been a loss of innocence in markets, even if not all policy-makers perceived it. (Philip Snowden, the former British Chancellor of the Exchequer, is supposed to have said when his successor announced that sterling was leaving the gold standard: 'Nobody told me I could do that!')

The important lesson from this experience is that private capital flows will help to stabilise fixed exchange rate systems only if market participants believe exchange rates are sustainable and will be supported by official policy. Where these preconditions are lacking, capital flows are more likely to be a source of vulnerability to a fixed rate system.

Floating exchange rates were the default option when governments and central banks found themselves unable to remain on the gold standard. Floating allowed countries to adopt monetary policies geared to stimulating demand and made it easier for central banks to act as a lender of last resort to the domestic financial system. But it also allowed currency depreciation that was seen as 'exporting' unemployment to other countries. In that sense, it contributed to the beggar-my-neighbour policies of the 1930s and to the political consequences they spawned. The lesson from the floating of the 1930s seemed to be that rules were needed to prevent exchange rate flexibility from degenerating into a vicious circle of competitive depreciation.

The Bretton Woods conference represented the first successful attempt to consciously design an international economic system. (Earlier, unsuccessful, attempts were the Brussels conference in 1920, The Genoa conference of 1922 and the London conference of 1933.) The Bretton Woods system reflected lessons drawn from both the fixed and floating period. The floating rate period seemed to teach that exchange rates should be viewed as matters of mutual concern, since individually determined exchange rate policies could be inconsistent and unstable. The gold standard experience seemed to show that fixed exchange rates were more stable, but required a credible domestic adjustment mechanism, a cooperative international environment, and an absence of destabilising capital flows.

The Bretton Woods system worked well so long as capital flows were modest, international inflationary and deflationary pressures were limited, and countries accepted an obligation to direct domestic macroeconomic policies towards achieving external balance. These preconditions began to fray in the 1960s. Capital flows increased as exchange restrictions were dismantled, and new instruments and markets were developed. Inflationary pressures intensified, especially during the long expansion of the 1960s. And countries, especially the one at the core of the system, became increasingly unwilling to subordinate domestic goals to the disciplines of the balance of payments.

The collapse of the Bretton Woods System was due to an inability to agree on how to sustain fixed rates in the face of divergent policy preferences and mounting speculative pressure. It was not due primarily to a conscious adoption of floating as a superior option. The introduction of greater flexibility for the major countries was accompanied by attempts to frame rules to guard against competitive devaluation (IMF, 1974). It was also accompanied by recognition that many countries would continue to opt for a managed exchange rate, whether through the continuance of a declared parity or in some other way. The revision to the Articles of Agreement of the IMF that gave legal effect to the end of the Bretton Woods system authorised virtually all types of exchange rate regime, except a peg to gold.

How has the system evolved over the past thirty years or so of eclecticism? And how have developments compared with expectations? Perceptions of the answers to these questions have shaped the responses to the issues to be analysed in the remainder of this chapter. Six points can be made:

First, contrary to what some had feared when the Bretton Woods system collapsed, there has been relatively little evidence of competitive exchange rate practices. Partly as a result, the trend towards greater liberalisation in international trade and capital flows has continued without significant interruption. Any perceived need to retain administered influence over exchange rate relationships in order to avoid policy inconsistencies has thus diminished.

Second, exchange rates among the major currencies have been much more volatile than most observers expected. Early advocates of floating rates (for example, Friedman, 1953; Meade, 1951) had painted a picture of smooth and gradual movement of exchange rates in response to divergences in national policies. In practice, fluctuations among the major currencies, in both real and nominal terms, have been substantial (see Figure 4.1).

A third feature of exchange rate developments, which partly explains the second, has been the dramatic growth in capital flows. In fact, capital market developments are now the principal driver of short-term changes in the exchange rates. Deep and liquid capital markets have the capacity to discount into today's price all factors that affect expectations of flows of payments in the future. They can quickly expose inconsistencies between the markets' and the authorities' perceptions of an equilibrium exchange rate.

Fourth, the floating period has reminded observers of the importance of having a domestic monetary anchor to contain inflation. As late as 1970, many policy-makers saw monetary factors as secondary in the inflation-generating process. This was no longer the case a decade later. The core country (the United States) had by then experienced an upsurge in inflation facilitated by loose monetary policies and the absence of an exchange rate constraint. For other countries too, floating removed constraints on monetary and credit expansion and contributed to the Great Inflation of the 1970s. The realisation that floating needed a domestic monetary anchor led to the search for substitutes for unfettered discretion as a means of conducting monetary policy.

Fifth, the past twenty years have seen a much greater incidence of banking and currency crises than was experienced in the earlier post war years. They have proved harder to prevent, more difficult to manage, and more costly than would have been imagined earlier. While the main sufferers have been emerging market countries, industrial countries have not been immune.

Sixth, there has been a much greater variety of exchange rate regimes. At various times, countries have experimented with wider bands, crawling bands, asymmetric bands, basket pegs (disclosed or undisclosed) and various other forms of exchange rate management or pegging. It has become clear that the degree of fixity or flexibility of an exchange rate lies along a spectrum, rather than being described by a few fixed points.

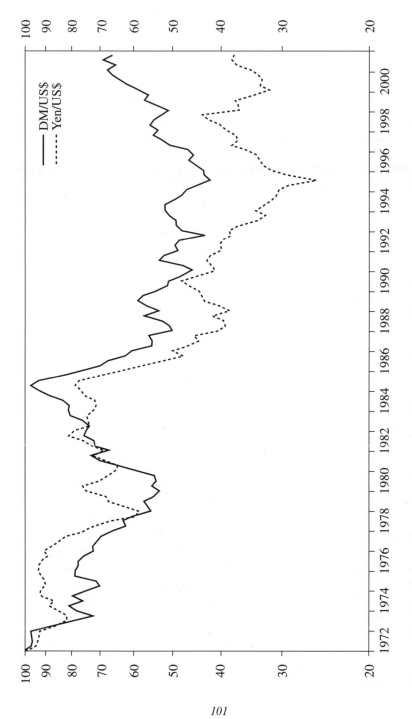

Figure 4.1 Nominal exchange rates against the US dollar (1971 Q4 = 100; on a semi-logarithmic scale)

Consideration of these features has led observers to draw conclusions about the appropriate choice of exchange rate regimes for the 21st century. While some still believe that a balance can be struck between fixity and flexibility (for example through 'target zones') many have concluded that free capital flows make intermediate regimes inherently unstable. Some have gone even further and questioned whether the advantages to small and medium-sized countries of having their own currencies outweigh the costs. Those that have favoured exchange rate flexibility have concentrated on such issues as: how to exit from a fixed rate peg? and how should one manage domestic monetary policy once a rate is floating? There is universal acceptance that all regimes other than fully fixed exchange rates need a monetary anchor. There is also an increasing realisation that an exchange rate regime cannot be stable unless the means are in place to prevent or contain financial crises. Against this background, I turn now to a consideration of the questions raised at the beginning of this chapter.

IS THERE A 'DISAPPEARING MIDDLE'?

There is now a growing group of economists that believe intermediate exchange rate regimes, in an environment of capital mobility, are inherently unstable. A representative opinion is that of Summers (1999): '. . . in a world of freely flowing capital, there is shrinking scope for countries to occupy the middle ground of fixed but adjustable pegs'.

The theoretical starting point for this argument is the well-known proposition of the 'impossible trinity'. A country cannot have, at the same time, a fixed exchange rate, an independent monetary policy and free capital mobility. And since most countries are neither willing nor able to maintain restrictions on capital flows, so the argument goes, the choice must be made between a fixed exchange rate without monetary autonomy, and monetary autonomy with a floating exchange rate.

As a more practical matter, advocates of the 'disappearing middle' point to the fact that most currency crises in recent years have been due, at least in part, to failed attempts to defend fixed-but-adjustable exchange rates. The narrow margins of the EMS succumbed to speculative attack in the wake of German reunification; Mexico was forced off its peg in 1994; and many countries of East Asia were obliged to abandon attempts to defend managed exchange regimes when these came under sustained attack in the late 1990s.

These are powerful arguments, but their theoretical underpinnings do not always stand up to close scrutiny. Take the theory of the impossible trinity. It is undoubtedly true that *if* a country faces free international capital flows, and *if* it wishes to fix its exchange rate, it cannot also have an independent monetary policy. Equally, if it wants an independent monetary policy, it will have to have a floating exchange rate. But in economics, the existence of corner solutions does not typically exclude interior solutions. Why should it not be possible to have *some* additional autonomy for monetary policy by giving up *some* degree of stability in the exchange rate?

On a more practical level, although fixed rate regimes have proved susceptible to crises, there are plenty of examples of fixed rates being used successfully to bring down inflation rates and promote economic convergence. The ERM operated this way for much of its life, and most of the countries that succumbed to currency crisis in Latin America and South-East Asia had previously quite a positive experience with pegging.

Something extra is needed to move convincingly from the impossible trinity to the disappearing middle. Only by filling in this part of the argument is it possible to identify more precisely which exchange rate regimes are stable and which are likely to prove unsustainable. The answer seems to lie in the equilibrium properties of foreign exchange markets under different exchange rate regimes. To examine these properties, it is helpful to recognise that there are not three regimes (fixed, flexible and pegging) but a spectrum. Not all points that lie between the two ends of this spectrum have the same characteristics. And not all are equally vulnerable to crisis.

Frankel (1999) identifies nine separate regimes, running from most fixed to most flexible (see Table 4.1).

Like Lawrence Summers, Frankel considers that the extremes of this spectrum are more stable than the intermediate regimes. Specifically, he notes the view that countries will be increasingly pushed to regimes 1–3 or 9, with regimes 4–8 being hard to sustain. He is far from alone in reaching this type of conclusion.

Table 4.1   A classification of currency regimes

---

1. Currency Union
2. Currency Board
3. 'Truly fixed' exchange rate peg
4. Adjustable peg
5. Crawling peg
6. Basket peg
7. Target zones.
8. Managed float
9. Free float

Source: Frankel (1999).

To examine the validity of Frankel's taxonomy, and specifically his assessment of which regimes are viable and which are not, consider first the prototypical intermediate regime, a fixed-but-adjustable exchange rate with relatively narrow bands (No. 4 in Frankel's list). A number of characteristics of such a regime contribute to its vulnerability to crisis. First, the possibility exists of a discrete change in the exchange rate of significant size. If expectations of such a change become firmly held, they will become difficult to counteract through interest rate differentials. Thus, an incentive to capital flows will be created. Second, the direction of a possible discrete change in an exchange rate can often be predicted with a high degree of confidence. And third, there is a self-fulfilling element to the actions of market participants when they position themselves to respond to an anticipated rate adjustment.

The anatomy of the consequent developments has been developed in the now-familiar literature on currency crises, initiated by Krugman (1979). In a 'first generation' model, market participants make assumptions about what the balance of payments will look like under current macroeconomic policies, and compare this with the capacity of the authorities to finance it. When the available reserve stock becomes uncomfortably low relative to prospective financing needs, they begin to sell the suspect currency. This further weakens the financial position of the currency in question, inducing further sales, and precipitating the crisis.

In more sophisticated models, the triggering mechanism for the crisis is not the current account position but the balance sheet of the public or private sector. If either is heavily indebted, the consequences for domestic financial stability of raising interest rates to stem a capital outflow may be severe. And precisely because market participants perceive that higher rates would be politically or economically unsustainable, they sell the suspect currency.

Other models capture multiple equilibria. Under certain assumptions, speculative attacks can be mounted and succeed, even when there is no disequilibrium in underlying policies (Flood and Garber, 1984). The most intuitive way of thinking of this is to consider a devaluation as setting off a process of inflation that eventually validates the original currency movement. Complicating factors may be related to weaknesses in the domestic financial system.

Under both first and later generation models, the greater efficiency of capital markets has the effect of foreshortening the process by which a crisis develops. If capital markets are well informed and efficient, unsustainable trends or inherent vulnerabilities will be spotted early, and their consequences translated into contemporaneous price movements. Insofar as capital markets have become more efficient, they have clearly reduced the authorities' ability to sustain disequilibrium prices and policies.

Does this mean that none of the intermediate regimes identified by Frankel should be regarded as sustainable? To answer this question, it is useful to consider how the equilibrium properties of the foreign exchange market change as one moves away from regime 4 (fixed but adjustable) in the direction of greater fixity or greater flexibility.

One way of moving to greater fixity is to limit the possibility for flexibility in the rate, and to tie monetary policy ever more closely to that of the country to which the currency is pegged. A currency board can be established, with rules enshrined in legislation, or even the constitution, governing the creation of domestic money. The problem is, it may not be easy to convince markets that such rules will be respected when they confront political and economic pressures. The experience of Argentina is a case in point. When markets sense an inconsistency between a monetary rule and economic realities, they are apt to speculate against the monetary rule. And the more they do, the greater the cost of sticking to the rule. Probably, the only way to convince markets that an exchange rate will not be changed is to give up even the means to make adjustments. This was an important lesson taught by the experience of the European Monetary System.

At the fixed end of the spectrum, therefore, nothing much short of currency union is fully credible. But it would not be correct, in my view, to be equally categorical as one moves from a regime of pegging with a narrow band toward greater flexibility. It may be possible to 'loosen' a pegging system without going all the way to free floating.

A regime with a fixed peg that can be altered by government decision is vulnerable because of the possibility of a large or discrete move in one direction. Two factors influence the probability of such a situation arising: the width of the band around parity; and the sustainability of the authorities' commitment to retain the regime. The wider the band, the greater, other things equal, the authorities' capacity to defend it without changing the central rate. And the smaller, correspondingly, is the prospective change in the market rate for any adjustment in central parities.

The sustainability of the regime can be enhanced by increasing the flexibility with which it functions. Possible ways of doing this are to allow the central parity to move over time (to 'crawl'); to express the parity in terms of a basket of currencies instead of a single currency; and to stand ready to make timely adjustments in declared parities. Automatic or discretionary adjustments in parities can help prevent a disequilibrium from becoming too great. And a 'basket' peg can reduce the risk that a parity will become inappropriate as a result of movements in third party exchange rates. This latter factor was instrumental in destabilising Asian currencies and the Argentine peso, when the dollar appreciated in the late 1990s.

This argument suggests that a fixed-but-adjustable exchange rate regime can be made more stable by a suitable combination of widening the band, using a basket peg, and making timely adjustments in the central rate. Is this the end of the story? Unfortunately not. A wider band or more frequent parity adjustments may strengthen the resilience of a pegging regime but they weaken its presumed economic benefits. A pegging regime is usually pursued in order to influence market perceptions that might otherwise cause undesired movements in the rate. If the exchange rate band is too wide, or if the authorities are too ready to alter the parity in the face of market pressure, the impact of specifying a parity will be diluted. In the limit, if the band were adjusted automatically to reflect market movements, it would become virtually indistinguishable from floating.

There is also an important political economy aspect to exchange rate management. There is not much point in having a fixed rate if it does not involve resisting market pressure at least some of the time. Resisting market pressure involves taking some risks and incurring some costs. These may be in the form of exchange market intervention, domestic policy changes (for example raising interest rates), or verbal commitments by political leaders. Whichever the precise form, once costs have been incurred to defend a parity, the stakes have been raised. It becomes even less palatable to make an adjustment. The market then has to judge how likely it is that the authorities will be forced into an adjustment. Then, as Morris and Shin (1999) demonstrate, each action by market participants to anticipate the possibility of a parity change raises the cost of defending the exchange rate, and each act of defence by the authorities raises the costs of abandoning the defence.

However, as Morris and Shin go on to observe, 'Whatever the perceived benefits of maintaining a currency peg, and whatever their official pronouncements, all monetary authorities have a pain threshold at which the costs of defending the peg outweigh the benefits of doing so'. Private market participants are aware of this. Thus 'the more prevalent are the actions which increase the pain of holding the peg, the greater is the incentive for an individual actor to adopt the actions which increase the pain. In other words, the actions which tend to undermine the currency peg are mutually reinforcing' (Morris and Shin, 1999).

Where does all this leave the theory of the 'disappearing middle'? Certainly, without suitable qualification, the theory is too broad. It is not true that *only* the polar options of full fixity and free floating are sustainable. It is possible to envision intermediate exchange rate regimes that, suitably managed, have stable equilibrium properties. However, there are clear risks that intermediate regimes will be managed in such a way as to create a *de facto* peg, that becomes vulnerable to speculative attack. This danger can be limited by avoiding any formal commitments to an exchange rate, and limiting any actions used to influence the exchange rate to those that have a justification on domestic grounds as well. For example, pursuit of domestic inflation objectives should help stabilise exchange rates without providing a target for speculators to aim at. Morris Goldstein (2001) characterises such a regime as 'managed floating plus'.

WHICH REGIME IS APPROPRIATE FOR WHICH COUNTRY?

The analysis so far suggests that certain exchange rate regimes are likely to be unstable, while others represent feasible choices. Unstable ones are those with tight exchange rate pegs in an environment of mobile capital where there is a high likelihood of policy divergences or economic shocks. In such circumstances, countries will find it impossible to achieve simultaneously the policy goals of tightly managing their external exchange rate, retaining freedom of domestic macroeconomic management and enhancing access to an integrated international capital market.

Potentially sustainable exchange rate regimes can be grouped under four headings:

(a) Fully fixed rates (that is where a separate domestic currency has been abandoned, or the market assesses the probability of a change in the rate within any relevant time frame as effectively zero).
(b) Pegging regimes in which the market is unable to exploit expectations of exchange rate changes (that is where effective capital controls exist).
(c) Managed floating regimes, or soft pegs, in which market expectations of a step change in the exchange rate never become strong enough to generate a currency crisis.
(d) Free floating regimes.

Of these, (a) and (d) represent polar regimes of full fixity and free floating. Between these two extremes are two possible regimes which fall clearly on either side of the 'disappearing middle'. One is to have a fixed peg with narrow margins, and to support it with exchange controls. China is the country that comes closest to this regime at the present time. The other is to allow much greater exchange rate flexibility, but to manage it through actions designed to contain undesired exchange rate volatility.

Which of these four regimes is likely to be appropriate for which country? In assessing their relative advantages for countries in different economic circumstances, it is useful to start by a consideration of the characteristics of the different regimes.

A regime in which the domestic currency is credibly pegged to an external anchor will result in a convergence of inflation rates (at least in traded goods) toward those in the anchor country. This will be beneficial if a large part of the foreign trade of the country concerned is denominated in the anchor currency, and/or if the country wishes to publicly signal its intention to give up an autonomous monetary policy (say, because such autonomy has been misused in the past). On the other hand, a fully fixed exchange rate will be less beneficial if trade and investment patterns are more diversified (because trade-weighted exchange rates can vary, and a trade-weighted basket peg is a less credible anchor for policy purposes). Fixed exchange rates also prevent the authorities from using monetary policy to absorb macro-economic shocks, and limit their capacity to act as lender-of-last resort to the banking system.

A floating exchange rate has contrasting characteristics. It can permit more flexible adjustment to fluctuations in exchange rates among partner countries (that is maintaining a more stable trade-weighted exchange rate). It can also allow real exchange rates to vary more easily when required by shifts in capital flows or the terms of trade, and it can allow monetary policy to absorb macroeconomic and financial shocks. On the other hand, exchange rate flexibility will be less desirable if it is viewed by the market as removing a bulwark against inflationary policies, or if the exchange market has disequilibrium properties that cause systematic overshooting.

To cite these characteristics is to make evident the fact that the appropriate choice of exchange rate regime will depend on the circumstances of individual countries, which in turn are likely to evolve through time. Small open economies will value exchange rate stability more than larger and more closed ones. And pegging to a single currency is better for countries with a concentrated pattern of trade than for those with a more diversified one. The use of the exchange rate as an anchor for monetary policy depends on the credibility of alternative anchors. A country with a history of high inflation will typically find it harder, at least initially, to bring down inflation solely through the use of a discretionary monetary policy.

Against this background, what can be said in concrete terms about the choice facing particular groups of countries? A first point is that for many countries the attractiveness of greater flexibility has undoubtedly increased. Those that have been driven from previous pegs are usually unwilling to put the additional constraints in place to improve the resilience of a fixed rate. Moreover, returning to a fixed rate with a currency board, and thus tying domestic monetary policy even more closely to the exchange rate, has generally been seen as having other problems. It is hard to find a 'correct' rate that would be believed by the market; and it is perceived as dangerous to restrict the capacity to support impaired domestic financial systems. As a consequence, such a regime will not find it easy to achieve the credibility that is one of its supposed advantages. So, relatively large countries moving away from the 'unsustainable middle' have usually (though not always) gone in the direction of greater flexibility. They have avoided explicit exchange rate commitments, while nevertheless often retaining the possibility of using policy to influence the rate. The number of countries that have moved from pegging to floating over the past six or seven years is by now quite substantial. It includes Mexico, Brazil, Thailand, Indonesia and Korea, among others.

For most of these countries, flexible exchange rates are working quite well. The exchange rate can take the strain of shifting market confidence without provoking a currency crisis. And the articulation of inflation targeting regimes has for many seemed to provide a satisfactory anchor for monetary policies and for price expectations of market participants. The alternative of fixed exchange rates protected by capital controls is not attractive for countries that see their future as linked to progressive integration into international capital markets.

But for countries that have adopted flexibility, there remains the question of how freely they should allow their currencies to float. Where foreign exchange markets are well-developed, and there exist a broad range of other capital market instruments, it may be possible to approach rather closely the free-floating end of the spectrum. But there needs to be a significant measure of market confidence in the political and economic stability of the country, so that stabilising capital flows are called forth when the exchange rate begins to move significantly in one direction or the other.

Concern about whether these conditions are met has meant that relatively few have floated completely freely. Many have made it clear that they wished to avoid undue volatility in their exchange rate, and have been prepared to adjust domestic policies (particularly interest rates) to resist unwanted appreciation or depreciation. Foreign exchange intervention has often been used to maintain external competitiveness by moderating currency appreciation, as well as to accumulate reserves to resist potential downward pressures later.

One justification for managing a floating exchange rate is the volatility of capital flows. It is far from clear that capital flows always perform the stabilising function of smoothing the process of adjustment to disturbances. Markets that are thin, or subject to informational or other failures cannot be counted upon to produce an optimal equilibrium. Excessive volatility and overshooting are a real risk. To the extent this is so, it provides a rationale for authorities continuing to try and influence the exchange rate.

Not all countries have chosen to move away from the 'unsustainable middle' in the direction of greater flexibility. Some have chosen a different route. Argentina, Hong Kong, Estonia and Bulgaria, for example, have elected to have a currency board. Others have gone even further and dollarised their economies, abandoning the domestic currency (Ecuador, El Salvador). Except in the case of Hong Kong, for which special circumstances apply, the abandonment of discretion over domestic monetary policy has usually reflected a recognition that the credibility of domestic monetary policy is very weak. The (borrowed) credibility of an external anchor is therefore needed. However, simply pegging to a foreign currency is not enough to do the trick. Markets would recognise that a peg can be abandoned. Something more is needed to demonstrate the authorities' commitment not to change the peg. A currency board provides an economic mechanism to prevent the divergence of monetary policy from that pursued in the anchor country. If, further, the rules under which the currency board operates are enshrined in legislation, or even the constitution, additional barriers to discretion are erected.

Of course, so long as a separate currency remains in existence, the markets may suspect that operating guidelines may be adapted, legislation repealed, or the constitution amended. Such concerns seem to persist with respect to the Argentine peso. This constitutes an argument for going even a step further and dropping the domestic currency altogether. The case in favour of this approach is that countries following it can avail themselves of a medium of exchange of unquestioned stability. Of course, in doing so, they lose not only the freedom to manage domestic monetary policy, but also the seignorage that having a separate currency brings.

What about the use of exchange controls? These have been seen as a potential means of suppressing speculative pressure and thus giving the authorities time to either take measures to restore a sustainable payments position, or else to undertake an orderly change in the value of the currency. But there are counterarguments. The case against exchange controls is that:

(i)   they interfere with 'desirable' capital movements as well as 'undesirable' ones;
(ii) they are ineffective in a world where there are multiple channels through which market participants can take positions;
(iii) they permit policy-makers to delay needed policy actions to address policy fundamentals; and
(iv) they encourage corruption in their administration.

These drawbacks to capital controls are valid, particularly over time, and lead to the conclusion that it would be unwise to base a permanent regime on them. There are qualifications, however. Short-term controls on capital may be able to provide temporary relief at relatively modest cost. And the more that measures affect the *price* rather than the *availability* of foreign exchange, the less the distortions are likely to be. Finally, for a country that already has substantial exchange controls, it may be wise to phase them out gradually, in line with the capacity of the domestic financial system to adapt to a more competitive environment.

Reflecting considerations such as these, Malaysia imposed temporary controls along with its decision to repeg its exchange rate in 1998; Chile has used a tax-like mechanism to restrain capital inflows, and China is moving toward capital account convertibility gradually, while retaining a fixed rate for its currency. Some other countries in Asia use informal restrictions to limit the capacity of market participants to 'short' their currency, though this approach will probably work well only in a cohesive social environment.

HOW TO 'EXIT' FROM A FIXED EXCHANGE RATE?

Even if it has become harder to sustain an intermediate exchange rate regime, the fact remains that many countries still do. And, although less necessary now, fixed exchange rates have often been successfully used to bring down inflation. Among countries that have used an exchange rate anchor in this way are Israel, Brazil, Mexico, several transition economies, as well as members of the European Exchange Rate Mechanism (ERM). But it is now recognised, however, that a fixed exchange rate regime, with narrow margins around parity, can be vulnerable to speculative attack. This gives rise to the question of how to 'exit' from such a regime, if possible before an exchange market crisis forces the issue.

(i) Moving from Pegging to Flexibility

In exiting from a pegging regime, a kind of 'catch-22' operates. When conditions are calm, the peg operates smoothly, and there is no incentive to contemplate a change. However, when the peg comes under attack, the authorities feel obliged to defend it. Abandoning an exchange rate under pressure is seen to have potential adverse consequences of both an economic and a political nature. Economically, a sudden step change in the value of the currency may give rise to a hard-to-control cycle of price increases and depreciation. It may also contribute to a domestic financial crisis if financial contracts implicitly assume the continuance of the peg (for example if domestic financial institutions have significant currency mismatches in their portfolios). Politically, devaluation under pressure is inevitably seen as a defeat for government policy.

For both reasons, pegged exchange rates are rarely abandoned as a deliberate act of policy. More usually, a forced exit takes place after a debilitating period of painful resistance. It is not too much to say that memories of such experience are among the most powerful reasons why policy-makers and others are so reluctant to recommend a fixed rate regime.

Yet there are examples of countries that have successfully adapted fixed rate regimes (Chile, Colombia, Israel, Poland). What are the considerations that need to be taken into account in designing an 'exit' strategy? Eichengreen et al. (1998) note that the first requirement is to begin to consider the question of exit when the currency is still strong. If the process of exiting from a peg begins when market forces are broadly in balance, there need be no abrupt movement in the exchange rate, and therefore no sudden and difficult economic adjustments. By remaining in control of the situation, the authorities can retain credibility, and avoid giving the impression of powerlessness before the forces of the market.

A second requirement is gradualism. One possibility is to introduce more flexibility into the pegging regime by broadening the width of exchange rate bands. This enables a greater role for market forces in determining the rate, and provides an indication of whether the existing rate is perceived as sustainable. In turn, the authorities can experiment with techniques other than intervention to influence the exchange rate and gauge their effect. Other means of loosening the peg can also be employed, such as using a basket instead of a single currency peg, and allowing the central rate to move over time (a crawling peg).

Third, it is necessary to develop the institutional mechanisms that are needed to support a greater role for market forces in determining the exchange rate. These include a network of dealers, the capacity to make forward contracts, adequate settlement arrangements, and so on. All of these are important to give the market the necessary depth, breadth and liquidity. It is also important to have such institutional mechanisms in place to avoid unnecessary rate fluctuations occurring for purely technical reasons.

Fourth, since greater flexibility in financial asset prices will expose financial institutions to new risks, it is important that appropriate supervisory oversight is in place. The movement away from a pegged exchange rate will usually be accompanied by a relaxation of foreign exchange controls and a more rapid growth in financial intermediation. Experience has shown that rapid financial liberalisation, unaccompanied by commensurate upgrading in risk management practices, can lead to, or reveal pre-existing weaknesses in, financial structures. For this reason, strengthened domestic financial supervision is an essential part of an exit strategy from a repressed financial system.

Finally, any move away from pegging arrangements for the exchange rate requires an alternative (and credible) anchor for monetary policy. Since the exchange rate will no longer provide the measure of the authorities inten- tion to pursue a domestic monetary policy consistent with exchange rate stability, an alternative constraint on policy is needed. This subject is treated in a little more detail below.

(ii) Exiting to Currency Union

Of course, the 'exit' from a pegging arrangement does not have to be toward exchange rate flexibility. It could also be in the other direction, toward a currency board, dollarisation, or currency union. What considerations apply deciding whether and how to make this kind of shift?

A great deal of analysis surrounded these issues in the period leading up to the Maastricht Treaty on Economic and Monetary Union in Europe (Crockett, 1994; Giovannini, 1995). One strand of thought (the so-called 'monetarists') held that the adoption of a single currency would force con- vergence of inflation rates. Thus, elaborate preconditions were unneces- sary: so long as the institutional structure of monetary union was robust, a currency union would not be threatened by sustained macroeconomic divergences.

The majority view that was eventually adopted ('economists') held that the needed convergence should precede monetary union, in order to avoid tensions that could create divergences in economic performance, post- union, and possible political backlash. As a result, the Maastricht Treaty proposed five, by now well-known, 'convergence' criteria:

(i)   budget deficits under 3 per cent of GDP;
(ii)   public debt levels under 60 per cent of GDP;
(iii) inflation rates not more than 1½ per cent above the average of the three best performing countries;
(iv)   long-term interest rates within 2 percentage points of the average in the three countries with lowest rates;
(v)   exchange rates within the normal ERM bands for two years prior to entry to union.

It is possible to quibble with the precise specification of these criteria, and at the time many did (Goodhart, 1991). It is also possible to argue that structural factors relating to flexibility in factor and product markets are equally important in facilitating monetary union. Still, at a general level, each of the Maastricht criteria contains an important insight into the financial conditions that make for a smooth transition from a pegged to a fully-fixed exchange rate.

First, a strong fiscal and debt position (conditions (i) and (ii)) is necessary because, once currency union has occurred, inflation is no longer an option to deal with burdensome debt service obligations. If markets come to doubt the sustainability of the fiscal position (as witness the case of Argentina in mid-2001), risk-premia on outstanding debt can rise, threatening a vicious circle and unsustainable debt dynamics in the country concerned.

Second, similar inflation rates are desirable when exchange rates are pegged, because there is probably inertia in the inflation-generating process. In other words, it will take time for inflation rates to converge, even when currencies are locked. If inflation rates are too far apart when exchange rates are fully pegged, the country with the higher inflation rates will experience a loss of competitiveness that may be hard, and painful, to reverse by subsequent relative deflation.

Third, the criterion of similar long-term interest rates on government debt in essence measures the degree of market confidence in the sustainability of monetary union and the creditworthiness of the participating governments. If markets continue to harbour doubts about either factor at the outset of monetary union, the prospect of a costly crisis is enhanced.

Fourth, the criterion of a stable exchange rate prior to currency union provides a 'track record' of exchange rate stability that can be assumed to enhance the credibility of monetary union.

Beyond the 'Maastricht' criteria, there are a number of other preconditions for monetary union that will be particularly important for emerging market countries contemplating a hard peg to a major currency. The importance of flexibility in factor and product markets has already been mentioned. In addition, it is crucial to have a well-capitalised and well-supervised banking system, since the capacity of the authorities to act as lender-of-last resort is severely circumscribed in the absence of monetary policy independence. Finally, a strong reserve position is necessary for a country that seeks to manage a national money in a currency board arrangement with an outside currency.

WHAT MONETARY REGIME FOR A FLOATING CURRENCY?

It is widely recognised that, where monetary policy is not conditioned by the need to observe an external constraint, such as the exchange rate, an alternative 'anchor' is needed. This is not simply to provide the monetary authorities with a guide of what to do, but to give market participants a basis for their expectations of the future evolution of financial conditions. These expectations, in turn, play back into the exchange rate. Some monetary authorities have sufficient credibility that an explicit anchor is not needed. Their past actions are an adequate guide to what they are likely to do. The Federal Reserve is in this position. But others need something more concrete, especially when they have had a history of high and/or variable inflation. For a while, it was thought that focussing on monetary aggregates would provide a necessary anchor. But in practice the demand-for-money function turned out to be not stable enough.

More recently, in the industrial countries, a remarkable consensus has emerged on the virtues of inflation targeting as a monetary regime. (Bernanke et al., 1998; King, 1997). Inflation targeting is now followed by New Zealand, Canada, the United Kingdom, Sweden, and Australia. It has also been advocated by influential observers for the three largest monetary areas of the United States, Japan and the eurozone (Meyer, 2001; Ito, 1999; Svensson, 2000).

So far, it has to be said, the record of inflation targeting has been remarkably good. This has led many emerging market countries to emulate the inflation-targeting framework. In this group are Brazil, Thailand, Mexico, South Africa, Chile, Israel and the Czech Republic.

The current popularity of inflation targeting regimes is due to the fact that they complement floating exchange rates by providing a framework for monetary policy that stabilises inflation and inflation expectations. Their initial success in the countries that have adopted them has added powerfully to their appeal. But it is perhaps appropriate to make three points. First, inflation targeting has not yet been tested under adverse circumstances, for example, a severe stagflationary supply shock, such as a major energy price increase. Second, the conditions necessary for the effective implementation of inflation targeting may be more demanding in some countries than in others. And third, inflation targeting may not be very effective in avoiding asset price bubbles and the consequent misallocation of investment resources.

Inflation targeting requires a number of preconditions. First, the central bank must be able to forecast prospective price developments over the relevant time frame (that is the period it takes for policy actions to have their effect). Second, the instruments at the command of the central bank must have a predictable effect on inflation. And third, the central bank must have the necessary autonomy to follow a consistent policy of achieving the inflation objective that is set.

Each of these conditions may be harder to achieve in an emerging market country than in one with a more sophisticated financial structure. Prices in emerging markets tend to be more volatile and less predictable, partly due to the economic structure of these countries. Changes in interest rates, the principal instrument in the hands of the authorities, are less effective in influencing aggregate demand and inflationary pressures. And the autonomy of the central bank is less well-established than in many industrial countries. Add to this the danger that capital flows (in either direction) have a greater tendency to be destabilising, and the conclusion is that floating exchange rates *cum* inflation targeting may not result in the same degree of stability of inflation in emerging markets as in the industrial world. Nevertheless, they may still be the best game in town.

Is there anything else an emerging market can do to improve the stability properties of a floating exchange rate regime? The answer seems to be 'not much'. However, it may be worth considering ways in which the two basic notions of currency floating and inflation targeting are implemented in practice. Morris Goldstein (2001) has emphasised the importance of protecting the banking system from the effects of exchange rate volatility by establishing strict regulatory rules over currency mismatches in bank portfolios. In addition, given the volatility of capital flows in emerging markets, there may be a case for attempting to offset some of their effects on the exchange rate, without necessarily establishing a rigid peg. And given the elasticity that inevitably affects the implementation of an inflation targeting approach, it may be worth paying attention to other indicators, such as the pace of credit growth and asset prices, as well as straightforward inflation forecasts, in making decisions on monetary policy.

THE EXCHANGE RATE SYSTEM OF THE FUTURE

I noted at the outset of this chapter that pretty much the full range of exchange rate regimes had been tried during the twentieth century. What are the prospects in the twenty-first? Will there be a trend, as some (Fischer, 2001; Rogoff, 2001; Alesina and Barro, 2001) have speculated towards a reduced number of currencies? If so, will this come about through currency unions, or the spread of dollarisation? Will the remaining currencies float freely or be managed? Or will the view that an independent country should have its own currency continue to hold sway?

Answers to these questions are inevitably speculative. Perhaps the best way to cut into them is to consider how exchange rate relationships among the major currency blocs (dollar, euro and yen) are likely to evolve, then to assess how other countries might position themselves in relation to the 'core'.

(i)   Exchange Rate Relationships in the G3

It is hard to imagine that the dollar, euro and yen will do other than float reasonably freely against each other for the foreseeable future. Even those who have stressed the advantages of a single world currency (Cooper, 1984) recognise that this is bound to remain a utopian idea for some time to come. The reasons lie both in economics and in governance. From an economic perspective, fiscal and structural policies will diverge in the three areas, and the exogenous disturbances to which each is subject will be different. Exchange rate flexibility will therefore continue to be important to help accommodate these divergences without putting excessive pressure on domestic adjustment mechanisms. Perhaps even more persuasive, however, are political arguments about governance. It is difficult to see how Japan, Europe and the United States could agree on an institutional structure to manage a single currency, or a locked exchange rate. This may change, but not in the foreseeable future.

What about the mechanisms for collective management of exchange rates in the G3? Perhaps, the best known is the 'target zone' proposal (Williamson, 1993; Williamson and Miller, 1987). Advocates of target zones argue that exchange rates have been excessively volatile and have tended to overshoot equilibrium values. This has caused economic costs, through uncertainty and resource misallocation. These costs are felt not only by the G3 countries themselves, but also by other countries. The answer, in the view of target zone advocates, is to agree on boundaries within which the equilibrium rate could be presumed to lie, and to direct policies toward preventing (or limiting) any movement outside those boundaries.

The target zone proposal has been refined over time, but has not yet attracted majority support either from the economics profession or from the policy-making community. There are both negative and positive reasons for this. On the negative side, it is hard to agree on an exchange rate band that would constitute 'equilibrium', and perhaps even harder to agree on how to stop the exchange rate moving outside this band. If a strong economic performance in a given country is causing its exchange rate to appreciate towards the edge of its band, should monetary policy be eased to bring about a weakening? Could the burden of adjustment be placed on fiscal policy? Would sterilised intervention be sufficiently powerful to do the trick? Doubts on these scores lie behind the scepticism of many economists about the practicability of the target zone proposal.

There are also more positive reasons for favouring exchange rate flexibility among the G3. When the economic performance of one major region of the world economy strengthens (for example, the case of the United States in the latter half of the 1990s) exchange rate appreciation serves the valuable function of stimulating demand in the rest of the world, and restraining inflation in the rapidly growing region.

I conclude from the foregoing that reasonably free floating among the major countries is likely to remain the norm for some time to come. This attitude is only likely to change if exchange rate variability becomes excessive, or if exchange rate movements begin to cause severe adjustment problems. Even in such a case (by no means impossible to imagine), the response is more likely to be an intensification of existing ad hoc cooperation. By ad hoc cooperation, I mean actions such as those of the Plaza and Louvre agreements of the 1980s, whereby the authorities of the major countries signal their views on exchange rates by a combination of public announcements, concerted intervention, and a coordinated adjustment of other policies. The establishment of announced exchange rate bands seems unlikely.

If my conjecture is correct, and G3 exchange rates continue to float without formal constraint against each other, this should not be confused with complete neglect of exchange rate factors. Central banks will always take exchange rates into account in formulating domestic monetary policy. Moreover, they consult regularly, at the BIS and elsewhere, on the interactions and implications of their policies. Still, the bottom line as far as the rest of the world is concerned, is that non-G3 countries will have to formulate their own exchange rate regimes against a background of floating relationships at the 'core' of the system. How will they do this?

(ii)   Exchange Rate Regimes for Non-core Countries

If the hypothesis of the 'disappearing middle' has validity, the increasing integration of goods and capital markets will make it harder, as the 21st century proceeds, to maintain adjustable pegged regimes. Non-core countries will therefore face the following choices in their exchange rate regime:

(i)   independent floating (free or managed);
(ii)   using another country's currency (dollarisation or euro-isation);
(iii)   regional currency union.

Clearly, decisions on this matter will be driven by both economic and political considerations. From an economic perspective, the framework for choice has been set by the literature on optimum currency areas (Mundell, 1961; Kenen, 1969). Broadly speaking, this literature suggests that a currency union is likely to be beneficial when:

(i)   there is a large degree of trade integration (because the advantages of exchange rate certainty and reduced transactions costs will be greater);

(ii)   when the regions within a currency union are not subject to asymmetric external shocks;
(iii) when there exist income transfer mechanisms within the currency area to cushion regional disparities in economic activity.

For a considerable period, the practical application of the optimum currency area literature did not seem to point to much of a case for currency unions. Only in the European Union could the conditions be argued to exist, and even there many economists (Krugman, 1992; Eichengreen and Frieden, 1994) doubted whether Europe was really an optimum currency area. They pointed to the possibility of asymmetric shocks (German reunification was often cited in this connection), to the lack of mobility of factors of production, and to the absence of income transfer mechanisms.

In my view, however, the conditions cited for the success of monetary union are too restrictive. Looking several decades ahead, other regions of the world may well be able to follow the path of the European Union. It will take considerable time and require institution-building, but it would be a mistake to see the obstacles as insuperable.

Why do I hold this view? Firstly, intra-regional trade integration is growing. The potential advantages of currency union are therefore becoming greater. Secondly, the costs of independent monetary policies (and independent exchange rate movements) are increasingly troublesome for economies in the same region (Mercosur and SE Asia come to mind). Thirdly, 'asymmetric shocks' may be less of a problem in practice than in theory. Most asymmetric shocks are policy-induced, and indeed often arise from monetary policy divergences. The formation of a monetary union can cause business cycles to become more synchronised, thus diminishing the magnitude of such shocks. And finally, the need for cross-border income transfers to cushion the effects of regional disparities itself depends on the existence of asymmetric shocks, which I have argued is exaggerated.

In fact, currency unions are more likely to be opposed (or favoured) for reasons related to politics and governance, as much as economics. A currency union means giving up an important element of domestic economic sovereignty, and finding satisfactory means to pool decision-making authority in the monetary sphere. The creation of a monetary union, as European experience shows, is a long and intricate process of creating common institutions in a variety of dimensions. In the case of Europe, it went hand in hand with broader economic and political integration. Even so, progress toward the eventual realisation of a common currency proceeded in stages.

If my conjecture in this section is right, and the next decades see movement towards the creation of additional currency unions, this would still leave several major questions about the global exchange rate regime:

(i)   What would be the relationship of the currency unions with the 'core' G3 currencies?
(ii)   What about countries that, for economic or political reasons, choose to stay outside currency unions?

One can imagine a regional currency union having a tight 'currency board' type relationship with one of the major currency units. This is indeed the case with the African currency unions (based on the franc, and now the euro) and the Caribbean currency union (based on the US dollar). This makes sense in the light of the trade and investment orientation of the countries concerned. For others, however, it is difficult to see much alternative to relatively free floating. This would probably be the case if a currency union were to be formed in Mercosur or in East Asia, where trading patterns are quite well diversified.

Finally, what about the large number of countries that will not easily fit into any conceivable currency union? Should they float or tie themselves increasingly closely to one of the major currencies? Or should they indeed abandon their own currency and 'dollarise'? The case for dollarisation is quite powerful in countries with a long history of inflation and weak central bank credibility. Dornbusch (2001), however, argues that it can be extended to other countries that have close trade and investment links with a major currency bloc. Mexico and Canada are often cited in this connection. I suspect that dollarisation for Mexico and Canada would not be an option, for political reasons, unless they were given representation on the Federal Open Market Committee, which seems unlikely. For similar reasons, Switzerland is also unlikely to 'euro-ise'. Nevertheless, countries that have an overwhelming share of trade and investment with one of the major currency blocs are likely to manage their currency in such a way as to have a stable rate of exchange with that currency.

To conclude, any evolution of the international exchange rate regime seems likely to be slow and gradual. The currencies at the core of the system are likely to continue to float against each other. Some peripheral currencies may disappear, either because they have 'failed' to perform the functions of money, or because they are merged into regional currencies. The larger non-core currencies will face the dilemma of how to conduct their monetary and exchange rate policies so as to achieve the optimal trade-off between domestic and external stability. For them, the best option currently available is probably managed floating with inflation-targeting.

REFERENCES

Alesina, Alberto and Robert J. Barro (2001), 'Dollarisation', *American Economic Review*, May, 381–5.
Bernanke, Ben S., Thomas Laubach, Frederic S. Mishkin and Adam S. Posen (1998), *Inflation Targeting, Lessons from the International Experiences*, Princeton: Princeton University Press.
Cooper, Richard N. (1984), 'A Monetary System for the Future', *Foreign Affairs*, 63 (1), Fall, 166–84.
Crockett, Andrew (1994), 'The Role of Convergence in the Process of EMU', in Alfred Steiner (ed.), *30 Years of European Monetary Integration from the Werner Plan to EMU*, New York: Longman.
Dornbusch, Rudiger (2001), 'Fewer Monies, Better Monies', *American Economic Review*, May, 238–42.
Eichengreen, Barry (1992), *Golden Fetters: The Gold Standard and the Great Depression, 1919–1939*, New York: Oxford University Press.
Eichengreen, Barry (1994), *International Monetary Arrangements for the 21st Century*, Washington DC: Brookings.
Eichengreen, Barry and J. Frieden (1994), 'The Political Economy of European Monetary Unification', in Eichengreen and Frieden (eds), *The Political Economy of European Monetary Unification*, Boulder, CO: Westview Press.
Eichengreen, Barry, Paul Masson, Hugh Bredenkamp, Barry Johnston, Javier Hamann, Esteban Jadresic and Inci Ötker (1998), 'Exit Strategies: Policy Options for Countries Seeking Greater Exchange Rate Flexibility', International Monetary Fund, Washington, DC, Occasional Paper 168.
Fischer, Stanley (2001), 'Exchange Rate Regimes: Is the Bipolar View Correct?', *Journal of Economic Perspectives*, 15 (2), Spring, 3–24.
Flood, Robert P. and Peter Garber (1984), 'Collapsing Exchange Rate Regimes: Some Linear Examples', *Journal of International Economics*, August.
Frankel, Jeffrey A. (1999), 'No Single Currency Regime is Right for All Countries or at All Times', NBER Working Paper No. 7338, September, Cambridge.
Friedman, Milton (1953), 'The Case for Flexible Exchange Rates', *Essays in Positive Economics*, Chicago: University of Chicago Press.
Giovannini, Alberto (1995), 'European Monetary Reform: Progress and Prospects', in A. Giovannini (ed.), *The Debate on Money in Europe*, Cambridge, Mass.: MIT Press.
Goldstein, Morris (2001), *Managed Floating Plus and the Great Currency Regime Debate*, Institute for International Finance, mimeo, October.
Goodhart, Charles A.E. (1991), 'The ESCB after Maastricht', FMG Special Papers, sp. 0044.
Hume, David (1752), 'Of the Balance of Trade', reproduced in Eugene Rotwein (ed.), *David Hume: Writings on Economics*, London, Nelson, 1955.
International Monetary Fund (1974), 'Decision No. 4232 (74/67): Guidelines for the Management of Floating Exchange Rates', Washington, DC: IMF.
Ito, Takatoshi (1999), 'A target for the Bank of Japan', *Financial Times*, 19 October.
Kenen, Peter B. (1969), 'The Theory of Optimum Currency Areas: An Eclectic View', in Robert A. Mundell and Alexander K. Swoboda (eds), *Monetary Problems of the International Economy*, Chicago: University of Chicago Press.
King, Mervyn (1997), 'Changes in UK Monetary Policy: Rules and Discretion in Practice', *Journal of Monetary Economies*, 39, June, 81–97.

Krugman, Paul (1979), 'A model of balance of payments crises', *Journal of Money, Credit and Banking*, August, 311–25.

Krugman, Paul (1992), *Currencies and Crises*, Cambridge, Mass.: MIT Press.

Meade, James E. (1951), *The Theory of International Economic Policy: the Balance of Payments*, Oxford: Oxford University Press.

Meyer, Laurence (2001), 'Inflation Targets and Inflation Targeting', Speech at the University of California, San Diego Economics Round Table, San Diego, California, 17 July.

Morris, Stephen and Hyun Song Shin (1999), 'Risk Management with Independent Choice', Bank of England, *Financial Stability Review*, November, 141–50.

Mundell, Robert A. (1961), 'A Theory of Optimum Currency Areas', *American Economic Review*, September, 657–65.

Rogoff, Kenneth (2001), 'Why not a global currency?', *American Economic Review*, May, 243–47.

Summers, Lawrence (1999), 'Testimony before the Senate Foreign Relations Subcommittee on International Economic Policy and Export Trade Promotion', 27 January.

Svensson, Lars (2000), 'The First Year of the Eurosystem: Inflation Targeting or Not?', *American Economic Review*, Papers and Proceedings, 90, May, 95–9.

Williamson, John (1993), 'Exchange Rate Management', *Economic Journal*, 103 (416), January, 188–97.

Williamson, John and Marcus H. Miller (1987), *Targets and Indicators: A Blueprint for the International Coordination of Economic Policy*, Policy Analysis in International Economics series, No. 22, Washington, DC: Institute for International Economics, p. 115.

Discussion of 'Exchange rate regimes in theory and practice'

Jose Viñals

The chapter by Andrew Crockett provides a very fine blend of the theoretical and practical issues surrounding a question which in the past has been very controversial and which is likely to remain so in the future: the choice of exchange rate regime. The chapter not only provides a very comprehensive and well-structured review of the subject but also advances interesting ideas.

The author is quite right when he states that concerning the choice of exchange rate regime strong opinions are expressed often based on weak theory. Yet it has to be recognized that this is due to the fact that we lack a sound micro-theoretic basis to assess the benefits and costs of alternative exchange rate regimes. Thus the most that can be done at this stage is to go the way the author went in his chapter: to identify a few key guideposts that can help us to better understand this thorny question by bringing together general economic principles and the lessons from the international experience with alternative exchange rate regimes.

Another point worth making is that while the chapter studies the choice of regime mainly from a country perspective, it is clear that the exchange rate regime is a key piece of the international financial architecture with significant implications, for example, for the degree of vulnerability of countries to crises, the incentives to promote an environment of free capital flows or the need to provide catalytic official financing on the international scene.

Although the chapter addresses a variety of very interesting questions, in my discussion I will concentrate on the following two: whether there is a 'disappearing middle' in the spectrum of available exchange rate regimes, ranging from full fixity to the full flexibility pole; and towards which pole should a country go provided that it decides to move away from the middle.

Concerning the debate over whether there is or is not a 'disappearing middle': my impression is that there is some semantic confusion in the literature stemming from how the so-called 'middle' is defined. If the 'middle' excludes managed floating, then judging by the choices made in the recent past by many countries the 'middle' would be less densely populated now-adays. However, if the 'middle' is defined to include managed floating – as the author quite correctly does – then the opposite is true.

Andrew Crockett's basic point – which I fully share – is that neither the so-called 'impossible trinity' nor recent experiences with pegged exchange rate regimes are enough to explain why there is a 'disappearing middle'. Indeed, there is nothing to prevent life inside the trinity. As the author states, what needs to be acknowledged is that fixed-but-adjustable exchange rate regimes are inherently unstable in a world of free capital flows. Nevertheless – as he notes – while this can explain why the 'more fixed' part of the middle is less attractive, it does not imply a bipolar choice: fully-fixed or fully-flexible. Specifically, as shown by recent experience, while for those countries willing to go towards more fixity nothing much short of a cur-rency union or similar is likely to be suitable, the same is not true for those willing to move towards more flexibility. Indeed, the 'more flexible' part of the middle is not likely to be destabilising if well managed.

These conclusions are acceptable subject to certain qualifications. In my view, the sustainable part of the middle is even more limited than the chapter seems to suggest, at least as far as advanced economies which are well integrated into world capital markets are concerned. In particular, no matter how flexibly managed, any exchange rate regime which is based on an explicitly and publicly announced exchange rate target is an invitation to speculators. However, the 'more fixed' part of the middle has a chance of succeeding as a transitional device for countries embarking in a project of regional economic and monetary integration provided that the system is designed to sufficiently encourage two-way risk. In these cases, the multi-lateral nature of the arrangement and the credibility of the end-point would exercise a stabilising effect even with free capital movements. All in all, however, except for these transitory arrangements, I think that the theory of what I would call the 'disappearing fixed part of the middle' broadly holds.

The author is also right to point out that there is no universal, nor eternal 'best' exchange rate regime and that the choice of regime depends on the specific circumstances faced by a country at a specific time. Still, it is inter-esting to note – as he does – that relatively large economies tend to move inside the 'middle' towards more flexibility – but not full flexibility – while others have gone towards the fixity pole by entering into a currency union, dollarizing or adopting a currency board.

Of particular relevance is the discussion in the chapter of the determi-nants of the degree of exchange rate flexibility in the case of those coun-tries which adopt a 'managed float'. Yet I think the chapter would have benefited from a sharper distinction between advanced and emerging economies. In the first group, spontaneous exchange rate flexibility is generally moderated by the reaction function of the monetary authorities – insofar as exchange rates affect price developments and monetary policy reacts to the latter – and, in some cases, by leaning-against-the wind strategies or even exceptional interventions. In emerging markets, instead, the interest in avoiding sharp exchange rate movements has to do with the authorities' concern with financial stability and with the sustainability of public finances. Indeed, the inability of these countries to borrow in their own currency and the lack of hedging instruments lead to significant degrees of dollarization of liabilities and severe foreign currency mismatches in the balance sheets of the private sector. In turn, the existence of significant stocks of foreign-currency-denominated public debt also makes public finances highly sensitive to exchange rate changes.

Finally, concerning the case of countries which have opted for moving towards the fixed pole, I think that the experience of the last few years tends to suggest that the more promising route is that of countries engaged in an economic and monetary integration process leading to a currency union, like EMU. In contrast, only under very special conditions would it be true that unilateral movements to establish a currency board or to adopt a major currency – like dollarization – is the appropriate course to take. As a result, I would take a less neutral position than that of the previous chapter. My view would be that while movements towards increased exchange rate flexibility are quite understandable and likely to be stability-enhancing if accompanied by an appropriate domestic monetary anchor, things are likely to prove in general more cumbersome when moving towards the fixed pole. In this other pole, I do not see much future in unilateral actions but rather in the formation or enlargement of currency unions whenever there is the political will to do so, and good enough reasons to think that such unions are economically appropriate *ex ante*, or will become so *ex post*.

5. Is foreign exchange intervention effective? The Japanese experiences in the 1990s

Takatoshi Ito[*]

1. INTRODUCTION

Foreign exchange interventions have been one of the most secretive activities of monetary authorities around the world. They have been always a source of controversy, both in the academic literature and in practice. Some have believed that intervention cannot be effective based on a popular monetary model of determining the exchange rate, and also argued that the size of intervention tends to be overwhelmed by the market size, especially for major currencies. Others have argued that in some instances, interventions seemed to be effective by changing the sentiment of the market through signalling the future changes of policy. Some models, they also argue, that take into account the risk difference between domestic and foreign bonds would show some influences of intervention through portfolio shifts among the private sector. A dominant view on effectiveness of intervention has changed the side a few times in the past decades. The monetary authorities tended to intervene heavily in the foreign exchange market during the transition from the Bretton Woods system which collapsed in August 1971 to the floating of major currencies in the beginning of 1973. Even after the floating began, some monetary authorities in large economies were believed to be intervening heavily in the foreign exchange market. In the early 1980s, the Jurgensen study (1983; also Edison, 1993), which benefited from obtaining data from the participating authorities as a part of the official-sector study, concluded that interventions, especially sterilized interventions, did not have much impact on the exchange rate.[1] Nonsterilized interventions have some effects, but only temporarily. However, the apparent success of concerted intervention following the Plaza Accord of September 1985 in driving down the overvalued US dollar aroused academic interest. A series of papers by Dominguez and Frankel showed some effects of interventions on the level, volatility, and risk premium of exchange rates (see Dominguez, 1990; Dominguez and Frankel, 1993a, b, c). They have emphasized the signalling effect of intervention that would work on expectation of institutional investors. Although effects of interventions have been debated extensively, no conclusive consensus has been obtained. (See Sarno and Taylor (2001) for a most recent survey, and Ramana and Samiei (2000) for the work on the effectiveness of intervention on the yen/dollar exchange rate before the disclosure.)

Except for the United States, information about intervention has not been disclosed publicly among the G7 countries. Although the authorities could exchange information for internal studies on intervention through Group of 10 (G10) or Bank of International Settlements (BIS), outside researchers could not have obtained data freely. In some cases, data were released to selected researchers for academic purposes only, with the condition that data would be destroyed after the research was concluded. Empirical studies of intervention have become a popular exercise as data on intervention have become available to researchers. The past empirical studies have mixed results on the effectiveness of foreign exchange interventions.

The Japanese authorities had not released data of intervention to nonofficials, even for academic research, although reported data to international organizations were occasionally used for internal studies in official circles, including G10 and BIS. Some researchers in the academic and private sector had to go to newspaper or wire services to create proxies (mostly zero-one dummy variables) for Japanese interventions.

In July 2001, the Japanese Ministry of Finance disclosed intervention records from April 1991 to March 2001. The intervention record in the future will be disclosed in the same format four times a year (MOF home page: www.mof.go.jp/english/e1c021.htm).

The rest of this chapter is organized as follows: Section 2 will describe the Japanese intervention record in the 1990s, including some institutional details of intervention operations in Japan. Section 3 will describe the yen–dollar rate movement in the 1990s, and intervention phases. Section 4 estimates profits/losses from intervention operations. Realized gains/losses from buying and selling the US dollars, the carrying profits/losses of large foreign reserves, and unrealized gains/losses at the end of sample period are estimated. Section 5 discusses the intervention strategy and intention. In Section 6, regression results are presented to show that Japanese interventions tended to be successful at least in the short run, for the second half of the decade. Section 7 examines the reaction function. Section 8 concludes the chapter.

2.   DATA DESCRIPTION AND INSTITUTIONAL DETAILS

In August 2000, the Japanese Ministry of Finance started to disclose data of daily intervention in the preceding quarters (that is, a delay in disclosure by one to four months). The historical data from April 1991 to March 2000 was released in July 2001. Interventions in the future will be also disclosed in the same format, four times a year. What exactly are disclosed and what are not can be summarized as follows. The disclosed data by the Japanese Ministry of Finance include the following information: (a) the day of intervention, (b) the yen amount and direction (sold/bought) of intervention for the day, (c) currencies that are involved in intervention. What is not disclosed, but would have been desired by researchers, are the following: (a) Exact time of the day (hour, minute, second) and how many times within the day; (b) market (Tokyo, London, or New York) where the intervention was carried out; (c) the exact exchange rate at which intervention was carried out.[2] Although it was never mentioned explicitly, it is understood that all interventions were carried out in the spot market, and no forward market intervention or interventions using the derivatives market has been used. Since the exact exchange rate that is applicable to a particular intervention action is not disclosed, the central rate of the Tokyo market of the day of intervention will be used in this study. Since the central rate is the rate at which most transactions took place, it can be regarded as a good proxy for the intervention rate.

Japanese intervention has been under the jurisdiction of the Ministry of Finance. Intervention decisions – not every detail, but broad decisions – have to be made by the Minister of Finance. Detailed strategies are formulated in the line of bureaucratic hierarchy from the Vice Minister for International Affairs, the Director General of the International (Finance) Bureau, and the Director of the department in charge of intervention and foreign reserves. Movements and conditions in the foreign exchange market are constantly monitored by the department in close consultation with the Bank of Japan. Intervention orders, when issued, are carried out by the Bank of Japan.

Financial bills (short-term government bills, with maturity of three months) are issued to the market to obtain yen cash that is used to purchase the foreign-currency-denominated assets in the intervention. Financial bills are rolled over, when foreign-currency-denominated assets are maintained as foreign reserves. Sales of the foreign-currency-denominated assets result in reducing outstanding financial bills by redeeming them upon maturity. The balance sheet of the Special Accounts of the Foreign Exchange Fund discloses these assets and liabilities. Strictly speaking, foreign reserves are

Table 5.1   Comparison of institutional aspects of intervention

	Japan	USA	Euro	UK
Decision	Ministry of Finance	Treasury (lead) and FRB	ECB in consultation with EcoFin Council	HM Treasury and BoE (as monetary policy)
Agent	BoJ	New York FED	ECB	BoE
Disclosure	April 1991– present (1–3 month delay). Day, amount, currency.	All since 1973? (1–3 month delay). Amount, day, time, currency.	Not disclosed.	Year 2000 to present. Day, amount.

not on the balance sheet of the Bank of Japan, but are a part of budgetary operations. Some of the profits from the Special Accounts are transferred to the general budget. The Japanese foreign reserves can be regarded as a huge investment fund managed by the Ministry of Finance. However, details of the assets and liabilities of the Account, such as composition of foreign currency assets by currency or by maturity, are not disclosed. At the end of March 1999, the Special Account lists about 32 trillion yen of foreign currency denominated securities and deposits.

The disclosure practice of foreign exchange market intervention varies from country to country. (See Table 5.1.) The monetary authorities of the United States are the most transparent. The decision of intervention is jointly made by the Treasury and the Federal Reserve Board, and carried out by the Federal Reserve Bank of New York (NY Fed), with a lead by the Treasury. The data of intervention, disclosed publicly from NY Fed, includes amounts, day and time of intervention. The data go back to the 1970s. The Bundesbank and other eurozone central banks did not disclose the intervention data publicly, but some data were released for academic research. After the euro was launched, decisions on intervention were transferred to the European Central Bank (ECB), with consultation with the EcoFin council. The ECB has not disclosed intervention data. The monetary authorities of the United Kingdom, HM Treasury and the Bank of England, started to disclose intervention data in 2000. No historical data have been disclosed publicly. Table 5.1 summarizes the disclosure practice among the major monetary authorities.

The disclosed amount of Japanese intervention on day *t* could be a result

Table 5.2   Time line of possible patterns of intervention in Day t

Case 1		Day *t*−1			Day *t*		
	Tokyo 9–17:00	London 9–17:00	New York 9–17:00	Tokyo 9–17:00	London 9–17:00	New York 9–17:00
Japan				**Intervention**		
US						**Intervention**

Case 2		Day *t*−1			Day *t*		
	Tokyo 9–17:00	London 9–17:00	New York 9–17:00	Tokyo 9–17:00	London 9–17:00	New York 9–17:00
Japan						**Intervention (by NYFed)**
US						**Intervention**

Case 3		Day *t*−1			Day *t*		
	Tokyo 9–17:00	London 9–17:00	New York 9–17:00	Tokyo 9–17:00	London 9–17:00	New York 9–17:00
Japan				**Intervention**		
US				**Intervention (by BoJ)**		

of intervention in the Tokyo market of day *t*, intervention in the European or US time zones of day *t* (in local time), either carried out directly by the Bank of Japan or carried out by other central banks on behalf of the Bank of Japan. With the disclosure constraint of daily aggregation, the best proxy for the exchange rate just before the intervention on day *t* is the New York close of day (*t*−1), and the proxy for the exchange rate just after the intervention is the New York close of day *t*. The time line for possible patterns of intervention within a day is shown in Table 5.2.

3.   MOVEMENTS OF THE YEN/DOLLAR EXCHANGE RATE IN THE 1990S

Movements of the yen/dollar exchange rate and intervention points are reviewed in this section in order to give an overall picture of the decade. Although some accounts of interventions may be in detail, a blow-by-blow account of interventions during the period of spectacular yen appreciation to 80 yen/dollar and back to 100 yen/dollar in 1995 will be important in designing a more formal analysis later.

Figure 5.1 shows the daily movements of the exchange rate (upper panel) and accumulated monthly interventions on the corresponding time scale (lower panel) for the period from April 1991 to March 2001. From the figure, it can be seen that the yen has fluctuated between 80 yen/dollar and 146 yen/dollar during the ten-year period. The yen has appreciated from near 140 yen/dollar in the spring of 1991 to 80 yen/dollar in April of 1995, then it turned around and depreciated to 146 in the summer of 1998. The yen/dollar rate then went from 146 to near 100 in the next two years. The yen depreciated back to 125 by the end of the sample period.

Interventions have been conducted from time to time, as the yen becomes weaker or stronger than the ten-year average. When the yen/dollar rate was near 140 yen/dollar in May–June, 1991, there were three days of interventions to sell the dollar (and buy the yen). The lowest (in terms of dollar value in yen) point of intervention was 139.20 and the highest point of intervention was 141.80. This round of intervention appears to coincide with the turnaround of the yen, because the highest intervention rate coincides with the highest in this period.

There was another round of interventions in support of the yen from January 1992 to August 1992. There were 23 days of interventions during the eight months. Interventions appear to have been carried out to stop the yen from becoming too weak again, losing the gains made in the second half of 1991. Interventions were conducted in a range between 126.50 and 134.50. The intervention started when the yen was at around 128. The first intervention of this round was quite successful in making the yen stronger (at around 125). However, after a month, the yen became weaker, hovering at around 130. Several interventions from February to April 1992 did not stop the yen from depreciating to 134. The yen trend turned around at 134.75. Even after the yen started to strengthen, interventions continued. Interventions were in small lots, typically below 50 billion yen in a day, and carried out sometimes infrequently and sometimes almost every day. Interventions continued until the yen reached less than 128. Therefore, this round of interventions can be understood to make sure that the yen/dollar would not weaken beyond 135, and, moreover, to make the yen appreciate to the 127 level.

The direction of interventions changed in April 1993. By then, the yen was considered to have appreciated enough. The intervention in support of the US dollar, or preventing yen appreciation, started when the yen appreciated beyond the 115 yen/dollar level on 2 April, 1993. The neutral zone – the yen band between the last yen-buying intervention and the first yen-selling intervention – turned out to be about 14 yen.

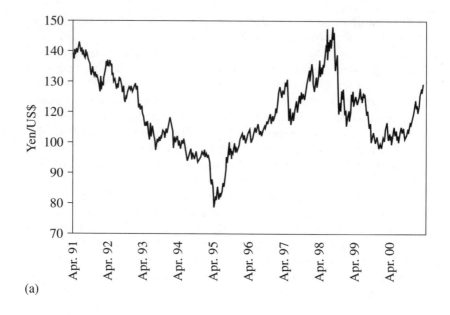

(a)

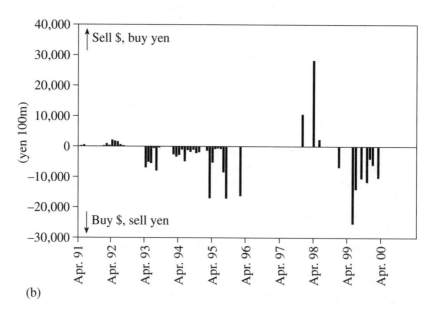

(b)

Figure 5.1   *(a) Yen/dollar exchange rate, 4 January 1991–30 March 2001,*
                Tokyo close; (b) amounts of intervention (monthly
                aggregation)

Interventions during this episode continued until the yen peaked at 100.50 yen/dollar on 17 August, when intervention sold more than 200 billion yen in a day. During the months from April to August 1993, the yen appreciation had occurred despite interventions to sell yen. In that sense, it appears numerous interventions during the five-month period were not particularly effective. On the other hand, if one interprets those interventions to be conducted to smooth the yen appreciation process, or to prevent an eventual defence line of 100, then the interventions from April to August were a success. Moreover, when exchange rate dynamics around intervention days are closely examined, a tendency is detected, in that interventions are prompted by a sudden yen appreciation (2 yen in the preceding day or two; for example 2 April, 19 April, 26 May, and 28 June), and that interventions stop yen depreciation at least for a day or so. One may conclude that *leaning-against-the-wind* operations from April to August were a failure in that the yen appreciated by 15 yen, *despite* repeated interventions. On the other hand, they were a success, in that each intervention tended to stop yen appreciation in the short run, that is at least a day or two, and that the yen appreciation was stopped short of a psychological barrier of 100, *because of* repeated intervention. Evaluations of intervention effects vary depending on what was the intent of interventions, which is not observable.

Even after the yen movement turned around on 17 August at just before the 100 level, intervention continued until the yen reached 104.5 on 7 September. In a broader sense, the intervention from August to September was to *lean in the wind*. Interventions were not employed between 7 September, 1993 and 15 February, 1994, when the yen fluctuated between 105 and 113 yen/dollar.

The 15 February, 1994 intervention seems to be prompted by a sudden appreciation of the yen overnight (by 2 yen) to 102. From this point on, the monetary authorities intervened at least several days in one month from February to November, or to be precise 55 days in 10 months, in the range of 96.45–105.10. It is hard to say whether the objective of intervention was to keep the yen from appreciating beyond 100 (in that case, it failed in late June 1994) or to make the yen appreciation smoother than otherwise.

Heavy interventions were conducted from late June to mid-July 1994, when the yen/dollar rate approached the level 100 again. During a period from 20 June to 1 July, yen-selling intervention was conducted for 11 days with a total of 538 billion yen. On 24 June, 136 billion yen of the Japanese monetary authorities, combined with the US intervention of US\$610 million worth of yen, were sold with an apparent intention to prevent the yen from appreciating beyond 100. The yen/dollar rate for the first time in its post-war history, broke into the double-digit number on 27 June.

However, after the 11–12 July intervention, the yen/dollar rate moved back above the 100 level. In mid-August, the yen/dollar rate broke the 100 level again. Interventions were conducted for six days in a row in an attempt to stop appreciation. These interventions were barely successful in bringing the rate back above 100. The interventions in September also made little impact on the level of the yen. The yen appreciated from mid-August to the beginning of November, despite 19 interventions, and became 96.45 yen/dollar on 3 November. On 2 November, Japanese intervention sold more than 100 billion yen, and the US intervention sold 800 million dollars worth of the yen, followed by another joint intervention – the Japanese selling 50 billion yen and the US 500 million dollars worth – on 3 November. These two days of joint interventions finally turned around the yen. The yen hovered just at 100 at the end of 1994. During 1994, interventions were conducted in 55 days, selling a total of 2.639 trillion yen.

No intervention was used from 3 November, 1994 to 17 February, 1995. The first intervention of 1995 was conducted on 17 February, when the yen/dollar rate was at around 97. During the period from 17 February to 18 April, intervention was conducted on 34 days, with a total amount of 2.3 trillion yen, in support of the US dollar. However, the yen gradually appreciated despite these interventions. During the month of March 1995, a battle over the yen was fierce, with the market pressuring the yen to appreciate beyond the 90 mark, while the authorities were attempting to defend the 90 yen mark. In March, the Japanese monetary authorities intervened on 21 days out of 23 business days. The US–Japan joint intervention was conducted on both 2 and 3 March. However, the yen steadily appreciated in these two days, to the level of 95 yen/dollar. On 6 March, the yen/dollar rate became 93, and on 13 March, just above 90. From 13 to 31 March, Japanese intervention was conducted for every day for three weeks, with a total amount of 1.3 trillion yen. The yen/dollar rate stayed in a narrow range of 88–90 yen, although the amount of intervention varied widely from one day to the next. It looked like the case that the intervention was conducted to keep the yen from appreciating beyond 88 yen per dollar. However, there was no resolve to push the yen back above the 90 level. Since the yen appreciated little by little despite the interventions, it would be difficult to argue that interventions were successful.

On 3 and 4 April, there were joint interventions by the Japanese and US authorities. (On 3 April, the Japanese monetary authorities sold 120 billion yen, and the US 750 million dollars worth of yen; and on 4 April, the Japanese 43 billion yen and the US 250 million dollars worth.) Despite this show of force, the yen did not depreciate, but stuck at 86 yen/dollar. The yen started to appreciate from the following day. On 10 April, the yen/dollar rate became 83 yen/dollar, and on 18 April, it became 81, despite repeated unilateral interventions by the Japanese authorities (on 6, 7, 10, 14, 17, and

18 April). The yen recorded the all-time high of 79.75 (for a few seconds), or 80.25 at the Tokyo close on 19 April. Incidentally, there was no intervention that day.

During the swift appreciation from 88 to 80 yen/dollar from 3 to 18 April, the Japanese authorities sold 500 billion yen, which was less than half of what was sold in the March intervention in a seeming attempt to defend 90. The very swift move of the yen in the first half of April may be puzzling. It was said that technical factors such as knock-out options and delta hedge strategies were responsible for the movement. Many, if not all, economists regarded the level of 80 yen/dollar, or movement from 100 to 80 in three and a half months, out of sync with fundamentals at the time.

From mid-April, the yen turned around, but did not depreciate significantly either. By mid May, the yen depreciated to the level of 87 yen per dollar. However, toward the end of May, the yen appreciated again. On 30 May, the yen reached the level of 82 yen per dollar. On 31 May, the joint intervention by the Japanese and US monetary authorities was conducted, and that brought the yen to the level of 84.5.

The Japanese intervention was conducted on 28 June, at the level of 84 yen/dollar. This was the first intervention under the direction of new Director General of International Finance Bureau, Dr Sakakibara. The second intervention by Dr Sakakibara was on 7 July, jointly with the US authorities, which depreciated the yen by about 2 yen, to the level of 86.8 yen/dollar at the New York close. (The intervention amount was not particularly large. The Japanese sold 580 billion yen, and the US sold 330 million dollars worth of yen.)

Toward the end of July, the yen depreciated to the 88 yen/dollar level. On 2 August, a large-scale joint intervention was carried out. The Japanese authorities sold 676 billion yen, and the US authorities sold 500 million dollars worth of the yen. The joint intervention on 2 August was accompanied by policy measures, for example to liberalize the restriction of pension funds investment abroad. The joint intervention caused the yen to depreciate by 3 yen, and the yen/dollar level was restored to the 90s' level, for the first time in four and half months. Sakakibara recalls the day: 'We intervened aggressively in Tokyo. The yen/dollar rate started at 87 in the Tokyo market, but finished at around 90 due to our intervention to push up the level by the close. Later in the day, the concerted intervention was carried out in New York. Intervention amounts were the highest in history . . . After the Tokyo market closed and before the New York market opened, Minister Takemura phoned Secretary Rubin and reported the market condition in Tokyo, and consulted on interventions in New York. I was glad that Secretary Rubin regarded highly of the [Japanese policy] measures announced and interventions carried out in Tokyo . . . And, concerted interventions in New York finally broke the level of 90' (Sakakibara, 2000, p. 124).

Additional interventions were carried out on 11 August (Japanese unilateral) and on 15 August (Japan–US–Germany, joint). These interventions were quite effective, and the yen reached 97 yen/dollar. These interventions were to lean into the wind.

In September, final pushes to restore the level of 100 were attempted. On 6 September, the Japanese authorities intervened with 226 billion yen, to bring the yen to 98.9 by the New York close. On 8 September, a record high of 858 billion yen was sold by the Japanese authorities to break the 100 level. Sakakibara recalls the moment as follows: 'In the afternoon of the 8th, we bought dollars more and more, but the yen/dollar rate did not move just below 100 for 30 minutes to one hour . . . In the end, we used electronic broking. At last, the yen/dollar rate went over the 100, and posted 100.20 on the screen. Cheers broke out in the dealing room of the Ministry' (Sakakibara, 2000, p. 129).

Interventions under Sakakibara's direction, those between 28 June and 22 September, have distinctive features that should be contrasted to the previous interventions. First, these interventions were *not* prompted by sudden yen depreciation of the preceding day or two. They seemed to be motivated by dissatisfaction with the current level. The intervention was conducted to change actively the then prevailing level of the yen/dollar rate, while the previous interventions were conducted in an attempt to defend a certain level. In short, the previous interventions were a lean-against-the-wind type, while the Sakakibara interventions were a lean-in-the-wind type. Second, the frequency of intervention was less but the per-day amount of intervention was larger than before. Sakakibara himself noted the difference, emphasizing that it was a deliberate choice. Talking of interventions by his predecessor, he wrote 'The market was accustomed to interventions, because they were too frequent. The interventions were taken as a given. Most interventions, including joint interventions, were predictable, so that interventions, even joint ones, had only small, short-term effects, and could not change the sentiment of the market' (Sakakibara, 2000, p. 119). Sakakibara then attempted a 'change of intervention philosophy and technique. For this, all I [had] to do was to make [the] decision and convince the Vice Minister and the Minister of this. For one, the frequency of interventions was reduced substantially, and the per-intervention amount is increased, in order to push up the level [of the dollar vis-à-vis the yen]' (ibid., p. 120).

One more intervention was conducted on 22 September. That seemed to have been prompted by a sudden yen appreciation. In the first half of 1995, before 21 June, interventions were conducted in 35 days with selling 2,359 billion yen, while in the second half of 1996, after 21 June, interventions were conducted in only 8 days, selling 2,000 billion yen. The per-intervention yen was much higher under Sakakibara's direction.

After September, the yen/dollar rate stayed at around 100 for the rest of the year, and then depreciated, without interventions, to the 107 level by February 1996. When the yen appreciated back toward 104, a series of interventions was conducted. However, five days of interventions in the last ten days of February did not produce any measurable impact on the rate. It was quite unlike Sakakibara's interventions of 1995, in that this time it seemed to be prompted by yen appreciation just before intervention, and despite interventions, the yen/dollar rate did not move. Sakakibara claims that for these interventions he detected that yen appreciation pressure had been building, and absorbing those pressures by interventions was important to prevent potential yen appreciation. Therefore, even though the yen did not depreciate, despite a total of 1,603 billion yen interventions, he would still claim a success (see Sakakibara, 2000, p. 138).

This kind of detailed information is quite important in designing the empirical analysis. First, interventions by Sakakibara may be different from others in how they were prompted by the market movement and how effective they were in influencing the yen/dollar rate. Therefore the reaction function and the effectiveness function may have a structural break at the point Sakakibara assumed the Director General post. Second, how to judge the effectiveness of interventions is difficult, because intentions of interventions vary from one person in charge to another, or depending on a depreciation or appreciation phase.

Intervention did not take place from February 1996 to the end of 1997, as the yen steadily depreciated. When the yen depreciated over the level of 130, interventions in support of the yen were carried out in December 1997. It was five and half years since the last yen-buying intervention, and it was a year and half since the last intervention in the opposite direction. The last yen-selling intervention point was 105.70 (Tokyo central rate), and the rate at which yen was bought this time was 127.00 yen. This implies that the neutral band, the difference between the yen-selling intervention point and the yen-buying intervention point was more than 21 yen. Three days of interventions did not cause yen appreciation. In fact, the yen gradually depreciated to 129 over the three days of interventions that were intended to appreciate the yen. However, the yen depreciated to the 130 level in January 1998. When the yen depreciated to 135 and then appreciated back to 132 in April, heavy intervention was conducted. Interventions on 9, 10 April bought a total of 2.8 trillion yen, a record amount in the 1990s. However, this pushed down the dollar by only 1 to 2 yen/dollar. It was not a failure, but not a great success considering the large size of intervention.

The yen depreciated to 137 in May, and to the 140s in early June without being challenged by interventions. When the yen depreciated to 143 on 15 June a joint intervention was pulled off, and quickly brought the yen to the level of 136 (a jump of 7 yen) on June 16. The yen stayed at around 140 until August, when it depreciated back to the upper 140s range, again. However, no intervention was conducted. The yen gradually appreciated in September, and then appreciated sharply by 10 yen on 7 October, to 120 yen/dollar, without intervention. This is considered to be a result of hedge funds unwinding yen-carry trade positions.

It is remarkable that a relatively small number of interventions was conducted in 1997 and 1998, although the yen/dollar rate fluctuated widely. A large part of the fluctuations may reflect worsening Japanese financial systems. Two large financial institutions failed in November 1997, and another large financial institution was failing in 1998. The systemic vulnerability invited selling and short-selling of Japanese assets and currency during the summer of 1998. However, those speculative positions were unwound quickly after the Russian debt crisis and de facto default in August and the near collapse of Long-term Capital Management (LTCM) in September, 1998. With these changing fundamentals, interventions were ruled out.

The yen continued to appreciate and reached 110 by the end of the year. The direction of intervention switched again in 1999. On 12 January, the Japanese authorities sold the yen which had an effect of depreciating the yen from 109 yen/dollar on the previous day to 112 yen/dollar. This intervention seemed to be quite effective. The yen trend was reversed, and the yen depreciated toward 123 yen/dollar in May 1999, when it started to appreciate again.

This time, the authorities seemed to be less tolerant on appreciation compared to the January intervention at around 110. In June, four interventions were conducted, pushing the yen from 118 to 122, with the selling of 2.9 trillion yen. Despite the large size of interventions, the yen depreciation was modest. This may be due to a relatively high yen/dollar level to conduct yen-selling interventions. Not very many market participants considered that the yen would depreciate further into the high 120s.

The yen gradually appreciated from the 120 level in July 1999 to 102 by the end of the year, despite 9 interventions, with the selling of 3.9 trillion yen. On 3 January 2000, the yen became 101, and threatened to reach the critical 100 level. The intervention of 4 January depreciated the yen to 103, and set the trend of subsequent depreciation. There were three more interventions in March and April, to make sure the yen depreciation trend remained. The yen depreciated to 126 yen/dollar by March 2001, the end of this sample period.

From the quick review of yen fluctuations and intervention points and amounts in the 1990s, there are several observations that can be helpful in designing a more formal analysis. First, intervention styles were different before and after June 1995, which was a deliberate choice of the new Director General Sakakibara who assumed office in June 1995. Second, the period of yen appreciation in the first half of 1995, from 100 to 80 yen/dollar, despite repeated, numerous interventions seemed to be a very extraordinary period. Third, looking back at the 1990s, dollars were bought (the yen was sold) when the dollar was cheap (the yen appreciated), and vice versa. The middle point in switching the direction was at around 125 yen/dollar. Fourth, on many, but not all, occasions, an intervention seemed to be prompted by a sharp move of the yen/dollar rate on the preceding day. However, some interventions were conducted without sharp changes, especially the early ones by Sakakibara. Of course, not all sharp changes in the yen/dollar rate resulted in interventions. Fifth, in some cases interventions worked in the sense that the yen moved (within a day) in the intended direction, but in some cases there were no measurable movements (within a day). Sixth, evaluations of the effects of intervention are much more difficult for the medium term effect (over several days or longer).

4.   WERE INTERVENTIONS PROFITABLE?

As noted in the previous section, all of the dollar-purchasing (yen-selling) interventions were conducted below the 125 level, while all of the dollar-selling (yen-purchasing) interventions were conducted above the 125 level. Table 5.3 shows the buying and selling operations aggregated in the 5-yen brackets.

In a sense, the Japanese authorities bought the dollar low and sold high. This indicates that the Japanese monetary authorities are profitable fund-managers, and that meant a 'stabilizing' speculator, in the sense of Milton Friedman. In a broader sense, the fluctuations of the yen/dollar rate would have been more than the reality, had the interventions not been conducted.

In this section, the profits made by the Japanese authorities are estimated. Profits from interventions can be categorized into three factors:

(i)   realized capital gains, that is buy low/sell high strategy;
(ii)   profits/losses from the interest rate differential, namely the difference between the interest costs of borrowing in yen and the interest gains from holding the dollar assets; and
(iii) unrealized capital gains (inventory of dollar asset values mark-to-market at end March 2001) compared to the average cost of acquiring the inventory.

Table 5.3   Intervention by exchange rate brackets

Rate (central rate)		Direction	Number of days	Sum of amounts 100 million yen
At or above	Less than			
140	145	Sell US$	3	2,736
135	140	Sell US$	1	139
130	135	Sell US$	8	30,581
125	130	Sell US$	20	15,338
120	125	Buy US$	2	17,109
115	120	Buy US$	4	21,568
110	115	Buy US$	17	13,815
105	110	Buy US$	28	38,310
100	105	Buy US$	50	63,977
95	100	Buy US$	35	27,257
90	95	Buy US$	9	5,406
85	90	Buy US$	16	20,718
80	85	Buy US$	7	3,680
		Subtotal, Sell US$	32	48,794
		Subtotal, Buy US$	168	211,860
		Total	200	260,654

Notes: In addition to these Yen/$ interventions there were 1 Sell$/BuyDM, 1 BuyDM/Sell yen, 5 Sell $/Buy Rupiah, 5 Buy Euro/Sell Yen interventions.
Lowest Point of Sell (Central rate, Tokyo) US$ 126.50.
Highest Point of Buy (Central rate, Tokyo) US$ 122.65.

First, let us calculate the capital gains and the average inventory costs. The dollar-purchasing (yen-selling) interventions amounted to 21,186.1 billion yen, with purchasing values of 203.4 billion dollars, when the daily yen amount was converted to the dollar at the central rate of the Tokyo market. The dollar-selling (yen-purchasing) interventions amounted to 4,879.3 billion yen, with selling values of 37.4 billion dollars. Over the ten-year period, the average yen/dollar rate for the dollar-selling intervention was 130.38 yen (4879.3/37.4), and the average yen/dollar rate for the dollar-purchasing intervention was 104.17 yen (21186.1/203.4). Therefore, the realized capital gains are estimated as 981 billion yen (= 37.4 billion dollars × (130.38 − 104.17)).

Subtracting the 37.4 billion dollars that are sold from the 4,879.3 billion dollars that were bought, the inventory (foreign reserves from the 1990s interventions) at the end of sample period can be estimated. This amounts to 4,841.9 billion yen. The difference between the mark-to-market as of 30 March 2001 (New York close), that is 126.25 yen, and the average inventory cost, 104.17, is the unit profit per dollar. This amounts to 3,665.2 billion yen. These calculations are shown in Table 5.4.

What is more difficult is to estimate the interest profits/losses. What is clear is that the Japanese authorities made profits on this department too, because for most of the 1990s, the Japanese interest rate was much lower than the US interest rate. We assume that in every quarter, the 3-month interest rate of government securities (Financial Bills) are paid out to the balance of accumulated intervention in yen, while the 3-month interest rate of the US Treasury bills was earned on the balance of accumulated dollar denominated assets. With this approximation, the interest profit is estimated as 3,975 billion yen. Details are presented in Table 5.5. This is probably an underestimate as it assumes that the profits from the interest differentials are paid out to the general account from the special account (recall Section 2); in other words, compounding is disregarded.

To recap, the Japanese authorities are estimated to have earned: (i) realized gains of 981 billion yen; (ii) interest profits of 3,975 billion yen; and (iii) unrealized gains of 3,665 billion yen. A rough estimate of 8.6 trillion yen was earned during the ten years. So, indeed, the interventions were profitable.

5.   TIMING, INTENTION AND STRATEGY: FIRST APPROACH

In order to evaluate whether the intervention worked, it is important to make working assumptions about the exchange rate level that would have existed without intervention and on the intentions of the monetary authorities.

The intention of the monetary authorities can be classified into the following four categories. When the authorities are aiming at putting a brake on the recent trend of the exchange rate movement, that is called the lean-against-the-wind interventions. This type can be further subdivided into an intervention that is intended to reverse the trend and an intervention that is intended only to slow down the speed (smoothing). For example, when the yen has appreciated, the intervention to sell the yen is regarded as a lean-against-the-wind operation. When the trend is reversed (that is, the yen depreciated due to intervention), the reversing intervention is regarded as being effective. If the yen did not depreciate, but the rate of appreciation became smaller after the intervention than before, then the intervention was effective as a smoothing operation, but not as a reversing operation.

There is another type of intervention. When the yen has depreciated, the intervention of selling yen can be conducted to push the yen further into depreciation. This strategy is commonly called a lean-in-the-wind operation.

Table 5.4 Calculation of realized and unrealized gains

	Intervention in billion yen (A)	Intervention in US$ billion (B)	Average exchange rate (yen/$) (C)	Realized gains (in billion yen) of buying $ 37.42371 at 104.17 and selling $ at 130.38	Unrealized gains (in billion yen) of selling (203.4–37.4) billion dollars evaluating at 126.25 yen against inventory cost of 104.17
Subtotal, Sell US$	4879.4	37.42371	130.38	981.14	3665.25
Subtotal, Buy US$	21186.0	203.38800	104.17		
Calculation	See Table. 5.3	Note (1)	(A)/(B)	$=37.42371 \times$ $(130.38–104.17)$	$=(21186–4879.4) \times$ $(126.25–104.17)$

Notes:
(1) For each intervention day, the exchange rate of Tokyo market (central rate) is applied to calculate the US$ equivalent. Then all intervention days, separately for sell US$ and for buy US$, are aggregated.
(2) In calculating unrealized gains, the NY close on 30 March 2001 is used. The yen/dollar rate was 126.25 yen/dollar.

The intervention goes with the market trend. When the level is considered to be undesirable (say, the yen is too overvalued), but the market is on the way to correct the level, a lean-in-the-wind operation is conducted to hasten the return to a normal level. If the authorities' intention is to accelerate the recent change in the same direction, the operation is considered successful if the rate of yen depreciation is higher after the yen-selling intervention than before. If the authorities' intention was just to make sure that the direction would continue, then the yen depreciation after the yen-selling intervention is enough to call it a success.

In order to judge the level of effectiveness, the yen trend before intervention on day t is defined as the change in the yen/dollar rate (New York close) from $t-2$ to $t-1$. Then the effect of intervention is contained in the change in the yen/dollar rate (New York close) from $t-1$ to t. Categorization of the intervention effects measured by these 'before' and 'after' effects is shown in Table 5.6.

The most common type of intervention was lean-against-the-wind interventions when there was yen appreciation. There were 119 of them, and only on about half of the occasions were they successful in reversing the trend (that is, appreciation the day before, and depreciation on the day of intervention). (Recalling Section 3, most of the failures come from the period of the first half of 1995, when the yen appreciated from 100 to 80, despite continuous interventions.) However, if the standard for success is relaxed to be less appreciation due to intervention, then almost 70 per cent of the time interventions were successful.

There were 19 cases of lean-against-the-wind operations in an attempt to stop yen depreciation. Of the 19 interventions, 10 of them reversed the trend, and 17 of them were successful in slowing down yen depreciation.

When the yen was depreciating, there were 49 interventions to sell the yen to depreciate it further. These lean-in-the-wind operations were not particularly successful. From a total of 49 times, the yen depreciation accelerated only 11 times. More than half of the time, the yen appreciated rather than depreciated on the day of yen-selling interventions that followed some yen depreciation. This may be counter to the conventional wisdom that it is easier to go with the market rather than against the market.

The lean-in-the-wind interventions in an attempt to appreciate the yen totalled only 13 cases, but were successful in accelerating the yen appreciation, or at least maintaining yen appreciation, in more than 60 per cent of the cases.

The tabulation is only suggestive, and not conclusive in evaluating effects of interventions. First, the table is created only from days when the intervention was conducted. For example, a sharp yen appreciation may be followed by some yen depreciation (correction of overshooting), even without

Table 5.5   *Calculation of interest income*

Year	Qtr	R $ %	R Y %	$ balance (million $)	Y balance (billion yen)	Interest gains (billion yen)	Accumulated gains (billion yen)
1991	2	5.6	5.5	−4.0	56.3		
	3	5.6	5.5	−4.0	56.3	0.0	0.0
	4	4.8	5.4	−4.0	56.3	0.1	0.1
1992	1	4.0	4.9	−14.4	190.9	0.5	0.6
	2	3.8	4.4	−54.2	709.4	1.1	1.7
	3	3.1	3.6	−59.2	773.2	1.2	3.0
	4	3.1	3.1	−59.2	773.2	0.4	3.3
1993	1	3.0	3.1	−59.2	773.2	0.6	3.9
	2	3.1	2.4	97.8	−938.1	2.7	6.6
	3	3.1	1.6	179.6	−1780	7.6	14.2
	4	3.1	1.6	179.6	−1780	7.9	22.1
1994	1	3.3	1.6	233.5	−2340.4	11.4	33.5
	2	4.1	1.6	313.6	−3154.3	20.6	54.1
	3	4.6	1.6	347.5	−3488.2	25.6	79.8
	4	5.4	1.6	384.1	−3844	35.9	115.6
1995	1	5.9	1.6	582.2	−5639.4	60.1	175.7
	2	5.8	1.6	653.7	−6244.5	55.1	230.8
	3	5.5	0.9	920.4	−8802.9	99.3	330.1
	4	5.4	0.4	920.4	−8802.9	117.3	447.3
1996	1	5.1	0.4	1073.2	−10406.6	134.4	581.7
	2	5.2	0.4	1073.2	−10406.6	139.7	721.5
	3	5.2	0.4	1073.2	−10406.6	141.6	863.0
	4	5.1	0.4	1073.2	−10406.6	144.0	1007.0
1997	1	5.2	0.4	1073.2	−10406.6	158.7	1165.7
	2	5.2	0.4	1073.2	−10406.6	156.4	1322.1
	3	5.2	0.4	1073.2	−10406.6	154.1	1476.2
	4	5.2	0.4	990.7	−9347.5	152.0	1628.2
1998	1	5.2	0.4	990.7	−9347.5	155.6	1783.8
	2	5.1	0.4	758.2	−6300.5	124.9	1908.7
	3	4.9	0.4	758.2	−6300.5	123.7	2032.4
	4	4.3	0.2	758.2	−6300.5	94.5	2126.9
1999	1	4.5	0.2	817.0	−6956.8	103.6	2230.6
	2	4.6	0.3	1025.0	−9456.4	141.6	2372.1
	3	4.8	0.4	1231.6	−11844.0	167.0	2539.2
	4	5.2	0.12	1377.6	−13349.2	183.2	2722.4

Table 5.5   (continued)

Year	Qtr	R $%	R Y%	$ balance (million $)	Y balance (billion yen)	Interest gains (billion yen)	Accumulated gains (billion yen)
2000	1	5.7	0.07	1527.6	−14921.4	230.5	2952.9
	2	5.9	0.05	1659.6	−16306.8	258.9	3211.8
	3	6.2	0.25	1659.6	−16306.8	266.5	3478.3
	4	6.2	0.41	1659.6	−16306.8	265.8	3744.1
2001	1	4.9	0.23	1659.6	−16306.8	230.7	3974.8

Notes:
(1) The dollar interest rate is the 3-month Treasury bill yield;
(2) the yen interest rate is the 3-month Financial Bill yield;
(3) the dollar balance of t is the sum of dollar balance of $t-1$ and the intervention amount (in dollars) in t, and the yen balance is the sum of yen balance of $t-1$ and the intervention amount (in yen) in t;
(4) interest income is the difference of income in dollars, that is dollar balance times dollar interest rate (then converted in yen) and payment in yen, that is yen balance times yen interest rate. The interest rate shown in the table is annualized, so that the calculation should use 1/4 of the rate shown in the table;
(5) accumulated gains of t is the sum of accumulated gains of $t-1$ and interest gains of t.

intervention. In order to evaluate the effectiveness of intervention, we need to assume some process on what the exchange rate movement would be without intervention. The tabulation above does not give us a good answer on this point. The next section uses regression analysis using all data, so that the exchange rate movement without intervention is estimated in the regression equation.

6.   EFFECTIVENESS OF INTERVENTION: REGRESSION APPROACH

A regression equation for the exchange rate movement is estimated using all daily data in the sample, April 1991 to March 2001. When there is no intervention, the exchange rate change (from $t-1$ to t) is assumed to be a linear function of the change of the day before (from $t-2$ to $t-1$) and the deviation of the current exchange rate from a long-run equilibrium rate. Here, knowing that about 125 yen/dollar was the dividing line between yen selling and yen purchasing, 125 yen/dollar is assumed to be a long-run equilibrium rate. (For a robustness check, the alternative of a long-moving average could be used, but major results would not change.)

Table 5.6 Were interventions successful? (given interventions were conducted April 1991–March 2001)

Direction	Before $s(t-1)-s(t-2)$	Number of interventions	After $s(t)-s(t-1)$	Benchmark (If no intervention)	Number of success	Rate of success (%)
Buy yen	Yen depreciation (lean-against)	19	Appreciation? (Reversal)	Random Walk	10	52.6
			Slower? (Smoothing)		17	89.5
Buy yen	Yen appreciation (lean-in)	13	Accelerating? (Push the trend)		8	61.5
			Not depreciation (Appreciation)	Random Walk	8	61.5
Sell yen	Yen appreciation (lean-against)	119	Depreciation? (Reversal)	Random Walk	54	45.4
			Slower? (Smoothing)		83	69.7
Sell yen	Yen depreciation (lean-in)	49	Accelerating? (Push the trend)		11	22.4
			Not appreciation (Depreciation)	Random Walk	19	38.8

When intervention is conducted on date t, the intervention variable, *Int* has the intervention amount (in 100 million yen), and 0 otherwise. When the US authorities intervened, the Japanese authorities also intervened. There was no 'unilateral' US intervention, although there were many of them by the Japanese authorities. The US intervention variable *IntF* (in 100 million yen) is used to capture the impact of joint intervention. (A similar exercise was conducted by Humpage (1999) using the intra-day intervention and exchange rate information for the US interventions.)

When the FED intervened, as always with the Japanese authorities, the FED intervention variable takes the intervention amount of the United States.

$$s_t - s_{t-1} = \beta_0 + \beta_1(s_{t-1} - s_{t-2}) + \beta_2(s_{t-1} - s_{t-1}^T)$$
$$+ \beta_3 Int_t + \beta_4 IntF_t + \beta_5 IntI_t + \varepsilon_t \qquad (5.1)$$

where $\varepsilon_t = v_t \sqrt{h_t}$ with $v_t \sim N(0,1)$, $h_t = \alpha_0 + \alpha_1 \varepsilon_{t-1}^2 + \alpha_2 h_{t-1}$

s_t: log of spot rate (NY close) of day t.
s_t^T: log of long-run equilibrium exchange rate, 125 yen.
Int: the Japanese intervention (in 100 million yen)
IntF: the US intervention (in million dollars)
IntI: the initial intervention (*Int*: if no intervention in 5 preceding business days; 0: otherwise)

Results are shown in Table 5.7. A hypothesis that the exchange rate movement without interventions follows a random walk cannot be rejected.

If the interventions by the Japanese authorities are effective, then we expect $\beta_3 < 0$. For example, if the yen-purchasing intervention (*Int* > 0) by the Japanese monetary authorities tends to appreciate the yen ($s_t - s_{t-1} < 0$), then the negative sign of β_3 should be obtained. It turned out that the Japanese intervention was effective in the full sample and the second half of the sample. Interventions during and after the Sakakibara regime tended to be effective, while the interventions in the first half were not effective. When the sample period is subdivided, it can be shown that the ineffectiveness comes from the 1994–95 period, when the yen appreciated from 100 yen/dollar to 80 yen/dollar. As was observed in Section 3, interventions in the first half of 1995 were quite frequent, but were not effective in halting the yen appreciation.

The US interventions (positive for yen purchasing) are judged to be effective when β_4 is negative. The total effects of the joint interventions are measured by $\beta_3 + \beta_4$. Since all of the US interventions were joint interventions, the magnitude of β_4 may contain any of the nonlinear effects of the joint interventions. The joint interventions by the Japanese and US

Table 5.7 Effectiveness of intervention

$$s_t - s_{t-1} = \beta_0 + \beta_1(s_{t-1} - s_{t-2}) + \beta_2(s_{t-1} - s_{t-1}^T) + \beta_3 Int_t + \beta_4 IntF_t + \beta_5 IntI_t + \varepsilon_t$$
where $\varepsilon_t = v_t \sqrt{h_t}$ with $v_t \sim N(0,1)$, $h_t = \alpha_0 + \alpha_1 \varepsilon_{t-1}^2 + \alpha_2 h_{t-1}$

s_t: spot rate (NY close) of day t.
s_t^T: long-run equilibrium exchange rate, 125 yen.
Int: Japanese intervention amount.
$IntF$:   FED intervention amount.
$IntI$:   Initial intervention (=Int, if no intervention in 5 preceding business days;
        =0, otherwise)

	Full sample: 01 Apr. 91–30 Mar. 01	First half: 01 Apr. 91–20 Jun. 95	Second Half 21 Jun. 95–30 Mar. 01
β_0	0.0001 (0.0002)	−0.0004 (0.0002)†	0.0003 (0.0003)
β_1	−0.015 (0.02)	−0.038 (0.036)	−0.023 (0.031)
β_2	−0.001 (0.001)	−0.0019 (0.0016)	−0.00065 (0.002)
β_3	−0.0000006 (0.0000002)**	0.0000037 (0.000001)**	−0.0000009 (0.0000002)**
β_4	−0.0000138 (0.000003)**	−0.000011 (0.000004)**	−0.000051 (0.000008)**
β_5	−0.0000017 (0.0000004)**	0.000001 (0.000003)	−0.0000012 (0.0000004)**
α_0	0.000003 (0.0000008)**	0.000006 (0.000003)**	0.000005 (0.000002)**
α_1	0.10 (0.01)**	0.10 (0.02)**	0.12 (0.03)**
α_2	0.84 (0.03)**	0.75 (0.07)**	0.78 (0.05)**
Adjusted R^2	0.035	0.020	0.08
OBS	2565	1098	1467

Notes:
Standard errors are given in parentheses.
† Statistically significant at the 10 per cent level.
* Statistically significant at the 5 per cent level.
** Statistically significant at the 1 per cent level.
Q(10) tests suggest no serial correlation.

authorities were effective in the first and second sub-periods as well as the full sample. The effectiveness of interventions (the magnitude of $\beta_3 + \beta_4$) was much higher in joint interventions than the unilateral interventions by the Japanese authorities.

The coefficient of β_5 shows the effectiveness of the first intervention in more than a week beyond just as one of the interventions. The use of such a variable is found in Humpage (1988). The full impact of the first intervention $\beta_3 + \beta_5$ is statistically significant in the full sample and in the second half of the sample.

In the second half of the sample period, it was estimated that $\beta_3 = -0.0000009$ and $\beta_4 = -0.000051$. The Japanese intervention of 100 billion yen moved 0.1 per cent of the yen/dollar rate, and the US intervention of 1 billion dollars (100 billion yen at 100 yen/\$) tended to have moved the yen by 5 per cent. The magnitude of the effects of the US interventions was much higher.

In sum, interventions were generally effective, except in a period when the yen appreciated from 100 to 80 in the first half of 1995. The failure of those interventions may be a result of the fact that yen appreciation forces at the time were so strong that repeated interventions could not stop them, or that the intervention strategy was not appropriate. The interventions after Sakakibara became the Director General tended to be effective. The first intervention in more than a week had a larger impact than subsequent interventions. The Japanese–US joint interventions were most powerful.

7.   REACTION FUNCTION

In this section, a reaction function of the Japanese monetary authorities is estimated. It has been casually observed in earlier sections that the intervention is conducted as a reaction to changes in the exchange rate in the short run and the deviation in level from the long-run equilibrium rate. A sudden, big change in the exchange rate tends to trigger intervention. This can be a daily change, or an accumulated change in a longer period, such as in a month. Another factor is the deviation from the long-term equilibrium rate. Recall that the dollar was never purchased when the value of the dollar was higher than 125 yen/dollar, and the dollar was never sold below the 125 yen/dollar level. This suggests intervention being dependent on the deviation from a level, say 125 yen/dollar, that the authorities regard as appropriate.

The reaction function is specified as follows: the intervention (amounts of yen) is a function of the change in the yen/dollar rate in the previous day, the change in the yen/dollar rate in the previous 21 (business) days, and the percentage deviation of the current (day before) level from 125 yen/dollar. Other factors may be relevant to today's intervention. Intervention may be correlated (once intervened, it is more likely to be intervened), and the intervention by the US Federal Reserve may prompt Japanese intervention the day after. In addition, whether there was a unilateral intervention by the Japanese authority or a joint intervention the day before may matter. The dummy variable to those possibilities are introduced. The following is the regression equation:

$$Int_t = \beta_0 + \beta_1(s_{t-1} - s_{t-2}) + \beta_2(s_{t-1} - s_{t-21}) + \beta_3(s_{t-1} - s_{t-1}^T)$$
$$+ \beta_4 Int_{t-1} + \beta_5 Int_{t-1}^F + \beta_6 ds_{t-1} D(Int_t \neq 0)_{t-1} + \beta_7 ds_{t-1} D \qquad (5.2)$$
$$(IntF_t \neq 0)_{t-1} + \varepsilon_t$$

Estimation is done for a whole period, the first half (before Mr Sakakibara became the Director General), and the second half. Estimated results are shown in Table 5.8. The findings are as follows.

First, there was a tendency to lean-against-the-wind, both in the very short run (the day before) and in the medium run. A positive coefficient of β_1 (β_2) implies that yen depreciation in the day before (cumulative yen depreciation in the preceding 21 business days) tends to prompt an intervention of buying the yen. The lean-against-the-wind tendency is observed in the full sample and both sub-samples (although it was not statistically significant in the first sub-sample). The difference between the two sub-samples in the estimates of β_1 means that interventions were not conducted so much in response to daily movement in the first sub-sample, while the daily change did influence the intervention decisions in the second sub-sample.

Second, a positive coefficient of β_3 implies that the more the yen/dollar exchange rate deviated from 125 yen/dollar, the more likely it was that the monetary authorities would intervene with a larger amount. This is consistently observed throughout the two sub-samples and the full sample. However, the intervention force to ensure the mean-reversion was larger in the second sub-sample, as the coefficient was about five times larger in the second sub-sample than in the first sub-sample.

Third, the predictability of the model as shown in adjusted R^2 varies over the period. The intervention was more predictable in the first sub-sample, while it was not in the second sub-sample. The excerpt where Mr Sakakibara explained his intervention strategy is confirmed in the result. Recall that there were many, continuous interventions in the first sub-sample, especially from 1994 to the first half of 1995.

Table 5.8 Reaction function

$$Int_t = \beta_0 + \beta_1(s_{t-1} - s_{t-2}) + \beta_2(s_{t-1} - s_{t-21}) + \beta_3(s_{t-1} - s^T_{t-1}) + \beta_4 Int_{t-1} + \beta_5 IntF_{t-1}$$
$$+ \beta_6 ds_{t-1} D(Int_t \neq 0)_{t-1} + \beta_7 ds_{t-1} D(IntF_t \neq 0)_{t-1} + \varepsilon_t$$

	Full sample	1 Apr. 91–20 Jun. 95	21 Jun. 95–30 Mar. 01
β_0	3.75	3.09	19.59
	(25.21)	(5.13)	(50.26)
β_1	10422.91	1053.77	13885.73
	(4637.75)*	(727.84)	(6281.99)*
β_2	1369.70	1462.71	1271.11
	(514.63)**	(387.74)**	(709.80)†
β_3	632.66	217.66	1044.12
	(153.94)**	(51.41)**	(366.13)**
β_4	0.08	0.45	0.11
	(0.03)**	(0.08)**	(0.05)*
β_5	0.19	−0.16	0.20
	(0.25)	(0.30)	(0.60)
β_6	8973.19	1656.74	41722.91
	(10590.21)	(7306.41)	(35801.49)
β_7	−11721.77	−1701.77	−40294.78
	(10516.36)	(9818.02)	(33200.06)
Adjusted R^2	0.026	0.345	0.025
OBS	2565	1098	1467

Notes:
Standard errors are given in parentheses. Q(10) test is rejected. Estimated by GMM.
† Statistically significant at the 10 per cent level.
* Statistically significant at the 5 per cent level.
** Statistically significant at the 1 per cent level.
$\beta_1 > 0$, $\beta_2 > 0$: Lean against the wind.
$\beta_3 > 0$, further the rate is away from 125 yen, more likely to have a larger intervention.
$\beta_4 > 0$, there is a tendency to have subsequent interventions.

8.   CONCLUDING REMARKS

In this chapter, the effectiveness of the Japanese interventions was examined from various angles. First, the history of the yen/dollar movement and intervention during the 1990s was reviewed. The intervention strategy employed by Sakakibara seemed to be distinctively different from his predecessors, as mentioned in his book. Second, the Japanese interventions during the 1990s produced large profits from realized capital gains, unrealized capital gains and profits from the interest rate differentials. The Japanese monetary authorities were judged as a successful, thus stabilizing, speculator, earning close to 9 trillion yen in ten years. Third, a regression analysis reveals that intervention during the second half of the 1990s in Japan produced intended effects on the yen. The US intervention in the yen/dollar market was particularly powerful.

There are more issues that should be examined in relation to interventions. In this chapter, the channel of effectiveness was not discussed at all. Effects through signalling are presumed, but not analysed. Volatility effects are also not analysed. These are left for future studies.

NOTES

*   Comments by Marcus Miller and other participants in the conference were quite helpful. The author gratefully acknowledges research assistance by Tomoyoshi Yabu. All the data used in this chapter are publicly available.
1.   Data were not released so that any academic follow-up studies were not possible.
2.   Some other technical details may be of interest to those who do micro-structure research of the foreign exchange market, for example, the distinction between intervention carried out by the Bank of Japan and that carried out by other central banks on behalf of the Bank of Japan, and whether it was carried out through interbank transactions or through voice/electronic brokers.

REFERENCES

Dominguez, Kathryn (1990), *Market Responses to Coordinated Central Bank Intervention*, Carnegie-Rochester Series on Public Policy, vol. 32, North Holland: 121–64.
Dominguez, Kathryn and Jeffrey Frankel (1993a), 'Does Foreign Exchange Intervention Matter? The Portfolio Effect', *American Economic Review*, December: 1356–69.
Dominguez, Kathryn and Jeffrey Frankel (1993b), 'Foreign Exchange Intervention: An Empirical Assessment', in J.A. Frankel (ed.), *On Exchange Rates*, Chapter 16, Cambridge, Mass.: MIT Press: 327–45.
Dominguez, Kathryn and Jeffrey Frankel (1993c), *Does Foreign Exchange Intervention Work?*, Washington, DC: Institute for International Economics.

Edison, Hali J. (1993), *The Effectiveness of Central-Bank Intervention: A Survey of the Literature after 1982*, Special Papers in International Economics, no. 18, Princeton, NJ: Princeton University, July.

Humpage, Owen (1988), 'Intervention and Dollar's Decline', Federal Reserve Bank of Cleveland, *Economic Review*, vol. 24, Qtr. 2: 2–17.

Humpage, Owen (1999), 'U.S. Intervention: Assessing the Probability of Success', *Journal of Money, Credit, and Banking*, vol. 31, No. 4, November: 731–47.

Jurgensen, P. (1983), *Report of the Worthing Group on Exchange Market Intervention*, Washington, DC: Treasury Department.

Sakakibara, Eisuke (2000), *The Day Japan and the World Shuddered: Establishment of Cyber-capitalism*, Chuo-Koron Shin Sha, April. (In Japanese.)

Sarno, Lucio and Mark P. Taylor (2001), 'Official Intervention in the Foreign Exchange Market: Is It Effective and, If So, How Does It Work?' *Journal of Economic Literature*, vol. XXXIX, September: 839–68.

Ramaswamy, Ramana and Hossein Samiei (2000), 'The Yen-Dollar Rate: Have Interventions Mattered?', IMF Working Paper, WP/00/95, International Monetary Fund.

Discussion of 'Exchange rate regimes in theory and practice' and 'Is foreign exchange intervention effective?'

Marcus Miller

Given the number of serious currency crises in emerging-market economies during the past 7 years, it makes no sense to talk about reforming the international financial architecture without addressing currency regimes.

(Goldstein, 2002)

The functioning of the global financial system depends, to a considerable extent, on the choice of exchange rate regime by its constituent members. The Bretton Woods system of fixed but adjustable exchange rate pegs against the dollar worked well 'so long as capital flows were modest, international inflationary and deflationary pressures were limited, and countries accepted an obligation to direct domestic macroeconomic policies towards achieving external balance' (Andrew Crockett, 2001, p. 5). But, with increased capital mobility, successive oil shocks and increased policy independence in the core economies, the system collapsed; and no alternative blueprint for exchange rates arrangements has been implemented since.

For the 21st century, Andrew Crockett predicts floating rates between G3 economies and increased adoption of regional currency unions by non-core economies. But for many countries that do not currently, and may not in future, join a currency union, there is an open question of how best to conduct their exchange rate policy. What are the options?

In a recent monograph advocating 'managed floating plus' as the best option for emerging markets open to international capital flows, Morris Goldstein (2002, p. 2) characterises Andrew Crockett as an adherent to the bi-polar view of exchange rate regimes, along with Barry Eichengreen, Larry Summers and Stanley Fischer. In his interesting discussion of past experience – and forecast of possible future developments – Andrew Crockett indicates that the phenomenon of the 'disappearing middle' is more a matter of political will than simple economic logic. He says 'It is possible to envision intermediate exchange rate regimes that, suitably managed, have stable equilibrium properties': but this is qualified by the observation that 'the incentives in managing a pegged rate system tend to push governments toward a regime in which destabilising properties take over . . . in which rates are kept in too narrow a band, the authorities are reluctant to make timely adjustments in rates, and hesitant to adapt domestic policies in a sufficiently forceful way to maintain the credibility of their commitment to the peg' (Crockett, p. 13).

INTERMEDIATE REGIMES: 'MANAGED FLOATING PLUS' AND BBC

Can intermediate systems be made more durable? Can the impediments to exchange rate adjustment be reduced? Economists at the International Institute for Economics believe that they can. Rather than Crockett's four 'potentially sustainable exchange rate regimes' running from full fixity to free floating, Morris Goldstein (2002), for example, argues that there are five horses in the race. As indicated by the rows of the table these include his own entrant, 'managed floating plus inflation targets and measures to limit currency mismatches', as well as that of his colleague John Williamson, who argues for a 'basket, band and crawl'. The criteria by which Goldstein reckons a regime may be rated are indicated by the columns: whether it provides a nominal anchor (column 1), whether it can cope with real shocks (column 2), whether it limits currency mismatches (column 3) and how well it can cope with sudden shift of external capital (column 4).

How do these entrants compare? While the two varieties of pegged exchange rate regimes at the foot of the table offer a nominal anchor against inflation, they can be faulted along the lines that Crockett indicates, namely they are insufficiently flexible in the face of real shocks. According to Goldstein, this is largely because they fail to provide incentives for limiting currency mismatches, with the consequence that any adjustment of the peg that may ultimately be necessary causes severe economic dislocation – as the East Asian and Argentine crises have demonstrated.

Floating exchange rates are useful in coping with both real shocks and shifts in sentiment in capital markets. But Goldstein does not recommend 'plain vanilla floating' for emerging markets, on the grounds that it will not generally constitute a credible check on inflation unless backed by inflation targets. He specifically recommends managed floating plus inflation targets and an 'aggressive policy to minimise currency mismatches' – to ensure that the flexibility they offer in coping with the real shocks is not circumscribed (see line 2 of Table 5.1D).

In between managing floating and adjustable pegs, there lies the option

Table 5.1D   Exchange rate regimes for emerging market economies

	Does it provide a nominal anchor?	Does it cope with real shocks?	Does it limit currency matches?	Does it cope with capital market shocks?
Plain vanilla floating	Probably not	Yes	Yes	Probably not
Managed floating plus[1]	Yes, thanks to to inflation targets	Yes	Yes	Yes
BBC (Band, Basket, and Crawl)[2]	Only if there are inflation targets	Yes	Yes	No
Adjustable peg	Yes	Yes, but usually with a lag	No	No
Currency board[3]	Yes	No	No	Yes, but may need capital controls

Notes:
[1] See Goldstein (2002).
[2] See Williamson (2000).
[3] See Williamson (1995).

labelled BBC for 'band, basket and crawl' endorsed by John Williamson (2000) after the East Asian crisis. This regime allows for adjustment to real shocks and also gives an incentive to avoid currency misalignment. But, in Goldstein's view, it may be faulted for not providing enough of a nominal anchor, nor sufficient flexibility to cope with capital market shocks.

Goldstein sums up, as follows: 'Adjustable peg and crawling band regimes are just too fragile for a world of large and sudden shifts in private capital flows and of sometime serious slippages in economic policy reform. Currency boards and dollarization solve some problems but are impotent in dealing with Argentina-type crises characterized by recession, an over-valued real exchange, limited flexibility of domestic costs and prices, and too much public debt to permit countercyclical fiscal policy. And plain vanilla floating has limited appeal to many emerging economies because of their balance sheet vulnerability to large exchange rate changes and because of their dissatisfaction with monetary targeting as a nominal anchor' (pp. 67–8).

MORE EXTRAS: CAPITAL CONTROLS, SOFT MARGINS

If Goldstein can add extras, what about adding features to other regimes to remedy some of their supposed deficiencies? Two in particular are worth considering: capital controls and soft margins. Argentina, for example, should surely have imposed capital outflow controls far earlier than it did, as a temporary measure to check private capital flight from a currency board that looked increasingly overvalued. Capital controls also can be a useful complement to the BBC regime, particularly Chilean-styled 'inflow controls' in a form of unremunerated reserve requirements,[1] as Williamson (2000) observes.

Goodhart and Delargy (1998) have argued that one of the factors helping economies to recover under the gold standard was the widespread expectation that the exchange rate would revert to its pre-crisis parity once the crisis was over: this avoided widespread insolvency such as that which occurred when the East Asian currencies were devalued, 'This is a feature that could be replicated by a target zone with soft margins: in a crisis, the currency could be allowed to depreciate perhaps with some internationally sanctioned right to suspend debt service until normality had been restored, but the expectation would be that the rate would return to its target zone as a part of the process of crisis resolution' (Williamson, 2000, p. 28)

Similar comments apply to a 'monitoring band' for the exchange rate, where there is no intervention near equilibrium but there is intervention triggered by exchange rate deviations outside the pre-set monitoring band. One of the main advantages of such an arrangement, as Velasco (2000) notes, is that if the authorities 'decide the market pressure is overwhelming, they can choose to allow the rate to take the strain even if this involves the rate going outside the band', that is it could make the BBC proposal more robust in the face of capital market shocks.

ASSET PRICE BUBBLES

In a recent paper, Corrado et al. (2002) show that such 'monitoring bands' are capable of reproducing the patterns of nonlinear mean-reversion found in an increasing number of empirical studies (Taylor and Peel, 2000; Kilien and Taylor, 2001, for example). But they also point out that 'leaning against wind' in this (non-linear) way is not sufficient to rule out bubbles – for which a wider back-stop band may be necessary. The interesting new evidence presented and analysed in the chapter by Ito (2001) suggests that *sterilized intervention* has in fact succeeded in acting as a backstop to check fluctuations in the yen at wide margins.

How and when sterilized intervention will succeed surely depends on the microstructure of foreign exchange markets: but so will the choice of exchange rate regime. Microfoundations for asset price bubbles in equity markets based on asymmetric information are studied by Abreu and Brunnermeier (2001), who also consider the role of public intervention acting as a co-ordination device. Could this be carried over to foreign exchange markets? The more likely a floating rate is to depart from its 'fundamental value' in this way, the more likely exchange rate policies involving public intervention – and the use of capital controls – are to command interest and attention.

NOTE

1. 'There is widespread agreement among economists that capital controls that alter the terms on which transactions can be undertaken (so-called price-related measures) are preferable to prohibitions and quantitative controls. This is because price-related measures allow agents to determine for themselves whether or not a particular transaction is worth undertaking, and such decentralization of decision making permits an aggregate target to be achieved at the lowest social cost' (Williamson, 2000, p. 45).

REFERENCES

Abreu, D. and M.K. Brunnermeier (2001), 'Bubbles and Crashes', mimeo, University of Princeton.
Corrado, L., M. Miller and L. Zhang (2002), 'Exchange Rate Monitoring Bands: Theory and Policy', CEPR Discussion Paper No. 3338.
Crockett, A. (2001), 'Exchange Rate Regimes in Theory and Practice', Chapter 4 this volume.
Goldstein, M. (2002), *Managed Floating Plus*, Policy Analyses in International Economics No. 66, Washington, DC: Institute for International Economics.
Goodhart, C. and P.J.R. Delargy (1998), 'Financial Crises: Plus ca change, plus c'est la meme chose', *International Finance*, 1, 2, 261–87.
Ito T. (2001), 'Is Foreign Exchange Intervention Effective?', Chapter 5 this volume.
Kilien, L. and M.P. Taylor (2001), 'Why is it so Difficult to Beat the Random Walk Forecast of Exchange Rates?', mimeo, University of Warwick.
Taylor, M.P. and D. Peel (2000), 'Nonlinear Adjustment, Long-Run Equilibrium and Exchange Rate Fundamentals', *Journal of International Money and Finance*, 11, 304–14.
Velasco, A. (2000), 'Exchange Rate Policies for Developing Countries: What Have We Learned? What Do We Still Not Know?', United Nations G-24 Discussion Paper Series, No. 5.
Williamson, J. (1995), *What Role for Currency Boards?*, Policy Analyses in

International Economics No. 40, Washington, DC: Institute for International Economics.

Williamson, J. (2000), *Exchange Rate Regimes for Emerging Markets: Reviving the Intermediate Option*, Policy Analyses in International Economics No. 60, Washington, DC: Institute for International Economics.

6. Customer trades and extreme events in foreign exchange

Mintao Fan and Richard K. Lyons*

1. INTRODUCTION

Professor Goodhart's impact has been substantial in many areas. One of those areas is a growing field that uses tools from microstructure finance to analyse exchange-rate behaviour (the 'microstructure approach' to exchange rates). This chapter is an introduction to one of the frontiers of that field. It addresses the trading of FX customers: investors, importers, exporters, corporate Treasurers, and so on. Past work within the micro-structure approach has focused on FX trading between banks, or 'inter-dealer' trading. It is true that most of the trading in FX is interdealer. Nevertheless, interdealer trading is in a sense derivative: it is the demands of non-dealer customers that represent underlying demand for currencies in the real economy. Data necessary for this analysis have become available only recently, in part due to the wholesale shift to electronic trading (and the data capture it permits).

Our main results include the following. First, we find that aggregate cus-tomer order flow in our sample (10–15 per cent of the market-wide total) shows little evidence of mean reversion.[1] Indeed, customer order flow cumu-lated over time is approximately a random walk. Second, aggregate customer order flow tracks exchange rate movements at lower frequencies (for example annual) rather closely. Third, when aggregate customer order flow is disag-gregated, we find that the parts behave rather differently. For example, our case study on the 10 per cent drop in the yen/$ rate that occurred in a single day in 1998 (around the time of the Long Term Capital Management col-lapse) shows that hedge funds were not the trigger of the collapse, but instead were net providers of liquidity (that is net buyers of dollars). The trigger was the portfolio shift of financial institutions like mutual funds, pension funds, and insurance companies. Fourth, we find that extreme exchange-rate move-ments at high frequency are generally associated with large net flows from financial institutions; in contrast, low frequency trends are associated with secular net flows from non-financial corporations.

The chapter is organized in five sections. In Section 2 we provide background on the available customer-trade data, including descriptive statistics. Section 3 introduces hypotheses from recent models of FX customer trading and puts them to the test. Section 4 is a case study of the behaviour of customer trades around the collapse of the yen/dollar rate in the fall of 1998. Section 5 examines other extreme movements in the dollar–yen and dollar–euro markets. Section 6 concludes.

2. BACKGROUND ON THE CUSTOMER TRADE SEGMENT

The role of order flow from non-marketmaker customers is central to microstructure theory. Indeed, customer flow is at the core of all the canonical models (for example Kyle, 1985 and Glosten and Milgrom, 1985, among others). In each of those models it is the customer orders that catalyze a market response. In this respect, it is not unreasonable to view different microstructure models as broadly similar: their basic implications for the relation between exchange rates and customer flow are the same (though the interim paths of price adjustment across models may differ).[2]

The importance of customer orders is obvious to practitioners as well. Any FX trader or trading-desk manager would agree. One trader we spoke with put it colourfully when he said that customer trades are the market's 'crack cocaine'. By this he meant that the customer orders are a catalyst, and a powerful one at that. In keeping with this notion of customer flow as the market's catalyst, proprietary information on those flows is a prime driver of proprietary trading at the largest banks. (Smaller banks see too little of the marketwide customer flow to make this information useful.) Embedded in this behaviour is the fact that banks find customer-flow information valuable for *predicting* exchange-rate movements. To date, work that adopts the microstructure approach to exchange rates has concerned itself with *explaining* movements, in the sense of accounting for movements using concurrent flow. That customer flow has predictive power as well (that is today's flow predicts future movements) adds a new dimension. It is this predictive dimension that most interests the practitioner audience.[3]

So why has previous literature focused so much on order flow between dealers? There are two reasons. The first is the simple fact that until the dataset described below became available, researchers had no alternative but to work with order flow between dealers. The second reason is that – despite the constraint on data availability – there is valid justification for focusing on flow between dealers. The justification relates to the differential transparency of customer–dealer versus interdealer flow. The reality of the FX market is that dealers do observe some order flow from interdealer trades – including trades in which they are not involved. Customer–dealer trades, on the other hand, are not observable except by the bank that receives them. Dealers therefore learn about other dealers' customer orders as best they can by observing other dealers' interdealer trades, and they set market prices accordingly. Although this learning from interdealer orders is consistent with empirical models in the existing literature (for example Evans and Lyons, 2002), the ultimate driver of that interdealer flow is customer flow.

Let us provide a bird's-eye view of how the customer-flow data of this chapter relates to the order flow data analysed in earlier papers. Volume in the major spot FX markets splits into three basic categories: customer–dealer trades, direct interdealer trades, and brokered interdealer trades. Figure 6.1 provides an illustration. The work of Lyons (1995), Evans (2003) and Evans and Lyons (2002), for example, uses data from the direct interdealer category. The work of Goodhart et al. (1996), Goodhart and Payne (1996), Payne (1999), and Killeen et al. (2001) uses data from the brokered interdealer category.

The customer data used in this study are qualitatively different from data used in other work on FX markets. In the past, data on customer orders in

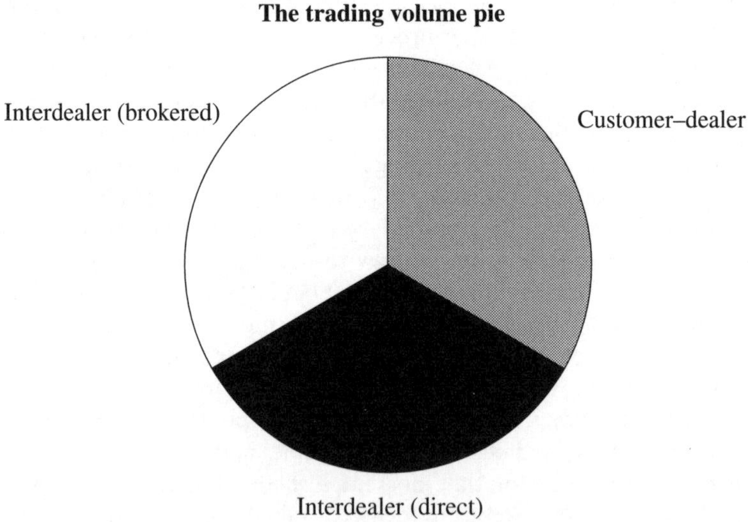

The trading volume pie

Interdealer (brokered)

Customer–dealer

Interdealer (direct)

Notes: In the 1990s, when empirical work on FX order flow began to develop, trades of the three basic types had roughly equal shares in total volume. By 2000, electronic interdealer brokers (principally EBS) had taken much market share away from direct interdealer trading. The BIS (2001) now estimates the brokered share of interdealer trading in major currencies at about 90 per cent.

Figure 6.1   Trading volume breakdown in the 1990s

the major markets have been difficult to obtain. The only possible source – given the market's current structure – is private banks themselves.[4] But in general these banks consider these data highly proprietary. Recently, however, we obtained customer trade data from a leading FX trading bank. (The bank, Citibank, is among the top three worldwide, with a market share in major-currency customer business in the 10–15 per cent range.) The bank made these data available only on a time-aggregated basis. Specifically, all the customer orders received by this bank worldwide are aggregated into daily order flows (executed trades only). The data set therefore does not include individual trades. Consequently, transaction-level analysis along the lines of that in Lyons (1995) is not possible.

Against this drawback, the data set has many advantages:

- Length: The data span more than five years, so analysis at longer horizons (for example, monthly) is possible.
- Markets: The data cover the two largest markets: $/euro and $/yen. (Before January 1999, order flow data for the 'euro' are constructed from flows in the constituent currencies against the dollar.)
- Transaction Types: The data include both spot and forward trades, but are netted of any trades in FX swaps (because FX swaps do not have net order flow implications).
- Components: The data are split into three customer-type categories, corresponding to three categories commonly applied by practitioners: non-financial corporations, unleveraged financial institutions (for example mutual funds), and leveraged financial institutions (for example hedge funds and banks' proprietary trading desks).

The last advantage provides considerable statistical power for uncovering the underlying causes of order-flow's impact on price. Are all orders equal in their price impact? Or might some order types – say the orders of hedge funds – convey more information than others? Our ability to disaggregate order flow to answer these questions brings us closer to a specification of the underlying information sources.

Figure 6.2 provides a visual description of the relative importance of these three customer categories.[5] The sample is January 1993 to June 1999. For the euro, the total trading volume across the three customer categories is roughly balanced. For the yen this is not the case: non-financial corporate trading is less than half that for the other two categories. (These breakdowns may be specific to the data-source bank, however.) For both markets, the daily order flow from nonfinancial corporations is the least volatile. Though not included in the figure, cumulative order flow over the whole sample displays quite different characteristics across the three

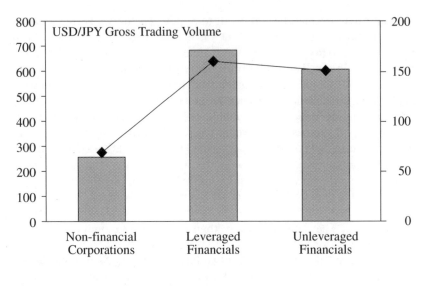

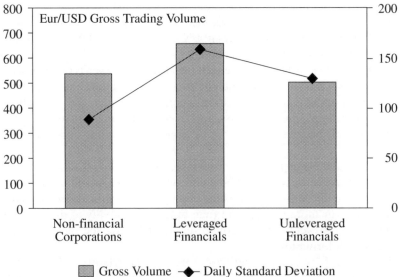

Notes: The sample for both currencies is January 1993 to June 1999. (Before the launch of the euro in January 1999, volume and order flow are constructed from trading in the euro's constituent currencies.) Gross volume is the mean daily volume measured in millions of dollars for USD/JPY and millions of euros for EUR/USD. Daily standard deviation measures the standard deviation of daily order flow.

Figure 6.2   Customer trades: relative transaction volumes and transaction volatility

customer categories. For the dollar–euro market, nonfinancial corpora-tions are the largest net sellers of euros and unleveraged financial institu-tions are the largest net buyers. (We return to this feature of the data in Section 5.) In the dollar–yen market, unleveraged financial institutions are the largest net sellers of dollars (though slight) and leveraged financial insti-tutions are the largest net buyers.

Order Flows versus Capital Flows

A slight digression on the link between customer order flows and balance-of-payments flows may be useful. It is important to recognize that balance-of-payments flows and FX transactions are not one-to-one. To understand why, consider an import of $100 million of Japanese goods into the US by a US multinational. (One could also use a capital-account transaction for this example.) Suppose the transaction is invoiced in yen, but the US multi-national pays the invoice from yen it already holds at its Japanese subsidi-ary. An import is logged, but there is no corresponding order in the FX market; the link is not one-to-one. In time, one would expect some adjust-ment of the multinational's 'portfolio', but that need not occur immedi-ately, and it need not involve order flow in the FX market (for example suppose the Japanese subsidiary responds by increasing its working capital borrowing in yen).[6] The bottom line is that balance-of-payments flows do not necessarily generate corresponding order flow in the FX market. If gleaning information from order flow is how dealers determine price, then portfolio shifts in the form of balance-of-payments flows will not be counted unless and until they generate order flow.[7]

3. HYPOTHESES AND TESTS

Let us sketch the basics of the model introduced by Evans and Lyons (2002) and use it to formulate testable hypotheses for customer order flow. (The empirical analysis in the Evans–Lyons paper examines interdealer order flow only.) One of the conceptual contributions of the Evans–Lyons model is its explanation for why interdealer flow cumulated over time can follow a random walk, while at the same time individual dealers close out their positions each trading day. Empirically, both of these features are true (to a first approximation) in the data.

Evans and Lyons (2002) consider a pure-exchange economy with two assets, one riskless and one risky, the latter representing foreign exchange. Each day, foreign exchange earns a payoff R, publicly observed, which is composed of a series of random increments, one for each day t:

$$R_t = \sum_{i=1}^{t} \Delta R_i \qquad (6.1)$$

The increments ΔR are i.i.d. Normal $(0, \sigma_R^2)$ and can be interpreted as the flow of public macroeconomic information (for example interest rate changes). The foreign exchange market has two participant types, dealers and customers. Within each day t there are three rounds of trading:

Round 1:   Dealers trade with customers (the public).
Round 2:   Dealers trade among themselves (to share inventory risk).
Round 3:   Dealers trade again with the public (to share risk more broadly).

The feature of their model that produces the result that dealer positions return to zero is their assumption that the public has a comparative advantage in holding overnight positions (that is the public is 'large' in a convergence sense relative to the risk-bearing capacity of the dealers). In equilibrium, the aggregate position of dealers is fully absorbed each day by the public. Put differently, for market-clearing in their model, any net trade by the public in round 1 must be reabsorbed by the public in round 3.[8]

This particular feature has strong implications for total customer flow. For example, it implies that marketwide, customer order flow each day should net to zero. Now, the data available to us on customer order flow represent the orders received by one bank, not the customer flow received marketwide, so this prediction is untestable. Suppose, however, that the single-bank data represent a random sample (10–15 per cent) of the marketwide customer order flow on any given day. In this case, the Evans–Lyons model predicts that:

H1:   For a single bank, customer order flow each day should differ from zero due to random sampling error only.
H2:   For a single bank, customer order flow each day should be uncorrelated with changes in the exchange rate.

Hypothesis 2 follows from the fact that the customer-order sample is assumed here to be random. (It should therefore contain on average as many realizations of the model's round 1 'shock' orders as it does end-of-day 'absorption' orders.)

It is also possible, however, that all customer orders are not equally informative of subsequent market movements. Suppose for example that customer order flows are not alike in terms of their market impact. One might imagine two categories of customers: high-impact customers and low-impact customers. If this were the right description of the world, then a bank's customer orders might not be representative of the customer-order population because the bank has a disproportionate amount of high-impact customers.

We turn now to plots of the customer flows, which provide a first glimpse of the possible link to exchange-rate movements. Figure 6.3 shows cumulative customer order flows and the level of the exchange rate in both the dollar–euro and dollar–yen markets.[9] Positive correlation is evident. Comparing these plots to those for cumulative interdealer order flow in Evans and Lyons (2002), one sees that the correlation in Figure 6.3 is not as tight at higher frequencies. At lower frequencies, say monthly, the relation is manifested clearly. These plots also have implications for the two hypotheses introduced above. These hypotheses stated that this bank's daily customer flow should differ from zero due only to random sampling error, and should therefore be uncorrelated with exchange-rate movements. These hypotheses are clearly rejected: cumulative order flow received by this bank is correlated with exchange-rate movements.

What could explain this positive correlation? One possibility is that it is not really there – the correlation is not statistically significant. But the correlation between these series is statistically significant (p-value below 1 per cent). Another possibility is that customer flow each day does not net to zero at the marketwide level. For example, collectively dealers may be maintaining non-zero positions. Though this would not be surprising from day to day, it would be quite surprising at weekly frequencies and lower (and these lower frequencies are more relevant for the correlation in Figure 6.3). Accordingly, we do not consider this a compelling reason to believe that rejection of hypothesis 1 is causing the positive correlation. Another reason why marketwide customer flow each day may not net to zero is that dealers *are* achieving their collective zero position, but do so by hedging with instruments that do not enter our sample (for example currency futures or options). The evidence suggests, however, that FX dealers use these methods of risk management rarely if at all (compare Naik and Yadav, 2000, for dealer hedging in other financial markets).

There remain at least two other possibilities consistent with marketwide customer flow each day netting to zero that can explain the correlation in Figure 6.3. (We offer these as suggestions for future work; we cannot settle the issue based on analysis presented here.) First, it is possible that the customers of this bank are on average better informed. For example, the bank that is the source of the data is one of the very top FX trading banks in the world, which may attract a disproportionate share of the most informative customer business. (More concretely, suppose the orders of hedge funds are the most informative and this bank receives more than its share of

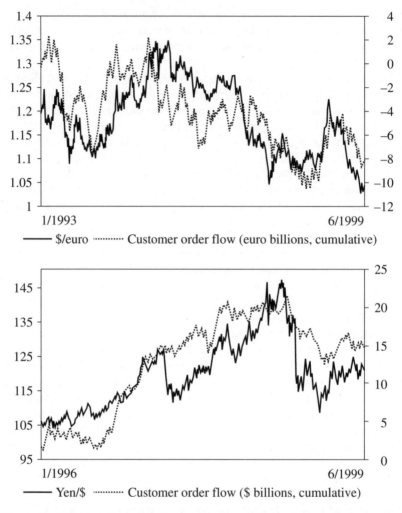

Notes: The plots show the spot exchange rate and cumulative customer order flow received by the source bank. The sample for the $/euro plot is January 1993 to June 1999. The sample for the yen/$ plot is January 1996 to June 1999 (the January 1993 to December 1995 period is not included due to the lack of Tokyo-office data). The spot exchange rate is expressed on the left-hand scale. The cumulative customer order flow is expressed on the right-hand scale (in billions of euros for $/euro and in billions of dollars for yen/$). Positive order flow in the case of the euro denotes net demand for euros (following the convention in that market of quoting prices in dollars per euro). Positive order flow in the case of the yen denotes net demand for dollars (following the convention in that market of quoting prices in yen per dollar).

Figure 6.3   Cumulative customer flow and exchange rates

hedge-fund orders.) A second possibility consistent with hypothesis 1 that can explain the correlation relies instead on this bank's sheer size. Suppose this bank's customers are the same as customers marketwide, but because the bank has such a large slice of total customer flow, its trades in the inter-dealer market generate disproportionate price impact. (A model along these lines could include a cost of 'monitoring' the trading activity of various banks; in this setting it may be cost-efficient to place disproportion-ate weight on the interdealer trades of large banks, despite their customers being no better informed than the average customer. See, for example, Calvo, 1999.) Further theoretical work will undoubtedly produce addi-tional explanations. As additional customer-flow data become available, empiricists will be able to distinguish between them.

4. CASE STUDY: THE COLLAPSE OF THE YEN/$ RATE, OCTOBER 1998

One of the most remarkable events in the post-Bretton Woods era of floating exchange rates is undoubtedly the remarkable drop in the yen/$ rate that occurred in October 1998. In a single day, the rate fell from about 130 to about 118, a change of roughly 10 per cent. On that day, bid-offer spreads were said to have topped one yen, that is 1 per cent or more in a market that usually trades with a spread of 1–2 basis points (and is argu-ably the second most liquid market in the world, behind the dollar–euro market). There was no identifiable macroeconomic news, at least not news that is usually associated with exchange-rate fundamentals. The financial news at the time was concentrated on the collapse of Long Term Capital Management (LTCM), a hedge fund whose positions around the world had become so illiquid that unwinding them became impossible without driving LTCM's capital below zero.

Major banks attribute the yen/$ rate's drop to 'the unwinding of posi-tions by hedge funds that had borrowed in cheap yen to finance purchases of higheryielding dollar assets' – the so-called yen carry trade (*The Economist*, 10/10/98).[10] This portfolio shift – and the selling of dollars that came with it – was forced by the scaling back of speculative leverage follow-ing the LTCM crisis. Though received wisdom suggests that this particular mechanism was at work, we still have little direct evidence. One paper, Cai et al. (2001), provides a first cut on the issue. They model volatility around the event using an aggregate order-flow measure and a comprehensive list of macro announcements. (Their aggregate order-flow measure is the same weekly data from the US Treasury used by Wei and Kim, 1997.) They do find that there is an independent role for order flow, even after accounting for an extensive list of public news. But their volatility model and aggregate flow measures cannot determine which players were pushing prices in which direction.

Here we adopt a case-study approach. We examine the behaviour of order flows by different players around the time of the event. Which institution types were doing the dollar selling? Identifying the sellers' types gives us insight into why the selling occurred (for example were they institutions that may have been 'distressed', in the sense of being compelled to sell due to institutional constraints like loss limits?).

Figure 6.4 plots the daily yen/$ exchange rate and cumulative order flow from each of the three customer segments. The one customer segment that jumps out as having clear connection with the yen/$ rate collapse is unleveraged financial institutions (denoted cum_inv). These institutions began strong selling before the exchange rate began to move. In total, they sold

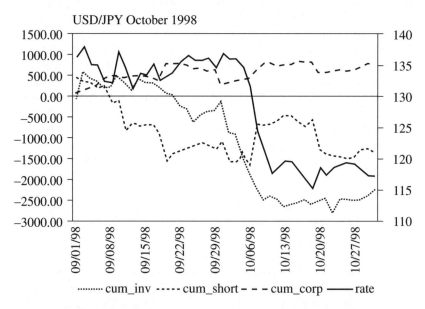

Notes: Left axis shows cumulative flows in millions of dollars (positive is dollar purchases). Right axis is yen per dollar. Note that the yen/dollar rate persisted at its new lower level following the sharp drop on 7 October. The series cum_inv denotes the cumulative order flow from unleveraged investors (for example mutual funds, pension funds, insurance companies, and so on). The series cum_short denotes cumulative order flow from leveraged investors (for example hedge funds). The series cum_corp denotes cumulative order flow from non-financial corporations.

Figure 6.4   October 1998 collapse of yen/$ rate: cumulative flow of the three customer types

about 2.5 billion dollars over the days preceding and including the collapse. It will be interesting in the future to identify which of these unleveraged financial institutions were the most important. Were they US institutions or Japanese? Did they become distressed in some way precipitated by the LTCM collapse, or is the 'distressed players' view of the event misguided? Another common view is that this type of institution was heavily affected by common risk management systems (as opposed to actual 'distress'). There is much room for future work to address these possibilities.

It is also possible that the portfolio shift of unleveraged financial institutions' was, in the end, not uncommonly large, but it occurred at a time when leveraged financial institutions were distressed, and were therefore not willing to provide liquidity that they would normally provide. The cumulative order flow from leveraged investors in Figure 6.4 is consistent with this (denoted cum_short). It shows that leveraged investors did not account for any abrupt selling at the time of the collapse (contrary to received wisdom). Rather, they appeared to have *provided* liquidity, buying about 1 billion dollars at the time the price was collapsing. In the weeks prior to the big rate move, however, leveraged investors in aggregate were indeed selling dollar positions, and may have been reluctant to get back into them. Finally, the cumulative order flow from non-financial corporations shows they were also buying dollars at the time of the price collapse (denoted cum_corp); their total buying was small, however – only about half the size of the buying by leveraged financial institutions, or 0.4 billion dollars.

What are some of the larger implications of this yen/$ case study? So abrupt a shift to a new exchange-rate level (without macro news) leads one to consider the possibility of path dependence. The type of path dependence we have in mind in this case is determined by the sequencing of trades by various customer types, and how that sequencing may have mattered for the ultimate exchange rate. For example, keeping the path of total customer flow the same, if it had been the unleveraged financial institutions that had gradually fled dollars in early September, rather than the leveraged institutions, might the new level of the yen/$ rate in late October have been different? Though path dependence of this kind is not a property of existing FX microstructure models, it is an interesting possibility for future work to consider.

Another larger implication of the case study is that liquidity in FX markets varies over time, sometimes quite substantially. Existing empirical estimates of order flow's price impact imply that the price impact from the relatively small portfolio shifts in Figure 6.4 should have been much smaller, perhaps a few percent, rather than the roughly 10 per cent change that occurred.[11] Though time-varying liquidity is also not a property of the early-vintage microstructure models, it is an issue that future work must consider. What triggers liquidity changes? Might what appears on the surface to be changing liquidity be due instead to changing order-flow composition?

5. OTHER EPISODES OF EXTREME PRICE MOVEMENT

Let us turn to some other examples of extreme exchange rate movements to determine whether the pattern shown above the yen/dollar rate in the fall of 1998 is representative. The rate move examined in the previous section is by far the largest daily move in our sample. Sticking with the yen–dollar market, we examine the remainder of the top five largest return days (either direction) in the yen market.

Figure 6.5, panels A–D, shows the flows in the days surrounding these other four large-return days for the two categories of financial institutions (leveraged and unleveraged). (Non-financial corporate flows are not presented in Figure 6.5 because they show no relationship to the exchange rate within these high-frequency windows.) The panels correspond to the following episodes in chronological order:

Panel A: flows around roughly 3 per cent drop in ¥/$ on March 31, 1995.
Panel B: flows around roughly 4 per cent drop in ¥/$ on June 17, 1998.
Panel C: flows around roughly 4 per cent drop in ¥/$ on September 1, 1998.
Panel D: flows around roughly 4 per cent rise in ¥/$ on September 9, 1998.

The figure shows that (high frequency) extreme events are typically associated with a large net flow from financial institutions. In three of the four cases, both of the financial institution types were in aggregate trading in the same direction as the exchange rate move on the day of the move. Though the net flow sizes are not as extraordinary as the returns on these days (given the distribution of daily net flows in the sample), they are substantial, and are likely to be positively correlated with the net flows received by other large banks (making the sizes on the left axis a downward biased measure of marketwide flow). The only one of the four days in which both categories did not go in the same direction as the exchange rate is September 1, 1998 (Panel C). In this case, the unleveraged financial institutions were going in the direction of the rate change (albeit only slightly), but the leveraged financial institutions were buying dollars strongly as the price of dollars fell. This case, then, looks (qualitatively) more like the

October 7, 1998, collapse of the yen/dollar rate: leveraged investors stepped in to provide liquidity, that is to oppose the price movement (at least this is true of the leveraged investors at this bank).

The word 'extreme' is typically associated with high frequency movements. But extreme events can also occur over time, in the form of secular trends that unexpectedly emerge. One such event is the secular depreciation of the euro since early 1995. This depreciation was particularly acute through 1999, the first official year of the euro's existence. (The impact on policy debates about EMU has been substantial.) Now, Figure 6.3 above suggested that customer flow data capture broad features of lower-frequency exchange rate trends. Is there a particular customer category whose qualitative behaviour corresponds most closely to the trend depreciation of the euro? The answer is yes. Figure 6.6 shows that the trend depreciation of the euro is closely associated with net flows from non-financial corporations. (The flows of the financial institution categories are not shown because they do not evince any low-frequency association.) The slope of the cumulative non-financial corporate flow is not only negative, it is becoming increasingly negative throughout (concave down). Is this a causal relation? We have to leave that to future work to determine. The association is quite striking in any event. Further work with more disaggregated data on the trades of nonfinancial corporations would be quite valuable. Note, finally, that this focus on non-financial corporations is in stark contrast to the focus on portfolio investment flows in the broader literature as a possible explanation for the euro's weakness.

Are the customers of the bank that provided the data representative of FX customers more generally? There are two parts to this question. First, are the shares of the three customer types in this bank's flow 'portfolio' representative of marketwide average shares? Second, within a given customer category (for example, leveraged investors), are this bank's customers representative of customers in that same category at other banks? Our conjecture is that the answer to the first question is no, while the answer to the second is a qualified yes. The reason we do not believe that the shares of this bank's customer types are representative of marketwide average is tied to our analysis of hypotheses 1 and 2. That is, one explanation for the positive correlations found in Figure 6.3 is that order flow from different customer categories may have different price impacts, and this bank's customer shares may be tilted toward high price-impact categories. Regressions of returns on contemporaneous order flows from the separate categories confirm that the different types have quite different price impact (statistically and economically), with the lowest price impact being from the non-financial corporations. The source bank suggests that (relative to the rest of the banking system) their order flow is in fact tilted away from non-

A: 31 March 1995

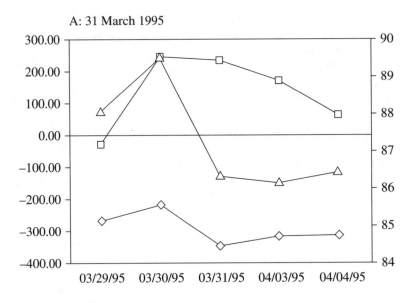

B: 17 June 1998

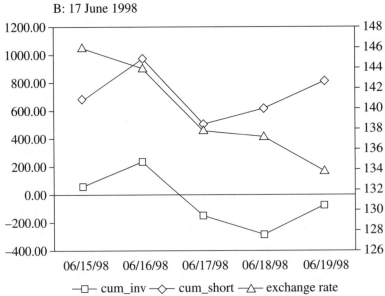

—□— cum_inv —◇— cum_short —△— exchange rate

Notes: Left axis shows cumulative flows in millions of dollars (positive is dollar purchases). Right axis is yen per dollar.

Figure 6.5   Top five big return days in US dollar–yen

C: 1 September 1998

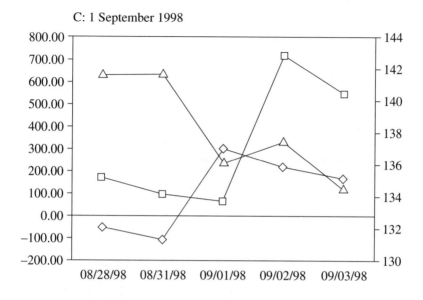

D: 9 September 1998

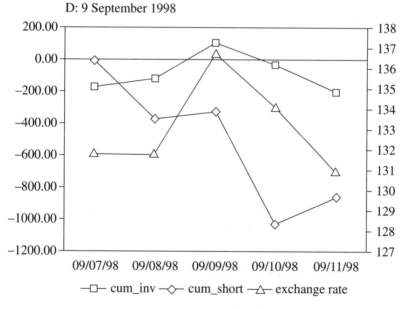

Figure 6.5   (continued)

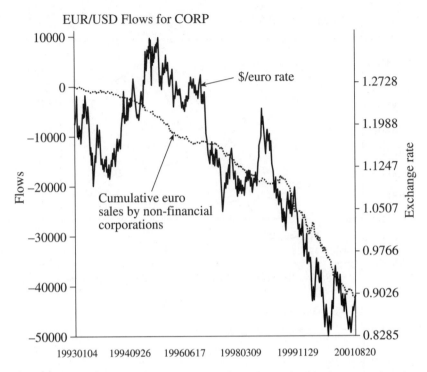

Notes: Left axis shows cumulative flows in millions of euros (positive is euro purchases). Right axis is dollars per euro. Before 1 January, 1999 flow is constructed from flows in the constituent currencies.

Figure 6.6   Non-financial corporate flows out of the euro, 1993–2001

financial corporations, which is consistent with our conjecture. Finally, we do believe that this bank's customers are representative of customers in that same category at other banks, as long as 'other banks' is taken to mean other commercial banks with substantial market share in the FX market.

6.   CONCLUSIONS

This chapter addresses the trading of FX customers: investors, importers, exporters, corporate Treasurers, and so on. Past work within the micro-structure approach has focused on FX trading between banks, or 'inter-dealer' trading. Though most trading in FX is interdealer, it is the demands of non-dealer customers that represent the underlying demand for currencies in the real economy. Data necessary for this analysis have become available only recently, in part due to the wholesale shift to electronic trading (and the data capture it permits).

Our main results include the following. First, we find that customer order flow (10–15 per cent of the marketwide total) shows little evidence of mean reversion. Indeed, customer order flow cumulated over time is approximately a random walk. Second, customer flow tracks exchange rate movements at lower frequencies (for example annual) rather closely. Third, when customer order flow is disaggregated, we find that the parts behave rather differently. For example, our case study on the remarkable drop in the yen/$ rate that occurred in October 1998 shows that hedge funds were not the trigger of the collapse, but instead were net providers of liquidity. The trigger was the portfolio shift of financial institutions like mutual funds, pension funds, and insurance companies. Fourth, we find that extreme exchange-rate movements at high frequency are generally associated with large net flows from financial institutions; in contrast, low frequency trends are associated with secular net flows from non-financial corporations. We consider the largely graphical analysis of this chapter as but a first step in a new arena for empirical work within FX microstructure, a research area that Professor Goodhart set in motion (see Goodhart, 1988; Goodhart, 1989; Goodhart and Figliuoli, 1991).

NOTES

*   We thank the following for helpful comments: Richard Adams, Andrew Rose and Mark Taylor. Lyons thanks the National Science Foundation for financial assistance.

1.   Order flow is not synonymous with trading volume. Order flow – a concept from microstructure finance – refers to *signed* volume. Trades can be signed in microstructure models depending on whether the 'aggressor' is buying or selling. (The dealer posting the quote is the passive side of the trade.) For example, a sale of 10 units by a trader acting on a dealer's quotes is order flow of -10.

In rational-expectations (RE) models of trading, order flow is undefined because all transactions in that setting are symmetric. One might conclude from RE models that one could never usefully distinguish the 'sign' of a trade between two willing counterparties. A large empirical literature in microstructure finance suggests otherwise (Lyons, 2001).

2.   By analogy, it is not unreasonable to view firms that trade on the NYSE as fundamentally the same as firms that trade on the NASDAQ, other things equal (that is similar cost of capital, similar relative valuation, and so on).

3.   For practitioner-oriented research on flow effects on exchange rates, see, for example Citibank's *Citiflows Global Flow and Volume Analysis* (various issues), Deutschebank's *Flowmetrics Monthly* (various issues), and Lehman Brothers' *Global Economic Research Series*, particularly the issue on 'FX Impact of Cross-Border M&A'. For evidence from practitioner surveys, see Gehrig and Menkhoff (2003). It is noteworthy that – unlike fundamental and technical analysis – order-flow analysis is not available to everyone: one needs sufficient order-flow data.

4.   Osler (2003) also obtains data on FX customer trades directly from a bank. Her focus is

stop-loss and take-profit orders. She shows that clustering of these orders at particular prices helps to explain two familiar predictions from technical analysis, namely that (1) trends tend to be reversed at support and resistance levels and (2) trends tend to gain momentum if support and resistance levels are breached.

5. A natural question is where the trades of central banks appear. The source of these data is reluctant to disclose the specifics. Though not reported in the table, the source bank does maintain a fourth category of customer called 'miscellaneous'. Though the trades within this category are quite small relative to the trades in the three main categories, the category is likely to include any central bank trades for which the source bank was the counterparty. (Central bank trades tend to be small relative to private trades.)

6. One could argue that in frictionless general equilibrium, starting from Pareto-optimal allocations, it is not clear why firms' ex-ante 'portfolios' are not instantaneously restored. As an empirical matter, this objection to the example is not so compelling: for many institution types, there are substantial (labour-intensive) costs of adjusting their net positions in the market. This may produce path dependence in portfolio allocation, even if the relation between realized order flow and price is unique.

7. A direction for future research in this area is to isolate categories of trades that fit neatly into a particular balance-of-payments category. For example, one could isolate equity mutual funds. In this case, one could be confident that their FX trades fit neatly into the category called international portfolio investment.

8. By public we mean non-dealers, which includes the proprietary trading desks at dealing banks (a type of leveraged investor, as already noted).

9. The yen plot begins in January 1996 because Citibank did not include customer-flow data from its Tokyo office in its database until late 1995. (The Tokyo office is especially important for Citibank's dollar–yen customer flow.) Note that this may account for the seemingly small share of non-financial corporate trading in total customer trading in dollar–yen shown in Figure 6.2: if non-financial corporations tend to trade via their regional office, whereas financial institutions tend to trade on a 24-hour basis worldwide, then the customer trades in the database before 1996 would be tilted toward the financial institutions.

10. A comprehensive description of events is provided in BIS (1999).

11. For example, Evans and Lyons (2002) find that net order flow of $1 billion produces a lasting price change of about 0.5 per cent. See also Furfine and Remolona (2001) for a transaction-level analysis of time-varying price impact in the US treasury bond market over the same period.

REFERENCES

Bank for International Settlements (1999), *A Review of Financial Market Events in Autumn 1998*, Publication of the Committee on the Global Financial System, October.

Bank for International Settlements (2001), *BIS 71st Annual Report*, June (at www.bis.org).

Cai, J., Y. Cheung, R. Lee and M. Melvin (2001), '"Once in a generation" yen volatility in 1998: fundamentals, intervention, and order flow', *Journal of International Money and Finance*, 20, 327–47.

Calvo, G. (1999), 'Contagion in emerging markets: when Wall Street is a carrier', University of Maryland working paper.

Evans, M. (2003), 'FX trading and exchange rate dynamics', NBER Working Paper 8116, February, *Journal of Finance*, forthcoming.

Evans, M. and R. Lyons (2001), 'Portfolio balance, price impact, and secret intervention', NBER Working Paper 8356, July.

Evans, M. and R. Lyons (2002), 'Order flow and exchange-rate dynamics', *Journal of Political Economy*, 110, 170–80.

Fujiwara, I. (2000), 'Liquidity and leverage risk in the dollar/yen market', typescript, Oxford: Nuffield College, June.

Furfine, C. and E. Remolona (2001), 'Price discovery in a market under stress: the US Treasury market in fall 1998', typescript, Bank for International Settlements, November.

Gehrig, T. and L. Menkhoff (2003), 'The use of flow analysis in foreign exchange: exploratory evidence', typescript, University of Freiburg (Germany), Department of Economics, August, *Journal of International Money and Finance*.

Glosten, L. and Milgrom, P. (1985), 'Bid, ask, and transaction prices in a specialist market with heterogeneously informed agents', *Journal of Financial Economics*, 14, 71–100.

Goodhart, C. (1988), 'The foreign exchange market: a random walk with a dragging anchor', *Economica*, 55, 437–60.

Goodhart, C. (1989), *'News' and the Foreign Exchange Market*, Manchester Statistical Society publication, October.

Goodhart, C. and L. Figliuoli (1991), 'Every minute counts in financial markets', *Journal of International Money and Finance*, 10, 23–52.

Goodhart, C. and M. O'Hara (1997), 'High frequency data in financial markets: issues and applications', *Journal of Empirical Finance*, 4, 73–114

Goodhart, C. and R. Payne (1996), 'Micro-structural dynamics in a foreign exchange electronic broking system', *Journal of International Money and Finance*, 15, December, 829–52.

Goodhart, C., R. Ito and R. Payne (1996), 'One day in June 1993: a study of the working of the Reuters 2000–2 electronic foreign exchange trading system', in *The Microstructure of Foreign Exchange Markets*, eds J. Frankel, G. Galli and A. Giovannini, Chicago: University of Chicago Press, IL, pp. 107–79.

Killeen, W., R. Lyons and M. Moore (2001), 'Fixed versus flexible: lessons from EMS order flow', NBER Working Paper 8491, September.

Kyle, A. (1985), 'Continuous auctions and insider trading', *Econometrica*, 53, 1315–35.

Lyons, R. (1995), 'Tests of microstructural hypotheses in the foreign exchange market', *Journal of Financial Economics*, 39, 321–51.

Lyons, R. (2001), *The Microstructure Approach to Exchange Rates*, Cambridge, Mass.: MIT Press (chapters at haas.berkeley.edu/~lyons).

Morris, S. and H. Shin (1999), 'Risk management with interdependent choice', *Financial Stability Review*, November, 141–50.

Naik, N. and P. Yadav (2000), 'Do market intermediaries hedge their risk exposure with derivatives?', typescript, London Business School, February.

Osler, C. (2003), 'Currency orders and exchange rate dynamics: an explanation for the predictive success of technical analysis', typescript, Federal Reserve Bank of New York, August, *Journal of Finance*, forthcoming.

Payne, R. (1999), 'Informed trade in spot foreign exchange markets: an empirical investigation', typescript, London School of Economics, January.

Wei, S. and J. Kim (1997), 'The big players in the foreign exchange market: do they trade on information or noise?', NBER Working Paper 6256, November.

7. Trading activity, volatility and transactions costs in spot FX markets

Richard G. Payne[*]

1. INTRODUCTION

In recent times, a fair amount of attention, from both academics and regulators, has been focussed on the links between the microstructures of securities markets and their 'stability'. The question at the heart of this attention is whether microstructure factors can help explain the onset and persistence of market turbulence. After the event of a 'market shock', do the design of a trading system or the natural responses of liquidity suppliers and demanders in a market tend to exacerbate and/or prolong the shock's effects?

Microstructure-level variables that are fundamental to investigations of this issue are liquidity and trading activity. Liquidity is an oft-discussed but rarely defined concept. In what is to come, we will use the following definition: a liquid market is one in which an agent can immediately trade a reasonably large quantity with relatively small price impact. Trading activity can also be measured in several different ways. More traditional measures of trading activity are simply counts of or aggregate volumes from recent transactions, regardless of whether trades were buyer or seller initiated. In what follows we employ one such measure – transaction frequency. However, a more relevant variable from a microstructure perspective, as emphasised in recent papers by Evans and Lyons (2002) and Chordia et al. (2001), is *order flow* – the difference between the aggregate number/volume of buyer initiated and seller initiated trades in a particular interval. Order flow is important as it indicates the balance of liquidity demand, either positive or negative, which is the key determinant of price changes in microstructure theory based on asymmetric information (Glosten and Milgrom, 1985; Kyle, 1985; Easley and O'Hara, 1987) or inventory control (Ho and Stoll, 1983). The most common measure of market turbulence is return volatility.

With measurements of these variables one can start to address questions such as the following. Is order flow 'destabilising' in the sense that one sees an excess of seller (buyer) initiated trades after price drops (rises), tending to lead to further price reduction (increase)? How is market liquidity affected by prior trading activity and return volatility? Does liquidity itself affect subsequent volatility and transaction frequency measures? What role does order flow have to play in these inter-relationships? The final three questions lead one to consider a dynamic system involving liquidity measures, transaction frequency and volatility in which price shocks may be propagated through time due to their effects on liquidity and trading. For example, if the natural reaction of liquidity suppliers to a price shock is to withdraw (at least temporarily) from the market then subsequent small shocks to the liquidity demand process will likely have large price effects – thus volatility will tend to cluster temporally.

We investigate these linkages using transaction-level FX data for the EUR/USD and the GBP/USD drawn from the Reuters D2000–2 electronic broking system.[1] The data covers the period from end September 1999 to end July 2000, a span of 10 months. We use percentage bid-ask spreads as a measure of liquidity for our trading venue. Clearly, given the definition above, spreads are at best a partial measure of liquidity. They measure the cost of instantly trading a small amount of currency. Ideally we would like to have a measure of D2000–2 order book depth to supplement our spread data but this is not available. However, note that recent research (Danielsson and Payne, 2001; Lee et al., 1993) has shown that spreads and depth are strongly positively correlated. We construct three measures of trading activity using the numbers of market buy and sell orders filled on D2000–2 – order flow is the number of market buys less market sells and transaction frequency is the sum of these two numbers. We also use absolute order flow in some regressions, where absolute order flow is simply the magnitude of the order flow measure. We do not have access to the size of the market buys and sells and hence cannot measure transaction volume accurately. Finally, our measure of volatility is derived from high-frequency return data. We construct *realised volatility* measures as in Andersen et al. (2001) for (relatively) low sampling frequencies by summing squares of high-frequency returns.[2] The basic sampling frequency for all of our analysis is hourly.

We start by investigating the effects of past price changes on order flow, seeking to establish whether there is any evidence that D2000–2 liquidity demanders tend to be momentum/positive-feedback traders or contrarian on average at the hourly sampling frequency. We find evidence (for the GBP/USD only) that D2000–2 traders tend to be contrarian in that they tend to buy after price falls and sell after price increases. Thus there is no evidence of destabilising, trend-chasing order flows. We go on to investigate the determination of bid-ask spreads, transaction frequency and volatility, respectively, where in all analysis both left- and right-hand side variables have had their diurnal patterns removed. The specification we estimate is motivated by and is similar to that estimated in an early FX microstructure paper by Demos and Goodhart (2000). These authors addressed similar issues to those under examination here but using indicative quote data and hence without measures of inside spreads or trading activity. We demonstrate that spreads tend to be lower in times of high transaction frequency but are larger when absolute returns are large. Transaction frequency is shown to be negatively affected by spreads and is larger in times of big positive or negative returns. Finally (a couple of measures of) volatility is shown to be positively related to both transaction frequency and spreads.

We provide evidence that the responses of volatility and spreads to trades vary with the level of order flow. The response of volatility to transaction frequency tends to be larger when those trades are not balanced and the negative effect of transaction frequency on spreads is attenuated when absolute order flow is large. These results could be interpreted in terms of asymmetric information microstructure theory. A large market order imbalance might suggest the existence of superior information in the hands of those demanding liquidity such that liquidity suppliers are less willing to lower spreads with volume and volatility increases as information enters prices.

Our regression results also emphasise the important nexus of causality involving volatility, liquidity supply and liquidity demand. An exchange rate shock leads to immediate increases in bid-ask spreads. Subsequently, increased spreads generate further volatility increases and these effects propagate through time due to persistence in the aforementioned variables. Our results thus point to the role of liquidity supply dynamics in generating volatility clusters.

Some of our results are similar to those in extant literature. In recent years, a number of papers have focused on the determination of bid-ask spreads in FX markets. Bessembinder (1994) estimates spread specifications with volatility and volume measures on the RHS, finding that volatility tends to increase spreads but the effect of trading volume depends on whether volume is expected or unexpected. Expected volume reduces spreads while unexpected volume increases them. Bollerslev and Melvin (1994) also concentrate on the determination of tick-by-tick indicative FX spread series in terms of exchange rate return volatility. It should be noted that such indicative spread data are poor proxies for firm spread data (like those we use in the current study), especially at the tick-by-tick level.

Goodhart and Payne (1996) estimate the same model as in Bollerslev and Melvin (1994) but using a short span of firm spreads. Any number of papers have focused on the evolution of exchange rate volatility (for example Baillie and Bollerslev, 1991; Dacorogna et al., 1993 and Andersen and Bollerslev, 1997) and studies of the low frequency covariation of volumes and volatilities in FX markets are also common. To our knowledge, however, no previous work has focused on the interactions between liquidity variables, transaction frequency, order flow and volatility in FX markets using a high quality, transaction level data set that allows accurate high-frequency measurement of these objects. Moreover, no-one has looked into the determination of FX order flows using such a long span of data. Recently, though, papers such as Chordia et al. (2001) have emerged that study lower frequency (daily) interactions between liquidity, order flow and trading activity variables in equity markets, demonstrating an important role for order flow. Our results complement those contained in Chordia et al. (2001).

The rest of the chapter is set out as follows. Section 2 provides a brief introduction to the data used in the chapter and Section 3 details our empirical specifications and results. Section 4 concludes.

2. DATA

The data used in this study are derived from the quoting and trading activity on the Reuters D2000–2 broking system. This is an order driven, interdealer system that allows (pre-trade) anonymous quoting and trading in a fairly large range of currency pairs. For up to six currency pairs at once, users can observe the best limit buy and sell prices available on the book (plus the size at these quotes) and can observe all transactions.

Our sample covers the period from the end of September 1999 until the end of July 2000. The original data set gives tick-by-tick information on the best quotes and all trades in EUR/USD and GBP/USD. The sample contains 484582 trades in EUR/USD and 579262 in GBP/USD. These numbers imply that D2000–2's coverage of the GBP/USD market is far superior to its coverage of the (much larger) EUR/USD market. Due to this, in what follows we will weight the GBP/USD results somewhat more heavily in our discussion. During the sample period the euro dropped in value from $1.05 to around $0.95 while sterling traded down from around $1.65 in 09/1999 to $1.5 in 07/2000.

For the purposes of the current study we convert the data from its tick-by-tick form to an hourly sampling frequency. At the hourly frequency we record the percentage exchange rate return, the number of trades, order flow, average (within hour) percentage bid-ask spreads and realised volatility. Prior to any estimations we remove all data from the GMT overnight period and from weekends (due to low D2000–2 activity) and also remove a number of days from the sample due to failure in the feed through which the D2000–2 data were collected.[3]

Summary statistics for these hourly data series are given in Table 7.1 and plots of the return series are given in Figure 7.1. The two returns series display the standard features of zero means, significant non-normality and small autocorrelations. Hourly trade frequency in the filtered data is similar for the two currency pairs and for both pairs hourly order flow is significantly positive. The two series with the strongest autocorrelations are the trades and spread series. Interestingly, and in contrast with many other studies using (indicative) intra-day exchange rate data, neither realised volatility series is strongly autocorrelated.

Some of the dependence in trades and spreads is, in part, attributable to the diurnal patterns that are present in these series. A similar pattern exists in the volatility series and also in the absolute value of order flow. Plots of the estimated diurnal patterns from these four series are given in Figure 7.2 for the EUR/USD. These patterns look very similar to those found in earlier studies (Andersen and Bollerslev, 1997; Andersen and Bollerslev,

Table 7.1   Summary statistics for raw data

Series	Mean	s.d.	EUR/USD JB	ρ_1	ρ_2	ρ_3
Return	0.000	0.197	5029.360	0.024	0.037	−0.024
Trades	252.690	149.706	235.679	0.494	0.118	0.054
Flow	2.454	38.498	616.443	0.022	0.041	0.011
Spread	0.032	0.052	5.6×10^5	0.636	0.266	0.096
Volatility	0.048	0.254	1.1×10^8	0.021	0.001	0.002

Series	Mean	s.d.	GBP/USD JB	ρ_1	ρ_2	ρ_3
Return	0.000	0.133	2173.648	−0.009	0.034	−0.022
Trades	243.439	161.083	696.457	0.537	0.253	0.122
Flow	4.478	26.933	620.599	0.007	0.062	−0.052
Spread	0.246	0.146	1.1×10^6	0.624	0.343	0.218
Volatility	0.021	0.085	2.0×10^8	0.022	0.008	0.015

Notes: Summary statistics for exchange rate data The column headed s.d. gives sample standard deviations. The column headed JB gives the Jarque–Bera statistic for each series. The final three columns give the first three sample autocorrelations for each series.

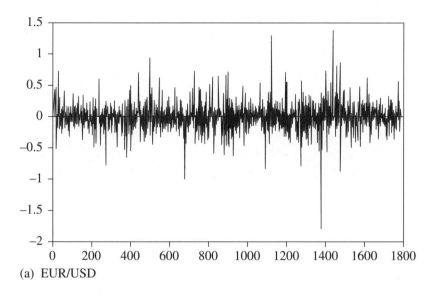

(a) EUR/USD

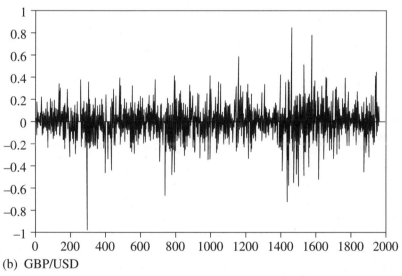

(b) GBP/USD

Figure 7.1 Exchange rate return plots

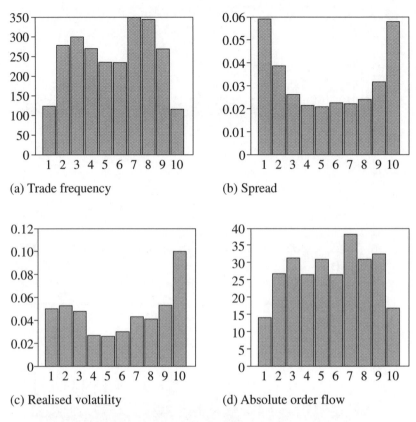

(a) Trade frequency

(b) Spread

(c) Realised volatility

(d) Absolute order flow

Figure 7.2   Diurnal patterns for EUR/USD data

1998) of indicative data. Prior to any estimations involving these series, we remove the diurnal patterns simply by scaling the kth intra-day observation on day t for series x by the average value of the kth intra-day observation taken across all t.[4]

Table 7.2 gives summary statistics for deseasonalised trades, spreads and volatility. Note that, by construction, the mean of these series must be unity. Interestingly, in all but one case, the first estimated autocorrelation for the deseasonalised data exceeds that for the raw data.

3.   RESULTS

We now present results from regressions of our transaction activity, liquidity and volatility variables on their own lags and on each other. We begin

Table 7.2   Summary statistics for deseasonalised data

Series	Mean	s.d.	EUR/USD JB	ρ_1	ρ_2	ρ_3
Trades	1.000	0.513	406.533	0.541	0.354	0.288
Abs. Flow	1.000	0.940	1985.077	0.105	0.072	0.070
Spread	1.000	1.354	1.2×10^6	0.688	0.351	0.194
Volatility	1.000	3.176	2.2×10^7	0.039	0.014	0.015

Series	Mean	s.d.	GBP/USD JB	ρ_1	ρ_2	ρ_3
Trades	1.000	0.621	2613.332	0.507	0.336	0.279
Abs. Flow	1.000	0.957	2964.600	0.110	0.133	0.056
Spread	1.000	0.552	1.0×10^6	0.647	0.405	0.291
Volatility	1.000	2.630	8.9×10^7	0.048	0.024	0.031

Notes: Summary statistics for deseasonalised exchange rate data The column headed s.d. gives sample standard deviations. The column headed JB gives the Jarque–Bera statistic for each series. The final three columns give the first three sample autocorrelations for each series.

with an analysis of the determination of order flow before investigating the interactions between transaction frequency, spreads and volatility.

3.1   Order Flow Determination

The first question we wish to address is whether D2000–2 order flow tends to be 'price stabilising' or 'contrarian' in that subsequent to price falls we see an excess of market buys over sells and vice versa, or whether order flow tends to be destabilising or momentum driven in the sense that flows tend to reinforce prior price movements – that is market buys follow price increases and market sells follow price falls. Recent evidence from daily US equity market data (Chordia et al., 2001) suggests a stabilising role for order flow.

We examine this question through a regression of order flow on five lags of flow and five lags of positive and negative return interaction variables.[5] The value of the positive return interaction variable (R_t^+) at t is just the maximum of the return itself (R_t) and zero whilst the negative return interaction variable (R_t^-) at t is the minimum of zero and R_t. We include these variables separately (as do Chordia et al., 2001) to investigate whether the return order flow relationship might be different in rising versus falling

Table 7.3   Determination of order flow

Regressor	EUR/USD	GBP/USD
Const.	4.0899**	3.8050***
FL_{t-1}	0.0153	0.0702**
FL_{t-2}	0.0388	0.0856***
FL_{t-3}	0.004	−0.025
FL_{t-4}	0.0348	0.032
FL_{t-5}	0.0075	0.0063
R^+_{t-1}	−8.0547	−47.7243***
R^+_{t-2}	9.6726	−5.435
R^+_{t-3}	3.0459	−9.146
R^+_{t-4}	7.3801	−0.0403
R^+_{t-5}	4.288	7.0173
R^-_{t-1}	10.5391	−25.4009***
R^-_{t-2}	−11.1928	−22.2169**
R^-_{t-3}	1.735	−11.3665
R^-_{t-4}	−20.9755***	−1.5598
R^-_{t-5}	6.8836	2.5831
$\bar{R}^2$	0.001	0.038
$Q(10)$	6.28404	11.091

Notes: ***, **, * indicate significance at the 1%, 5%, and 10% levels, respectively. The 5% and 1% critical values of the χ^2 (10) distribution are 18.3 and 23.2.

markets. Parameter estimates from this regression are presented in Table 7.3.

The results from this estimation for the EUR/USD are disappointing. Only one of the RHS variables is significantly different from zero even at the 10 per cent level indicating that past flows and past returns tell us little about the way in which order flow will evolve. However, for the GBP/USD data, there is highly significant evidence of two things. First, there is some positive autocorrelation in the flow series, although the coefficients are relatively small in magnitude. More importantly, there is evidence, from both the positive and negative return indicators, that order flow is contrarian. A positive return in the current hour tends to lead to reduced (that is more negative) order flows in the subsequent hour. Similarly a current negative return leads to significantly increased flows in the subsequent two hours.

Hence there is some evidence from our data that is in line with the equity market results in Chordia et al. (2001). FX traders tend to be net buyers subsequent to price drops and net sellers after price rises. Also, the fact that order flow is forecastable with past returns is interesting as, given the strong positive contemporaneous correlation between order flow and returns, it indicates a (small) degree of return forecastability.

3.2 Determination of Transaction Frequency

The main focus of this study is on the determination of and links between liquidity and volatility, with special attention paid to the role played by order flow. A key driving variable in the determination of liquidity and volatility is transaction frequency, as earlier studies on FX spreads (Bessembinder, 1994) and the volume–volatility relationship in financial markets (see the references contained in Karpoff, 1987) would imply. In this section we briefly look at the determination of transaction frequency itself to ascertain whether there is any feedback from liquidity or volatility. Hence we estimate a linear regression of trades on 5 lags of the dependent variable, lagged spreads and lagged volatility variables.[6] The results are presented in Table 7.4.

In line with the autocorrelation evidence for transaction frequency presented in Table 7.2, the table shows that the low displacement lagged dependent variables are generally highly significant for both exchange rates. Hence, even after removal of a diurnal pattern, intervals of high and low transaction frequency tend to cluster together. Also, there is negative feedback from spreads to trades. Subsequent to periods of high spreads, transaction frequency tends to be significantly reduced. Finally, for the GBP/USD, the effect of lagged volatility variables on subsequent trades is highly significant.

Table 7.4 Determination of trades

Regressor	EUR/USD	GBP/USD
Const.	0.3862***	0.4081***
TR_{t-1}	0.4753***	0.3803***
TR_{t-2}	0.0321	0.0700***
TR_{t-3}	0.0780***	0.0833***
TR_{t-4}	0.017	0.0193
TR_{t-5}	0.0265	0.0292
S_{t-1}	−0.0159***	−0.0397***
R^+_{t-1}	0.0473	0.5387***
R^-_{t-1}	0.045	−0.5329***
$\bar{R}^2$	0.305	0.277
$Q(10)$	8.62	8.14

Notes: ***, **, * indicate significance at the 1%, 5%, and 10% levels, respectively. The 5% and 1% critical values of the χ^2 (10) distribution are 18.3 and 23.2.

The volatility variables used in this analysis are the same positive and negative return interactions employed in the analysis of order flow.[7] The respective positive and negative signs on these variables suggest that when returns
either rise or fall fast, this tends to be associated with increased subsequent
transaction frequency.

This final result on the relationship between transaction frequency and
returns dovetails with the results on order flow and volatility. The transaction frequency results suggest that in periods after those with sharp price
movements, trading activity is greater and the order flow results tell us that
this increased trading activity is largely contrarian in nature. The result that
increased spreads tend to reduce subsequent transaction frequency simply
implies that those demanding liquidity are sensitive to the cost of imme-
diacy.

3.3   Determination of Bid-ask Spreads

Much of the recent time-series work on FX spread determination (at daily
and higher frequencies) is based on a specification first used in
Bessembinder (1994). This specification relates spreads in a given interval
to estimates/forecasts of volatility in that interval, expected trading volume
in the interval and unexpected trading volume. The theoretical basis for
such a specification is as follows; volatility and inventory carrying costs of
dealers are positively related such that increased volatility should increase
spreads; increased expected volume will likely be associated with reduced
spreads due to fixed costs of market making; unexpected volume, on the
other hand, is likely to reflect information arrivals and hence should
increase the information cost component of spreads. By and large, empirical studies based on this spread decomposition deliver results consistent
with this intuition (Bessembinder, 1994; Hartmann, 1999).

However, the preceding arguments, in our opinion, are not entirely convincing. The notion that increased expected volume should simply reduce
spreads is debatable. Surely the direction of trading activity will matter to
any liquidity supplier (on top of its magnitude). For example, from a liquidity supply perspective there is a large difference between the implications of
$20m in volume if that $20m is composed, on the one hand, entirely of
market buys and, on the other hand, of $10m of buys and $10m of market
sells. This type of effect might come from a standard asymmetric information story – one-sided market order flow suggests the existence of superior
information in the hands of those demanding liquidity and hence those
supplying liquidity worsen their terms of trade.

This argument suggests a role for the absolute value of order flow in the
relationship between spreads and transaction frequency. Specifically, we

hypothesise that, while the general effect of transaction frequency on spreads might well be negative, in times of largely one-sided trading this negative effect will be attenuated and may even become positive. As such, when market order flow is balanced, transaction frequency and spreads are negatively related but when absolute order flow is large it may be the case that transaction frequency and spreads are positively related.

To test our conjecture we regress spreads on 5 lags of the spread, current transaction frequency, the product of current transaction frequency and current absolute order flow and current values of the positive and negative return interactions. The results from this specification are given in Table 7.5.

Table 7.5 Determination of spreads

Regressor	EUR/USD	GBP/USD
Const.	0.6800***	0.4053***
S_{t-1}	0.8622***	0.6546***
S_{t-2}	-0.3591***	-0.069
S_{t-3}	0.2051**	0.0242
S_{t-4}	-0.1796***	0.0475
S_{t-5}	0.1241**	0.0101
TR_t	-0.4085***	-0.1129***
$TR_t \times AFL_t$	0.0447***	0.0109**
R_t^+	0.0502	0.2836***
R_t^-	-0.24	-0.2920***
$\bar{R}^2$	0.529	0.428
$Q(10)$	4.41	9.60

Notes: ***, **, * indicate significance at the 1%, 5%, and 10% levels, respectively. The 5% and 1% critical values of the χ^2 (10) distribution are 18.3 and 23.2.

First, we note the strong and significant positive dependence in spreads. Second, for both exchange rates there is a significant negative effect of current transaction frequency on current spreads – when trades are frequent then spreads are reduced. Presumably this is due to competition between liquidity suppliers in periods of intense and balanced trading activity. For the GBP/USD there is highly significant evidence of a positive effect from volatility to spreads.[8] Again, this is likely due to increased inventory carrying risk for those supplying liquidity. Finally, however, the coefficient on the interaction of trades and absolute flow is significantly positive in both regressions. Hence, when order flow is not balanced the negative effect of trades on spreads is attenuated, in line with the intuition above. Presumably periods of unbalanced flow are interpreted by liquidity suppliers as those where 'information asymmetry is high' and thus they are not as willing to reduce spreads when trades arrive.

3.4   Determination of Volatility

Finally, we examine the effects of trading activity and lagged liquidity on volatility. As in the previous subsection, we allow the effect of transaction frequency on volatility to vary with the absolute value of order flow. We hypothesise that unbalanced transaction activity should have a greater effect on volatility than balanced trading activity. Further, from the point of view of the liquidity–stability relationship discussed in the introduction, the effect of lagged spreads on volatility is interesting. If there is a positive relationship between spreads and subsequent volatility then one might argue that the actions of liquidity suppliers serve to amplify and perpetuate the effects of price shocks. Finally, we estimate regressions using two different volatility variables on the LHS. The first is a straightforward realised volatility measure formed as the sum of squared intra-hour returns. The second is a realised volatility measure constructed from the residuals of a regression of returns on order flow. We employ this second volatility measure to control for the strong contemporaneous effect that signed order flow has on returns (Evans and Lyons, 2002) as this will automatically generate a relationship between transaction frequency and return volatility. Hence, our specifications relate volatility on the RHS to lagged dependent variables, current transaction frequency, the product of current transaction frequency and absolute flow and lagged spreads. Results from the two estimations are given in Tables 7.6 and 7.7.

A first result from these tables is that, unlike any number of volatility estimations using indicative quote returns, the own dependence in our volatility measures is economically and statistically insignificant. There is little evidence of volatility clusters in our data at the hourly frequency. The effect of transaction frequency on volatility is significantly positive in all four regressions. Hence, even after having accounted for the effects of order flow on the return, trades engender volatility. The effect of trades on volatility is significantly larger, though, when volume is not balanced. When absolute order flow is large, trades increase volatility to a greater extent, presumably because unbalanced trading activity reflects differences in the information of liquidity suppliers and demanders. However, in purely quantitative terms this effect is not as striking as the similar effect in the spread regressions.

A final result is that in all four regression specifications the coefficient on

Table 7.6   Determination of volatility

Regressor	EUR/USD	GBP/USD
Const.	−0.1897	−0.2941***
V_{t-1}	0.0125	0.0073*
V_{t-2}	0.084	−0.0057
V_{t-3}	0.01	0.0081
V_{t-4}	0.0063	0.0084
V_{t-5}	0.004	0.0322
$TR_t \times AFL_t$	0.0031***	0.0038***
TR_t	0.7409***	1.0273***
S_{t-1}	10.3045***	0.1235***
$\bar{R}^2$	0.031	0.078
$Q(10)$	3.94	7.26

Notes: ***, **, * indicate significance at the 1%, 5%, and 10% levels, respectively. The 5% and 1% critical values of the χ^2 (10) distribution are 18.3 and 23.2.

Table 7.7   Determination of residual volatility

Regressor	EUR/USD	GBP/USD
Const.	−0.1799	−0.3216**
RV_{t-1}	−0.0049	−0.001
RV_{t-2}	−0.0035	−0.0008
RV_{t-3}	0.0004	0.0267
RV_{t-4}	−0.0009	0.0014
RV_{t-5}	0.0057	0.0209
$TR_t \times AFL_t$	0.0013	0.0050**
TR_t	0.6267***	1.0193***
S_{t-1}	10.5131**	0.1331**
$\bar{R}^2$	0.030	0.058
$Q(10)$	2.70	7.44

Notes: ***, **, * indicate significance at the 1%, 5%, and 10% levels, respectively. The 5% and 1% critical values of the χ^2 (10) distribution are 18.3 and 23.2.

the lagged spread is positive and highly significant. Thus when D2000–2 liquidity is poor, subsequently one is likely to see greater volatility. This lends credence to the idea that the effects of price shocks in these markets might be exacerbated by the responses of liquidity suppliers. If, as we saw earlier in this section, spreads increase in volatile periods and volatility is positively related to prior spreads then this will tend to distribute the effects of price shocks over time. More generally, if subsequent to a price shock, markets tend to thin out, then the likelihood of further jumps in price is increased.

4.   CONCLUSION

We have studied the determination of trading activity and liquidity measures using a new set of transaction level FX data on the EUR/USD and GBP/USD. Our main findings are as follows. There is evidence that order flow is contrarian in nature in that flow tends to be positive subsequent to drops in the exchange rate and negative after price rises. There is no evidence in our data of destabilising, trend-chasing order flows. We also show that the effects of transaction frequency on bid-ask spreads and on volatility are dependent on the composition of the transaction activity via order flow. When (absolute) order flows are large then the negative relationship between spreads and trades tends to get weaker while the positive response of volatility to trades is increased. Finally we demonstrate that liquidity, via bid-ask spreads, feeds back into the determination of transaction frequency and volatility – negatively in the former case and positively in the latter. Hence, while high spreads tend to reduce subsequent transaction arrivals, they increase subsequent volatility.

Thus, our results yield information on the relationship between key microstructure variables and market turbulence. The fact that order flow tends to be stabilising seems to indicate that those demanding liquidity in this market might play a role that damps down large price movements in one direction or another. However, the fact that there is a positive relationship between a variable that measures the quality of liquidity supply (the bid-ask spread) and subsequent volatility emphasises the role that liquidity suppliers have to play.

It is tautological to say that volatility should be linked to liquidity supply and transaction arrival as prices/quotes only change in financial markets when liquidity suppliers voluntarily alter their terms of trade or market orders drain extant liquidity supply. This points to the importance of gaining a more clear understanding of the dynamics of liquidity supply and demand. The current study, in a very limited fashion, contributes to this area of research but it is clear that further work is needed. Such work can only help us understand the onset and persistence of market turbulence.

NOTES

*   Thanks to Jon Danielsson and Charles Goodhart for helpful comments. Thanks to the Bank of England for providing the transactions data used in this study. Jinhui Luo provided helpful research assistance. All remaining errors are my own.

1.   These data were provided to us by the Bank of England.
2.   To be clear, if one wished to construct hourly realised volatility from 5 minute return data (that is volatility over the period from t to $t + 12$) one would compute $\Sigma_{i=1}^{12} r_{t+i}^2$.
3.   For the EUR/USD we define the overnight period to be the period between 4pm and 7am while for GBP/USD it is defined to be the period between 5pm and 7am.
4.   That is, we get rid of the diurnal pattern in $x_{k,t}$ by forming the following variable:

$$x_{k,t}^d = \frac{x_{k,t}}{\frac{1}{T}\Sigma_{t=1}^T x_{k,t}}.$$

5.   We experimented with alternative lag lengths without the results being qualitatively affected. Note also that the inference for this and all other specifications is based on heteroskedasticity robust estimates of the parameter covariance matrix.
6.   Note that we include the first lag of the spread and volatility, rather than their current values, on the RHS here. The reason for this is as follows. We view trading, either through transaction frequency or via order flow, as the main driving variable in the trades–volatility–spreads system, with volatility being next in line and spreads last. Thus, similar to the way one would identify a VAR using a recursive ordering, we allow transaction frequency to contemporaneously affect the other two variables and volatility to also contemporaneously affect spreads. Spreads only affect other variables with a lag and the effect of volatility on transactions is also only felt with a lag.
7.   Exactly the same result holds when we use the deseasonalised realised volatility measure on the RHS of this equation instead of these two interactions.
8.   The same result holds if you replace the positive and negative return interactions with a straightforward realised volatility variable.

REFERENCES

Andersen, T. and T. Bollerslev (1997), 'Intraday Seasonality and Volatility Persistence in Financial Markets', *Journal of Empirical Finance*, 4, 115–58.

Andersen, T. and T. Bollerslev (1998), 'Deutsche Mark–Dollar Volatility: Intraday Activity Patterns, Macroeconomic Announcements, and Longer Run Dependencies', *Journal of Finance*, 53(1), 219–65.

Andersen, T., T. Bollerslev, F. Diebold and P. Labys (2001), 'The Distribution of Realized Exchange Rate Volatility', *Journal of the American Statistical Association*, 96, 42–55.

Baillie, R. and T. Bollerslev (1991), 'Intra-Day and Inter-Market Volatility in Foreign Exchange Markets', *Review of Economic Studies*, 58, 565–86.

Bessembinder, H. (1994), 'Bid-Ask Spreads in the Interbank Foreign Exchange Market', *Journal of Financial Economics*, 35, 317–48.

Bollerslev, T. and M. Melvin (1994), 'Bid-ask Spreads and Volatility in the Foreign Exchange Market: An Empirical Analysis', *Journal of International Economics*, 36, 355–72.

Chordia, T., R. Roll and A. Subrahmanyam (2001), 'Order Imbalance, Liquidity and Market Returns', *Journal of Financial Economics*.

Dacorogna, M., U. Müller, R. Nagler, R. Olsen and O. Pictet (1993), 'A Geographical Model for the Daily and Weekly Seasonal Volatility in the

Foreign Exchange Market', *Journal of International Money and Finance*, 12, 413–38.

Danielsson, J. and R. Payne (2001), 'Measuring and Explaining Liquidity on an Electronic Limit Order Book: Evidence from D2000–2', Working Paper, Financial Markets Group, London School of Economics.

Demos, A. and C. Goodhart (2000), 'The Interaction between the Frequency of Market Quotations, Spreads and Volatility in the Foreign Exchange Market', in *The Foreign Exchange Market: Empirical Studies with High-Frequency Data*, eds C. Goodhart and R. Payne, Basingstoke, UK: Macmillan, pp. 335–52.

Easley, D. and M. O'Hara (1987), 'Price, Trade Size and Information in Securities Markets', *Journal of Financial Economics*, 19, 69–90.

Evans, M. and R. Lyons (2002), 'Order Flow and Exchange Rate Dynamics', *Journal of Political Economy*, 101(1) (February), 170–80.

Glosten, L. and P. Milgrom (1985), 'Bid, Ask and Transaction Prices in a Specialist Market with Heterogeneously Informed Traders', *Journal of Financial Economics*, 14, 71–100.

Goodhart, C. and R. Payne (1996), 'Microstructural Dynamics in a Foreign Exchange Electronic Broking System', *Journal of International Money and Finance*, 15(6), 829–52.

Hartmann, P. (1999), 'Trading Volumes and Transaction Costs in the Foreign Exchange Market: Evidence from Daily Dollar–Yen Spot Data', *Journal of Banking and Finance*, 23, 801–24.

Ho, T. and H. Stoll (1983), 'The Dynamics of Dealer Markets under Competition', *Journal of Finance*, 38(4), 1053–74.

Karpoff, J. (1987), 'The Relation Between Price Changes and Trading Volume: A Survey', *Journal of Financial and Quantitative Analysis*, 22, 109–26.

Kyle, A. (1985), 'Continuous Auctions and Insider Trading', *Econometrica*, 53, 1315–35.

Lee, C., B. Mucklow and M. Ready (1993), 'Spreads, Depths and the Impact of Earnings Information: an Intraday Analysis', *Review of Financial Studies*, 6(2), 345–74.

Discussion of 'Customer trades and extreme events in foreign exchange' and 'Trading activity, volatility and transactions costs in spot FX markets'

Mark P. Taylor

Exchange rate economics is one of the most challenging areas of our discipline, and it is one in which Charles Goodhart has made important contributions. For example, in his work on the interaction of chartists and fundamentalists, as set out in his inaugural lecture at the London School of Economics (Goodhart, 1988), he was one of the first economists to recognise explicitly that, although economic fundamentals may be important for the determination of long-run equilibrium in foreign exchange markets, short-run exchange movements may be dominated by the influence of other factors besides the list of standard macro-fundamentals.[1] Thus, Goodhart was one of the earliest economists to realise the importance of analysing the foreign exchange market from a perspective other than that employed by the traditional macroeconomic approach, and his subsequent work on microstructure built on this insight. Indeed, as Flood and Taylor (1996, p. 285) observe, it is because of the apparent importance of factors not on the standard macro list in determining exchange rate behaviour 'that new work on the microstructure of the foreign exchange market seems both warranted and promising'. From the other side of the Atlantic, Richard Lyons has been the leading pioneer in work on foreign exchange market microstructure, and it is therefore entirely appropriate that his intriguing paper with Mintao Fan should be presented at this conference in honour of Charles Goodhart.[2]

Fan and Lyons' chapter is an analysis of a new data base on non-market maker foreign exchange *customer* order flow, in contrast to previous studies, notably Evans and Lyons (2002), which have concentrated on *inter-dealer* order flow. The Evans and Lyons chapter is, in my view, an important landmark paper in foreign exchange rate analysis in that it demonstrates a strong empirical link between order flow and short-run exchange rate movements. Thus, Evans and Lyons show that inter-dealer order flow has high explanatory and predictive power for exchange rate movements for horizons of up to four months ahead.

On my reading of the Fan and Lyons chapter, the most important empirical findings are as follows. First, aggregate customer order flow tracks low frequency exchange rate movements closely – echoing the Evans–Lyons findings – and, second, that customer order flow cumulated over time is significantly correlated with exchange rate movements. This second finding is important because, as Fan and Lyons note, it *appears, prima facie, to contradict* the Evans–Lyons (2002) model which would predict a zero correlation. In the Evans–Lyons stylised model of market behaviour, there are three rounds of activity in the trading day:

Round 1:   Dealers trade with customers (public);
Round 2:   Dealers trade among themselves to share inventory risk;
Round 3:   Dealers trade again with public to pool risks more broadly.

Thus, the model predicts that customer order flow should net to zero at the end of each day and, therefore, if the customer order flow data for a particular bank represents a random sample, then that flow should each day be uncorrelated with changes in the exchange rate.

Fan and Lyons discuss a number of possibilities to explain their apparent empirical contradiction of this aspect of the Evans–Lyons model, but are apparently loth to discuss whether the model should be modified. In my view, one important issue raised by the chapter is whether the Evans–Lyons model should in fact be taken as axiomatic. Certainly, Fan and Lyons argue in their chapter that 'the ultimate driver of that inter-dealer order flow is customer flow', but it should be noted that this is an untested proposition. Interdealer trading account for some 90 per cent of worldwide foreign exchange market activity (Bank for International Settlements, 1999; Sarno and Taylor, 2001), and while much of this activity will be triggered by customer orders, with dealers unloading ensuing positions in the market, it seems hard to believe that the 'activity multiplier' (the total number of market transactions triggered by a single customer order) is of the order of nine or ten. Moreover, it may be that large market makers take considerable overnight positions rather than, as it were, laying off bets with the public. What is for certain is that this intriguing finding of the Fan–Lyons chapter warrants further empirical and theoretical investigation.

There are other interesting empirical findings in this very rich chapter which are worthy of note. For example, contrary to popular belief, Fan and Lyons adduce evidence to show that the drop in the yen that occurred around the time of LTCM's collapse in 1998 was perhaps not triggered primarily by the selling behaviour of hedge funds and that, indeed, hedge funds were net providers of liquidity in a market dominated by the port-folio shifts financial institutions such as insurance companies, pension funds and mutual funds.

Overall, as one would expect from the authorship of this chapter, it is a pioneering and highly interesting study. In common with Charles Good-hart's work in this area, it sheds new light on how the foreign exchange market is perceived by economists and raises a number of important questions.

As I mentioned in my comments on the Fan and Lyons chapter, the study of foreign exchange market microstructure was largely pioneered by Charles Goodhart. In recent years, much of this innovative and pioneering work has been done in collaboration with Richard Payne.[3] This chapter by Richard Payne maintains the high standard set in his joint work with Goodhart.

In common with the Fan and Lyons chapter, Payne's chapter provides an analysis of foreign exchange market order flow through an analysis of a new, transactions-level data base on the markets for dollar–euro and dollar–sterling drawn from the Reuters D2000–2 electronic broking system.[4] Research on foreign exchange market order flow is, especially in light of the Evans and Lyons (2002) chapter, in my view one of the most exciting areas of foreign exchange market research currently being under-taken. Payne's chapter is unashamedly empirical in its approach and uncov-ers a number of highly interesting research findings which both add to our understanding of the foreign exchange market and are likely to provide impetus for further research.

On my reading of the chapter, it would seem that at least part of this research effort might usefully be addressed to linking some of the empiri-cal regularities unearthed by Payne more closely to new and existing theo-retical work and perhaps also to previous empirical work. Taylor and Allen (1992), for example, show, *inter* alia, that chartist or technical analysis is widely employed in the major foreign exchange markets and, moreover, that 'oscillators' – also known as 'momentum indicators' or over-bought/oversold indicators' are widely used tools of technical analysis. Briefly, an oscillator generates a buy signal when the percentage change in the external value of a currency crosses a particular threshold within a given time period, thereby indicting that it has been 'oversold'. The wide-spread use of oscillators in the foreign exchange market would therefore tend to imply that there will be a preponderance of buy orders from dealers in the wake of sharp falls in the value of a currency – and this is exactly the 'contrarian' tendency which Payne observes in the data.

Among the several other interesting findings reported in the chapter, the link established between the absolute magnitude of order flow and the negative relationship between spreads and trades is particularly worth mentioning: when order flow is large in magnitude, the negative relationship gets weaker. Payne links this to theoretical work on informational asymmetry: if imbalanced order flow indicates a higher degree of informational asymmetry in the market, then traders may be less willing to reduce spreads when trades arrive. The idea that the direction as well as the overall volume of trading activity should affect the size of the spread is highly innovative, and it seems likely that Payne's work will spur further research activity in this direction.

NOTES

1. This early contribution on the influence of chartists in the foreign exchange market was made independently and in parallel with similar work by Frankel and Froot (for example 1990).
2. See for example Lyons' recent monograph (Lyons, 2001). For a recent survey of the literature on foreign exchange market microstructure, see Sarno and Taylor (2001).
3. See for example the collection of papers in Goodhart and Payne (2000).
4. See Sarno and Taylor (2001) for a description and discussion of electronic broking systems, including the Reuters system.

REFERENCES

Allen, Helen and Mark P. Taylor (1992), 'Chartist Analysis', in Murray Milgate, Peter Newman and John Eatwell (eds), *The New Palgrave Dictionary of Money and Finance*, London: Macmillan.

Bank for International Settlements (1999), *A Review of Financial Market Events in Autumn 1998*, Publication of the Committee on the Global Financial System, October.

Evans, Martin D. and Richard K. Lyons (2002), 'Order Flow and Exchange Rate Dynamics', NBER Working Paper 7317, *Journal of Political Economy*, 101(1) (February), 170–80.

Flood, Robert P. and Mark P. Taylor (1996), 'Exchange Rate Economics: What's Wrong with the Conventional Macro Approach?', in Jeffrey A. Frankel, Giovanni Galli and Alberto Giovannini (eds), *The Microstructure of Foreign Exchange Markets*, Chicago: University of Chicago Press for NBER, pp. 261–301.

Frankel, Jeffrey A. and Kenneth A. Froot (1990), 'Chartists, Fundamentalists and the Demand for Dollars', in Anthony Courakis and Mark P. Taylor (eds), *Private Behaviour and Government Policy in Interdependent Economies*, Oxford: Oxford University Press, pp. 73–126.

Goodhart, Charles A.E. (1988), 'The Foreign Exchange Market: A Random Walk with a Dragging Anchor', *Economica*, 55, 437–60.

Goodhart, Charles A.E. and Richard G. Payne (2000), *The Foreign Exchange Market: Empirical Studies with High-Frequency Data*, Basingstoke: Macmillan, and New York: St Martin's Press.

Lyons, Richard K. (2001), *The Microstructure Approach to Exchange Rates*, Cambridge, Mass.: MIT Press.

Sarno, Lucio and Mark P. Taylor (2001), *The Microstructure of the Foreign Exchange Market: A Selective Survey of the Literature*, Princeton Studies in International Economics No. 89, May, Princeton, NJ: International Economics Section, Department of Economics, Princeton University.

Taylor, Mark P. and Helen Allen (1992) 'The Use of Technical Analysis in the Foreign Exchange Market', *Journal of International Money and Finance*, 11, 304–14.

8. Competition and stability: what's special about banking?

Elena Carletti and Philipp Hartmann[*]

1. INTRODUCTION

The speciality of the banking system from the perspective of stability is a widely recognised idea (see for example Goodhart, 1987a and Goodhart et al., 1998). What is much less debated in the literature is the implications this special status has for market structures and competition policies. Similarly, not much research work has been dedicated to the implications different bank market structures and degrees of competitiveness have for bank stability and supervisory policies (see also Allen and Gale, 2000b and Canoy et al., 2001). In this chapter we want to look at two areas to address some of those questions.

First, we would like to discuss the institutional structure of competition policies, particularly of bank merger reviews. We want to analyse which government agencies are in charge of these reviews in different countries and what are the relative roles played by antitrust authorities and prudential supervisors. In this context we will also briefly look at how competition policy in banking more generally differs from that in other sectors. Second, since a whole variety of approaches emerges from this first set of issues, we then want to ask the question what the literature has to say about the relationship between competition and stability in banking. We will review the theoretical literature linking market structures with bank stability, supervisory tools and safety nets and then the empirical literature measuring the sign of the competition-stability nexus and testing hypotheses explaining it.

The chapter is structured as follows. The next section briefly recalls the argument about why banks are 'special' from a financial stability perspective, describes the three classic areas of competition policy and explains the relative importance of them for the banking sector. Section 3 discusses the relative roles of competition and supervisory authorities as well as competition and banking laws in bank merger reviews in the G-7 countries plus the European Union (EU). Section 4 first surveys theoretical models discussing the relationship between different market structures and bank liability side and systemic risk as well as the relationship between market structures and bank asset side risk. Second it surveys empirical and historical papers testing the so-called 'charter-value' hypothesis, risk diversification effects of mergers, relationships between consolidation and interbank linkages and cross-country comparisons of relative bank system efficiency and stability. The final section concludes.

2. COMPETITION POLICY IN BANKING: WHAT'S DIFFERENT?

It is widely assumed that banks and the banking system have a special status, mainly because they are regarded as more vulnerable to instability than other firms or sectors but also because less wealthy people may hold some non-negligible share of their wealth in various forms of bank deposits.[1] On the asset side, according to the traditional view banks specialise in assessing the relative viability and profitability of projects put forward by entrepreneurs and, based on their information production on these projects, they grant loans to the entrepreneurs. On the liability side, according to the traditional view banks are special in that they rely to a significant extent on (many small) short-term demandable deposits, which they pool and then invest in long-term loans to production firms. This maturity mismatch between assets and liabilities, together with the strong information content of their assets, makes banks play the additional role of providers of liquidity to depositors but – in the absence of deposit insurance – it also exposes them to the possibility of runs.[2]

Moreover, referring to more recent times banks are heavily involved in interbank lending markets and the payment system. Focusing on the wholesale side, they lend and borrow among each other in large amounts to cushion daily liquidity fluctuations. They are also heavily involved in conducting the large value payments resulting from their own and their customers' activities. In both ways, they are heavily linked to each other. For these physical exposures and for information asymmetries about their relative health, absent proper safety provisions there is a risk that the problem of one bank propagates to other banks, creating one form of systemic risk (the risk of interbank contagion). The other form of systemic risk is that aggregate shocks to the economy may deteriorate the viability of a larger number of relatively correlated projects at the same time, thereby bringing a larger number of banks simultaneously into trouble, since the typical bank contract does not allow for liabilities that are contingent on asset values.[3]

The vulnerability to runs and more recently to problems in the interbank market represents the source of concerns about bank instability originating from the liability side of the balance sheet. A second source of instability relates to bank risk-taking on the asset side. Because of their substantial financing from many small, relatively uninformed depositors and an often-existing public safety net in response to the previously mentioned vulnerability, banks can be prone to taking on 'excessive' risk in the choice of which projects to finance. The concern for a stable banking sector, together with that for consumer/depositor protection, provides the motivation for numerous special regulations and supervisory activities in this sector (including for example special bank licences, 'fit and proper' tests for managers, capital adequacy requirements, and so on) as well as safety net arrangements in the form of deposit insurance and lender of last resort facilities.

Whereas the stability considerations are widely known and well analysed in the economic literature, the same cannot be said for bank competition and antitrust policies in banking. In general, competition policy refers mainly to three different types of business practices, cartels, abuse of a dominant position and mergers. *Cartels* refer to any agreement and/or coordination of market behaviours (such as concerted practices) between firms, which have as objective or effect the prevention, restriction or distortion of competition. Examples of anti-competitive cartels are agreements that directly or indirectly fix purchase or selling prices or any other trading conditions, that share markets or sources of supply, that limit production, markets, technical development or investment. Cartels can be horizontal or vertical. The latter concern agreements between suppliers and producers and the former between producers and distributors. For co-operation to be prohibited, competition has to be negatively affected to a considerable extent.

Abuse of dominant position relates to any possible anti-competitive behaviour exerted by one or more firms occupying a dominant position in a market. A company holds a dominant position when it can behave independently from both competitors and customers, who have limited possibilities to react to such behaviour. The main examples of abuse are charging prices or imposing terms and conditions that are unjustifiably burdensome or work in a way that impedes market access by other competitors or induce them to abandon their operations. Being dominant is not in itself prohibited, what is prohibited is the abuse of a dominant position in the market.

A *merger* (or *concentration*) happens when two (or more) previously independent firms merge or when one firm acquires control over another (or several others), enabling it to exercise a decisive influence on its (their) operations. A merger is prohibited if it creates or strengthens a dominant position, which significantly impedes, directly or indirectly, the existence or development of effective competition. Alternatively, a merger may be authorised provided that it is amended in order to remove any adverse effects on competition. These so-called remedies are often 'structural' (in particular taking the form of divestitures) but could in principle also be 'behavioural' (for example forbidding future expansions). However, 'behavioural' remedies are often difficult to enforce.[4]

All the three elements of competition policy apply to the banking sector. However, given the market structures in this sector, cartels and mergers seem to play a greater role than abuses of dominant positions. The banking sector appears indeed fragmented in most countries, with potentially high concentration ratios only at the local level. However, in recent years a very large number of mostly national mergers has taken place (Group of Ten, 2001). Cartels in the banking sector include particularly agreements in the market for payment system services (services that exhibit some natural monopoly characteristics)[5] and agreements of tie-ins.[6]

One important question is to which extent competition policy is applied to the banking sector. More specifically, it is interesting to investigate whether the specificity of this sector in relation to the stability issues raised above and related regulations and safety net arrangements, has any link to competition or competition policy. If it is true, as sometimes argued, that too much competition is harmful in banking, since it reduces banks' margins and exacerbates the problem of excessive risk taking (see more below in Section 4), then competition should be restricted in banking and competition policy should follow less stringent criteria. One way to achieve this would be to make banking an exceptional sector or even transfer the responsibility for competition polices from antitrust authorities to banking supervisors. By looking at the development and design of competition policy in different countries we observe that competition policy in banking exhibits some peculiar features, indeed. For example, in the next section we will look at the institutional structure of bank merger reviews in the G-7 countries, asking whether competition or supervisory authorities have the lead in conducting the reviews.

It is also worthwhile mentioning here that in most countries competition policy was designed within an already existing regulatory framework and its application to the banking sector was not so straightforward. Even in the United States, where general competition law was introduced well before the banking laws,[7] some competition law considerations were brought into the banking sector only in the 1960s.[8] Before that time banking activity was not considered as a 'form of commerce' and, therefore, not subject to the general competition law. This reflected the view within the US Congress that excessive competition was harmful in the banking sector, creating an important source of bank failures.

In Europe fully-fledged competition laws controlling private economic power did not emerge nearly as early as in the US. The Treaty of Rome (1957), creating the European Economic Community, contained in articles

85 and 86 provisions designed to protect competition in the common internal market, that is to avoid distortions in trade between the member countries.[9] Whereas in theory the Rome Treaty did not contain anything preventing the full application of articles 85 and 86 to the banking sector, in practice the European Commission did not apply them in this regard before the early 1980s.[10] The prevailing idea was that banking was a special sector in which the conduct of business was heavily influenced by the monetary and financial policies of member state authorities, in particular by central banks and supervisory authorities in charge of financial stability and exchange controls (see for example Ghezzi and Magnani, 1998).

3. INSTITUTIONAL STRUCTURES OF BANK MERGER REVIEW POLICIES IN G-7 COUNTRIES

The specificity of the banking sector described above (leading to special licensing, regulation, supervision and crisis provisions) implies a different, more constrained business environment than in most other sectors. This can also lead to special characteristics how competition and antitrust policies work in the banking sector. In most countries not only competition authorities play a role in bank merger reviews, but also – to varying degrees across countries – bank supervisors have a direct involvement in the review process.[11] The economic rationale for this involvement will be addressed in greater depth below. At this stage it suffices to mention three potential reasons for it.

First, since a banking business requires a special licence from supervisors, granted upon the fulfilment of certain minimum capital requirements, 'fit and proper' tests of managers and so on, and a merger may create a new company or bring in new managers, it appears logical that banking supervisors have to check that the special corporate requirements according to banking laws and regulations would be fulfilled after the merger. Second, it is common practice in many countries that failures of (large) banks are dealt with through restructuring programmes, often involving the acquisition of the weak bank by a healthy one (or a merger), be it to avoid the systemic repercussions of a full-scale bankruptcy or to avoid the costs of it to the deposit insurance fund. Since prudential supervisors tend to have the best information about the situation, they usually play an important co-ordinating or even guiding role in such restructuring measures. Although many bank mergers are not related to failures and therefore the practical relevance of this argument may accordingly be lower, in the cases where they are it may still be easier for the supervisors to engineer a takeover when they have greater responsibility for mergers and acquisitions (M&As) in general (in particular for the competition review to control concentrations).[12] Finally, it may be that the very influential 'charter value hypothesis' (see for example the discussion of Keeley, 1990, and others below), saying roughly that a too competitive banking sector will be prone to instability, has convinced some countries to counterbalance the competition-oriented antitrust review with a stability-oriented supervisory review of bank mergers.

In the remainder of this section we are summarising the relative roles of competition and supervisory authorities in merger reviews in the G-7 countries.[13] We proceed by starting with the countries that have the strongest involvement of financial supervisors and the least involvement of competition authorities and finishing with the reverse cases. However, we recognise that this order can only be regarded as indicative, since our account is mainly based on the description of written rules on institutional responsibilities. The actual review practice may still exhibit some differences to the impression given by the formal legal and administrative rules regarding the actual influence of different authorities. Finally, this order may not always correspond to the relative weight given to competition considerations, since in some cases a supervisory authority may be bound by competition law or by competition considerations in the banking law.

Before starting with our country account of merger review responsibilities, it is necessary to point out that in European Union (EU) countries a two-layer regime is in place for the competition review of concentrations, in that all mergers with a 'community dimension' are examined by the Merger Task Force of the European Commission (in the DG Competition), whereas transactions without 'community dimension' are left to the competent national authorities alone. The dividing line between cases that are relevant for the EU as a whole and cases that are only of national relevance is drawn on the basis of the size and geographical dispersion of turnovers.[14] Therefore, the arrangements described below for the four G-7 countries belonging to the EU (France, Germany, Italy and United Kingdom) are only effective for bank mergers that do not reach the 'community dimension'. The other, that is larger cases are covered in the paragraph on the EU.[15]

France has exempted bank merger reviews (below the 'community dimension') from the general competition law and formal reviews by competition authorities. The main responsibility is rather with the 'Comité des établissements de crédit et des entreprises d'investissement', which is the one committee – out of a set of committees and commissions in charge of prudential supervision in the financial sector formally headed by the Governor of the Banque de France (or his alternate) – that deals with bank licensing. The criteria applied by this committee are determined in the banking law, in which supervisory and other public policy concerns prevail over competition considerations (if any). For example, the examinations consider particularly whether the new institution would act in a way compatible with the smooth functioning of the banking system and with a sufficient security for customers.

In *Italy* the general competition law applies to merger reviews in the banking sector, but the responsibility for the reviews is with the Banca d'Italia, which is also the prudential supervisor of this country. Actually, the supervision department conducts the merger review both from the antitrust and from the supervisory perspective (though in different sub-units). The Antitrust Authority is only required to give a prior non-binding opinion on all cases. Co-operation between both authorities is guided by a bilateral memorandum of understanding signed in 1996.

The *United States* has given authority to approve or prevent bank mergers to the relevant supervisory authorities (Federal Reserve Board, Office of the Comptroller of the Currency, Federal Deposit Insurance Corporation and Office of Thrift Supervision). However, the Antitrust Division of the Department of Justice independently reviews the mergers as well and reports its analysis to the supervisor(s) in charge. Even if the merger has been approved by the supervisors, the Antitrust Division can within one month appeal to the court when its analysis contrasts with the decision of the competent supervisor(s).[16] Also US banking law requires the supervisory agencies to take competition effects into account and not to allow anticompetitive mergers, unless 'the uncompetitive effects are clearly outweighed in the public interest' by the probable effect of the transaction in meeting the convenience and needs of the community to be served' (availability of banking services).

The *Canadian* approach is again different in that the banking laws assign the ultimate authority to block or approve a merger of financial institutions to the Minister of Finance. The minister takes this decision assessing the public interest upon receipt of two reports from the Competition Bureau, focusing on the competitive effects of the transaction, and the Office of the Superintendent of Financial Institutions, focusing on supervisory concerns. This implies – as confirmed in the Competition Act – that even if the Competition Bureau feels that a merger transaction should be modified or challenged before the Competition Tribunal, the tribunal can not make an order to this effect, if the Minister of Finance has issued a document to the Bureau of Competition stating that the transaction is '. . . in the best interest of the financial system in Canada'. However, within these constraints bank mergers in Canada are subject to similar competition reviews as the case for other industries.

Japan makes bank mergers subject to the same competition law as for other industries.[17] So bank mergers have to be approved by the Japan Fair Trade Commission, which is the sole authority implementing the Antimonopoly Act. The fragility of financial institutions (such as debt over-hang or even a high probability of bankruptcy) have practically no conse-quences under the competition law, which focuses entirely on preventing anti-competitive effects on the different banking markets. However, in con-trast to other industries, banks envisaging a merger have also to file an application for approval by the Financial Services Agency. This supervisory review is undertaken under the Banking Act, considering the availability of funds in a region and the convenience for customers, an adequate conduct of business (including for example the appropriateness of shareholders and managers) and the avoidance of disrupting the market (for example regard-ing fair competition among financial institutions). The competition and the supervisory review are conducted relatively independently with informal contacts between the two authorities. Formally the merging parties must fulfil the requirements by both.[18]

In *Germany* merger reviews are guided by special rules for banks within the competition law and by some paragraphs in the banking law. In apply-ing the competition rules the Federal Cartel Office can let a merger pass without explicit approval of the Federal Supervisory Office. However, if it wants to block one, it has to request the opinion of the supervisor, which is formally non-binding though. The Supervisory Office examines the cases from the perspective of the banking law and can block a merger if the new shareholders are not regarded appropriate or the management not qualified. As for other sectors, bank merger decisions can be subject to higher political review in that the Federal Minister of Economics has the option to overturn a blocking decision and approve a merger for 'reasons of the macroeconomy and common welfare' ('Ministererlaubnis'). In this case the minister has to ask the opinion of the independent Monopoly Commission. Generally, if Cartel Office and Supervisory Office come to different conclusions from their respective perspectives and cannot resolve their differences, then in practice the Economics (competition) and Finance (supervision) Ministers would have to find a solution.[19]

In the *United Kingdom* bank merger reviews are conducted under similar rules and procedures as for other industries. Cases raising significant com-petition concerns are subject to a report by the Office of Fair Trading to the Secretary of State for Trade and Industry, who can refer them to the Competition Commission for a formal investigation. However, even if the Competition Commission finds that the merger is 'against the public inter-est', the Secretary of State has de facto the power to overturn this view and permit an anti-competitive merger.[20] The Financial Services Authority and the Bank of England, considering prudential and general stability con-cerns, are consulted during this process.

Bank mergers in the *European Union* that reach the 'community dimension' are examined by the Merger Task Force of the European Commission, applying the 'Council Regulation on the Control of Concentrations between Undertakings' (EC Merger Regulation). This regulation, which applies to all sectors, empowers the Commission to investigate the companies involved and declare a merger on the basis of competition considerations 'incompatible with the common market'. In executing these powers the Commission is also entitled to request all necessary information from the competent national authorities. If the competent national authority is a supervisory agency – such as in France or Italy – then the Commission's main national counterpart is that supervisory authority. Even if de jure this seems not to qualify the Commission's focus on competition aspects in the review of bank mergers, the EC Merger Regulation states that 'Member States may take appropriate measures to protect legitimate interests other than those taken into consideration by this Regulation and compatible with the general principles and other provisions of Community law'.[21] This introduces a first possibility for the member states to interfere with the decisions of the Commission and pursue objectives other than those linked to competition policy.[22]

Perhaps more important for the case of bank mergers is another route through which EU member states can resist to the Commission's review policy. The so-called Second Banking Directive (European Council, 1989a, article 5) stipulates that national supervisory authorities have to be informed about 'qualifying' changes in equity holders and 'shall refuse authorization if, taking into account the need to ensure the sound and prudent management of a credit institution, they are not satisfied as to the suitability of the . . . shareholders'.[23] Another aspect of the national supervisory review is that the new corporate structure should not hinder efficient supervision. The formulation in the Directive (and potentially also the supervisory principle of efficient supervision) allows for different interpretations on the national level. It gives room for discretion to supervisors, for example regarding their attitude towards 'hostile' takeover bids or towards the tendency of new managements to distribute cash to shareholders after the merger (market pressures to do this are often observed).[24]

In sum, although the EU regime of bank merger review (for cases with 'community dimension') is strongly competition-oriented and although absent an EU-wide supervisory authority the Commission's institutional competence for large bank merger reviews may appear unshared, in practice EU countries have reserved a relatively large degree of discretion through the involvement of their national supervisors, looking at the mergers from a prudential perspective. This implies a risk, for example, that national supervisory authorities adopt a reluctant attitude towards cross-border bank mergers to preserve their control of prudential policies and promote 'national champions'. If going beyond certain limits, this could also reinforce the 'too-big-to-fail' problem on the national level with all the adverse consequences for market incentives.[25]

The differences of the relative roles of competition and supervisory authorities in various G-7 countries (and the EU) give rise to a number of possible interpretations. First, since part of the academic literature (discussed in the next section) has highlighted possible trade-offs between bank competition and bank stability the differences may reflect differential preferences across countries as to the weight given to financial sector competitiveness and financial stability in merger review decisions. Second, the differences may just reflect historically grown structures that were inherited from the past without a direct link to the efficiency–stability paradigm discussed in banking. However, this latter interpretation does not need to be disconnected from the former, since the historically grown structures may have been influenced by past experiences with financial crises or monopolistic banking systems.

Other relevant features that seem to be reflected in some way in the general merger review practice, that is applying to all sectors, in most G-7 countries are 'failing firm defence' or 'merger rescue' provisions. For example, the 'Horizontal Merger Guidelines' of the US Department of Justice stipulate that 'a merger is not likely to create or enhance market power or to facilitate its exercise, if imminent failure . . . of one of the merging firms would cause the asset of that firm to exit the relevant market'. These Guidelines are also used by the US Federal Reserve in its bank merger reviews and the 'convenience and needs' phrase, referred to above, in both the Bank Holding Company Act and the Clayton Act provides the legal basis for the failing firm defence in US banking.

Although not defined in a statutory way as in the US, the EU Commission has also developed in its case-law a 'rescue merger' concept, which is akin to the US 'failing firm defence' in that without a causal link between the merger and the reduction in competition/increase in concentration merger disapproval can be avoided.[26] Such provisions appear particularly relevant in the case of banking, where – as written above – supervisors often resort to co-ordinating a takeover or a merger of a failing bank instead of going through a potentially costly public liquidation. In particular, if the conditions for such a 'failing firm defence' are met, then such actions should be unproblematic even from the perspective of competition policy.[27]

However, in some countries there is also a broader notion of 'failing firm defence' that includes the consideration of other than pure competition considerations, namely more general social or economic objectives. For example, according to such a broader notion the merger review could weight potential anti-competitive effects from a merger against benefits, such as the preservation of employment, the preservation of technical achievements within a specific region or the availability of certain services in a specific region. The example of Canada, described above, illustrates that such a broader interpretation of the failing firm doctrine could potentially also include acceptance of anti-competitive merger effects to prevent harm to the financial system. We speculate that the fear of instability caused by bank failures may lead to the application of such a broader concept of 'failing firm defence'. Whereas the narrower concept of 'failing firm defence' could be read as avoiding any conflict between bank competition and bank stability, with this broader concept we enter the realm of having to weight competition and stability implications in bank merger reviews.

4.   SURVEY OF THE ACADEMIC LITERATURE ON COMPETITION AND STABILITY IN BANKING

We now turn to the issue of what scientific research has to say about the relationship between competition and stability. Academic and broader research interest in the issue has been triggered by the seminal article of Michael Keeley in the *American Economic Review* (1990), finding that the surge of bank failures in the US during the 1980s had (at least partly) been caused by various deregulation measures and market factors that reduced monopoly rents (denoted as 'charter value') and thereby increased the value of bank managers' put option on deposit insurance funds.[28] Similarly, Edwards and Mishkin (1995) argue that the excessive risk-taking observed in the 1980s in the US was banks' response to the erosion of profits due to competition from financial markets. This competition decreased their cost advantages in the acquisition of funds and undermined their position in the loan market.

Our aim is to review the existing literature on the relation between competition and stability, not to contribute to it here or to fill any gaps. The ultimate objective is to see whether an economic rationale for stability concerns and the special involvement of supervisors in the review of bank mergers can be identified. In the next sub-section we go through the theoretical literature and in the subsequent one through the empirical literature.

4.1   Theories on the Relation between Bank Competition and Bank Stability

We organise the survey of the theoretical literature according to the effects that competition, either in the deposit or in the loan market, has on the two sources of bank instability that we have outlined in Section 2. We first review the contributions analysing the effects of competition on banks' vulnerability to individual runs and systemic risk on the liability side. Then, we survey the contributions looking at the effects of competition on bank risk-taking behaviour on the asset side. In reviewing this literature, we also look at normative aspects concerning the roles played by regulation, supervision, closure policies and deposit insurance for the relation between competition and stability. Note that only few of the papers we will discuss endogenise aspects of industrial organisation in their analysis. The majority of them just compares the equilibriums achievable in different market settings without taking into account any strategic interaction among intermediaries.

Market structure and liability risk
The relationship between competition, liability risk and optimal regulation has been largely ignored by the banking literature. Most of the contributions on bank runs and systemic risk pay very little attention to the strategic interaction between banks, ignore the effects of different market structures on bank stability and on the efficiency and effectiveness of prudential policy measures. Most of the traditional models assume in fact that banks operate in a perfectly competitive environment or in a monopoly setting.[29] In both circumstances, runs or systemic crises emerge in equilibrium either as a consequence of co-ordination failure among depositors or as a rational response by depositors to the arrival of negative information about banks' future solvency. These models do not provide insights into the issue in which the market structure of the banking system is more likely to be unstable. Neither do they explore the effectiveness of safety net arrangements and of other regulatory measures in different market settings.

A few models address the relationship between competition and liability risk. Smith (1984) analyses this issue in a framework *à la* Diamond and Dybvig (1983) where banks compete to attract depositors that have different probability distributions over the dates of withdrawal. In the case when an adverse selection problem is present, that is when depositors only know their own probability of withdrawals, there may not exist any Nash equilibrium. The equilibrium contract, either pooling or separating, is indeed destroyed by the possibility of banks offering positive profit contracts to a specific segment of depositors. When this is the case, the banking system is not viable or in other words it is unstable. Thus, competition for deposits makes banks fragile in an environment characterised by adverse selection problems. The author argues that this problem can be resolved by appropriate regulatory measures, such as ceilings on deposit rates.[30]

Competition *per se* does not need to create instability. As shown by Matutes and Vives (1996), bank vulnerability to bank runs can emerge also independently of competition and can thus occur in any market structure. This result is obtained in a model *à la* Diamond (1984) enriched by duopolistic product differentiation, network externalities and bank failures. Matutes and Vives show that the distress probability of a bank is endogenously determined by depositors' expectations, which are self-fulfilling, given the presence of scale economies. A bank perceived to be safer commands a higher margin and a larger market share, which in turn makes it safer because of better diversification. The self-fulfilling character of depositors' expectations implies multiple equilibria. Possible equilibria include corner solutions, where only one bank is active, and even equilibria where none of the banks is active. This latter event is interpreted as a 'systemic confidence crisis'. It is due to a co-ordination problem among depositors, which arises for reasons similar to those encountered in the network literature, irrespective of the degree of competition in the deposit market. In the model the co-ordination failure can be solved by introducing deposit insurance. However, by ensuring that all banks remain in business, deposit insurance may preclude the realisation of desirable diversification and induce fiercer competition for deposits, which, in turn, increases the failure probability of banks. The net welfare effects of deposit insurance are ambiguous and cannot be assessed independently of the market structure.

Carletti et al. (2002) address more directly the effects of bank mergers on the competition and liquidity risk in the banking sector. They set up a model where banks compete for loans and engage in interbank lending in order to deal with liquidity shocks on the liability side *à la* Diamond and Dybvig. The competition effects of mergers, as measured by the level of post-merger loan rates, depend on the relative importance of increased concentration and potential cost reductions. Mergers lead to higher loan rates when the market power effect dominates and to lower loan rates otherwise. The stability effects of mergers, as measured by the probability that the interbank market experiences liquidity shortages and by the average size of shortages, depend on the structure of liquidity shocks, the relative cost of retail deposit financing as compared to inter-bank refinancing (determining reserve holdings) and the post-merger distribution of market shares (depending on the competition effects produced by mergers). The analysis displays various scenarios in which a merger raises either competition or stability concerns or both.

Market structure and excessive risk taking

We now review the theoretical literature on the effects of competition, either in the loan market or in the deposit market, on banks' risk-taking behaviour. This literature (the so-called 'charter value' literature very much inspired by Keeley's article) focuses in particular on the incentive effects of high charter values for bank risk taking. In a framework of relationship banking Besanko and Thakor (1993) show that increased competition induces banks to choose riskier portfolio strategies. In the course of the relationship with their borrowers, banks acquire private information that generates informational rents. As long as banks appropriate at least part of these rents, they have an incentive to limit their risk exposure so as to enjoy the value of the relationship. However, as soon as the banking industry becomes more competitive, relationship banking decreases in value and banks take more risk, particularly when deposits are backed by a risk insensitive insurance scheme. Boot and Greenbaum (1993) obtain similar results in a two-period model in which banks can acquire funding-related reputational benefits and improve their rents through costly monitoring.[31]

Other papers focus on how competition for deposits affects banks' risk taking and on how proper regulation can correct the perverse link between competition and excessive risk taking. Cordella and Yeyati (1998) address the relationships between competition for deposits, banks' risk-taking behaviour and different deposit insurance arrangements in a model of spatial competition where banks choose privately their portfolio risk. They show that with fixed-rate deposit insurance, enhanced competition increases deposit rates and risk through lower product differentiation and lower margins. In contrast, when deposit insurance premiums are risk-adjusted, deposit rates and asset risk are lower than under a flat-rate pricing scheme. Thus, when risk-based deposit insurance premiums can be implemented, banks can credibly commit to reduce asset risk, thus lowering the cost of funds and improving their overall performance despite competition on deposits.

Matutes and Vives (2000) examine the link between imperfect competition in the deposit market, banks' risk taking and deposit insurance in a model where banks are subject to limited liability and their failure implies social costs. A first result of the model is that in the absence of deposit insurance deposit rates are excessive (and thus bank asset risk high) when the failure costs are high and competition intense. A second result is that when deposits are insured through a flat rate scheme, competition leads to excessive deposit rates even without failure costs and banks take the maximum asset risk. Both deposit regulation (deposit limits or rate ceilings) and investment restrictions are needed to remove the perverse effect of competition. Finally, when deposit insurance premiums are risk adjusted, deposit rates and bank asset risk are lower than in an economy without deposit insurance. However, both may still be excessive so that it may still be optimal to introduce deposit regulations.

The relation between competition for deposits, excessive risk taking and regulation is also analysed by Hellman et al. (2000) in a dynamic framework where banks choose privately their asset risk and compete for deposits. In line with the charter value literature, competition erodes profits and therefore induces banks to gamble in their investments. A possible way to restore prudent bank behaviour is to introduce capital requirements. However, in a dynamic setting, they turn out to be a Pareto inefficient policy: As long as deposit rates can be freely determined, in a dynamic setting banks have incentives to increase them so as to expand their deposit base and earn a higher margin from gambling (market-stealing effect). Adding deposit rate controls as a regulatory instrument allows Pareto optimal outcomes in this model. By increasing charter values, deposit rate controls prevent the market-stealing effect, thus increasing banks' incentives to behave prudently.

An alternative regulatory instrument to create charter value and control banks' risk taking in competitive markets is analysed by Perotti and Suarez (2001). They develop a dynamic duopolistic model where banks compete in the deposit market and can invest in either prudent or speculative lending. Whenever a bank fails, the regulator has to decide whether to close the failing institution or to merge it with another bank, either an incumbent (rescue or merger policy) or a new entrant (entry policy). The two policies imply a trade-off between stability and competition. By reducing competition and increasing charter value, a rescue involves monopoly inefficiency but also prudent bank behaviour; in contrast, entry implies more efficiency but riskier bank behaviour. The optimal policy instrument is a combination of active rescues followed by entry. This creates *ex ante* incentives for banks to remain solvent to acquire failing institutions while at the same time limiting the ex post market power that surviving banks get through the rescue. Thus, the use of active merger policy and temporary entry restrictions can endorse stability.

Not all papers, however, find a clear negative link between competition and risk taking. In a model in which banks compete for loans and can use costly monitoring or credit rationing to deal with a moral hazard problem on the part of the entrepreneur, Caminal and Matutes (2002) show that a monopoly bank may face a higher risk of failure than a competitive bank. The idea is that a monopoly bank uses more monitoring and less credit rationing to deal with the borrower's moral hazard problem. This may induce a monopoly bank to grant larger loans than competitive banks and lead to a higher probability of failure, since loans are subject to multiplicative uncertainty. As a consequence, the relationship between market power and failure probability is ambiguous.

In a similar spirit, Nagarajan and Sealey (1995) show that the effects of competition on excessive risk taking depend on how charter values are determined. Their focus is on how regulatory policies, and in particular forbearance policy, affect charter values. When higher margins are the result of a forbearance policy that extends the expiration of equity holders' call option, they may not result in higher quality of bank assets. Conversely, high charter values provoke excessive risk taking when they are generated by a non-optimal forbearance policy.[32]

Summing up the discussion of available theories, whereas most papers find some trade-off between bank competition and stability, the claim that they are generally negatively related is not necessarily robust. First of all, there are scenarios in which increased loan competition reduces asset risk-taking or increases the ability of the interbank market to insure against liquidity shocks. Second, while ill-designed policies may generate or reinforce a trade-off between competition and stability in banking (for example risk-insensitive deposit insurance, static capital requirements or non-optimal forbearance), theory suggests that there are policy options that would ensure competitive and stable banking systems (for example risk-based deposit insurance, mixed approaches to failure resolution through mergers and so on).

4.2 Empirical Examinations of the Relationship Between Bank Competition and Bank Stability

Similar to the theoretical literature on the relationship between market structure/competitiveness and risk in banking, the empirical literature on this topic is also relatively small. We nevertheless review the few published empirical research papers we could find that come up with some figures on the issue at stake. Overall one can distinguish four types of studies: the first type regresses measures of bank risk on measures of bank market power, the second group of papers assesses the potential diversification or risk reduction effects of combining different businesses in a merger, the third type measures changes in bank stock return correlations as an indicator of the implications of consolidation for systemic risk and the fourth type discusses the relative efficiency and risk in bank sectors of different countries that are more or less competitive.

Did the erosion of banks' market power cause the increase in US bank failure rates during the 1980s?
In the seminal paper by Keeley (1990) two pooled estimations are undertaken. First, capital-to-asset ratios for 85 large US bank holding companies between 1971 and 1986 are regressed on their market-to-book asset ratio (Tobin's q, as a measure of market power or 'charter value') and a set of controls. The parameter of q in this regression is positive and highly significant, indicating that more competitive banking markets are associated with reduced capital cushions in banks. Second, interest rates on large certificates of deposits (CDs) for 77 large bank holding companies between 1984 and 1986 are regressed on q and a number of control variables. The parameter

for q is negative and very significant, indicating that reduced market power (lower q) is associated with higher risk premiums reflected in CD rates. Both estimations suggest that the erosion of 'charter values' in the US has contributed to the greater banking fragility during the 1980s.

Do mergers diversify risk and are larger banks less risky?
If bank mergers diversify risk, then any related increase in market power through concentration would be associated with lower risk and higher bank stability. Paroush (1995) provides a simple description of how asset-side risk concentration can be diversified through a bank merger. He then argues that the merger of Manufacturers Hanover Trust Co. and Chemical Bank in the US provides an example in which the loan concentration across four sectors (consumer, business, real estate and international loans) of the combined bank is lower than the concentration of loans in each predecessor bank.

Benston, Hunter and Wall (1995) test with data for 302 US bank mergers between 1981 and 1986 whether the behaviour of takeover bid prices reflects risk diversification as a motive for the acquisition or rather the increase of the deposit insurance put option value. They find some evidence that the pre-merger variance of target bank earnings and the pre-merger covariance between target and acquiring bank earnings are negatively related to bid prices, which is consistent with the former hypothesis but not with the latter (which would predict the opposite signs). However, they also caution that there is an older literature that argues that post-merger institutions change portfolios to take on new risks and transform the diversification benefits into increased cash flows at ultimately unchanged failure risk.

Craig and Santos (1997) also refer to this earlier literature and then compare the pre- and post-merger risk characteristics of 256 acquisitions by US bank holding companies between 1984 and 1993. They find that the sample banks show increased post-merger profitability and reduced post-merger risk, as measured by the standard deviations of the returns on equity and on assets, as well as the z-score measure of default risk (all up to 4 years after the transaction).[33] Only the coefficient of variation and the covariance of returns between acquirer and acquired show a more mixed picture, which the authors dismiss for statistical reasons.

Boyd and Runkle (1993) undertake simple univariate regressions to measure the sign of the relationship between bank size and bank risk. For 122 US bank holding companies and annual data between 1971 and 1990, they find that larger asset sizes in this group of already relatively large banks lead to insignificantly lower z-scores and to significantly lower standard deviations of the respective banks' stock price returns. The authors interpret these results as evidence that whereas larger banks benefit from diversification advantages (indicated by less volatile stock returns), these advantages do not translate into a (significantly) lower failure probability. An explanation for this is found in the significantly higher leverage of larger banks.

Boyd and Graham (1991, 1996) go a step further by asking the question whether large (supposedly more diversified) banks fail less often than small banks (below 1 billion dollars of assets) in the United States. To avoid a 'too-big-to-fail bias' they include in the failure category also banks that have received any form of government support to survive. It turns out that over the entire sample period of 1971 to 1994 the cumulate *number* of failures over all banks is 17 per cent for large banks and 12 per cent for small banks. When dividing the sample in three sub-periods they find that the annual failure rate for large banks is higher than the one for small banks for the earlier periods (1971 to 1978 and 1979 to 1986) whereas this picture is reversed for the more recent period, which also exhibits greater failure rates more generally (1987 to 1994). The authors emphasise that the results on the earlier periods may appear reversed when saved banks are not included in the failure category.[34]

On the basis of these diversification studies it seems somewhat difficult to draw firm conclusions on the competition-stability nexus in banking. However, there are some indications that in more recent times concentrations resulting from mergers in the US may have been associated with lower risk of individual banks after merger, which is in line with the predictions of the 'charter-value' literature. One reason for this result could be that the recent relaxation of branching restriction across US states has increased the diversification potential of mergers. However, other results indicate that larger banks do not necessarily fail less often than smaller banks.

Does bank consolidation increase interbank linkages?
In a background study to the Ferguson Report on financial sector consolidation (Group of Ten, 2001) de Nicolo and Kwast (2001) track the correlation of stock returns between 22 large and complex US banking organisations (LCBOs) from 1988 to 1999. They interpret these correlations as measures of direct and indirect interdependencies arising from the inter-firm on- and off-balance sheet exposures (including payment and settlement system linkages) and from correlated exposures to financial markets and non-financial sectors, respectively. Therefore these measures are taken as indicators of systemic risk. The authors show that these inter-LCBO stock return correlations increased over the sample period, particularly for more traditional institutions, as did the total market share of LCBOs in banking. In fact, they find these correlations themselves to be highly correlated with market shares, which is consistent with the idea that systemic risk in the US banking system has increased over time, partly as a

consequence of consolidation. While this study does not try to assess whether the consolidation observed was also associated with any (adverse?) effects on competition, its claim on increased interbank linkages through consolidation of LCBOs gives a different picture from the individual bank risks discussed in the context of the 'charter value' literature or the diversification literature.

Do countries with more competitive banking sectors face a greater risk of bank instability?

A few descriptive historical studies examine the efficiency and stability properties of banking systems in different countries during different periods, where competitiveness is often one factor in efficiency. For example, Bordo, Redish and Rockoff (1995) compare the Canadian and the US banking systems' performances between 1920 and 1980. They observe a much greater stability (in terms of failure rates) of Canadian banks as compared to US banks and speculate that this might have been partly related to the oligopolistic market structure of Canadian banking. However, an analysis of nominal and real deposit and loan rate levels in Canada and the US provides practically no evidence of higher monopoly rents in the former compared to the latter. However, due to their balance sheet structures Canadian banks were clearly more profitable than their US counterparts, suggesting that Canada had both a more stable and a more efficient (and not a less competitive) banking sector than the US during this period.

Capie (1995) studies the stability and efficiency of the UK banking system between 1890 and 1940. He finds this period to be very stable with no banking panic or financial crisis. Inter alia, this also reflects the milder effect of the Great Depression on Britain. Regarding market structure there occurred an on-going trend of banking consolidation leading from a system with many banks to an oligopoly, with the London clearing banks basically operating a price cartel and other restrictive practices. However, despite high prices for banking services to consumers Capie finds little evidence of abnormal profits, which leads him to the conclusion that they were also quite inefficient. Overall, the experiences with this episode seem to be consistent with the hypothesis that less competitive banking systems can be quite stable.[35]

Regarding more recent times, Hoggarth, Milne and Wood (1998) compare the relative performances of the UK and the German banking systems during the last decades. It turns out that banking profits in the UK were consistently higher than in Germany but also much more variable (similar to asset prices). Higher UK profitability can be explained by higher non-interest income and lower staff costs and greater German stability by lower and more stable inflation as well as less competition, particularly from foreign entrants. The experiences of these two countries could therefore be regarded as reflecting two cases, one less competitive but more stable system (Germany) and the other more competitive but less stable (UK). Staikouras and Wood (2000) undertake a similar exercise for Greece and Spain during the last decade, finding that Spanish banks as a whole are both more profitable and more stable than Greek banks, except that the sub-group of Spanish commercial banks is less stable. This leads them to think that the Spanish banking sector is more competitive than the Greek one, which still has a larger public involvement. This latter comparison is consistent with the hypothesis of no trade-off between competition and stability, similar to the comparison between Canada and the US above, whereas the Germany–UK comparison is consistent with the presence of a trade-off.

The main conclusion from this survey of the empirical literature is that there does not appear to be a single ever-valid relationship between competition and stability in the banking system. This conclusion is also well reflected in the main results of the Ferguson report (Group of Ten, 2001, ch. 0.2 and III) on the effects of consolidation in the financial sector. The 'key findings and policy implications' section of this report states that the 'potential effects of financial consolidation on the risk of individual institutions are mixed, the net result is impossible to generalise, and thus a case by case assessment is required . . . In part because the net impact of consolidation on individual firm risk is unclear, the net impact of consolidation on systemic risk is also uncertain' (p. 3). In a recent study of the Netherlands Bureau of Economic Policy Analysis about competition and stability in banking more generally (Canoy et al., 2001) the intricate relationship between these two market dimensions becomes also very clear. While the study focuses on 'trade-offs' between competition and stability, one main policy conclusion still is that 'many forms of competition do not endanger financial stability' (p. 161). In sum, it depends on the specific case and circumstances whether a change in competition (for example a merger or a concentration) is associated with an increase or decrease of risk in the banking system. In our view this insight about the complexity of the competition-stability nexus rather increases the importance to be placed on clear and well designed rules for the relative roles of antitrust authorities/competition policies and supervisory authorities/prudential practices regarding bank mergers.

5. CONCLUSIONS

In this chapter we have discussed the relationship between competition and stability in banking. We briefly described the application of classic antitrust tools to the banking sector and analysed in greater depth how the responsibility for bank merger reviews is shared between competition and supervisory authorities in G-7 countries and the EU. We then surveyed the theoretical and empirical literature on the link between bank competition and bank stability.

We found an amazing variety of relative responsibilities and national approaches regarding the institutional structure of bank merger reviews, with countries like France and Italy giving the lead on merger reviews to supervisory authorities and the European Union (for mergers with 'community dimension') and the United Kingdom to competition authorities. However, whereas the EU Commission's approach is very competition oriented, the Second Banking Directive preserves a relatively large degree of discretion to national supervisory authorities in the EU to block bank mergers, for example if they are not satisfied with the new shareholders. Regarding the legal basis for bank merger review procedures there is also variety, some countries dealing with the issue in the competition laws and others in the banking laws. Like mergers, cartel cases also play a greater role in the banking sector, in particular regarding payment systems that are characterised by natural monopoly features. However, despite the large number of bank mergers occurring in many countries during the last years, abuses of dominant positions have so far remained of rather low importance in antitrust practice.

The theoretical literature does not seem to be conclusive on the relationship between competition and stability. Theories of bank runs and systemic risk largely disregard the implications of different bank market structures for the safety of the sector. Theories based on the idea of 'charter value' argue that market power mitigates bank risk taking, since foregone future profits in the case of bankruptcy are higher. However, a more recent strand of literature suggests that stronger competition does not necessarily worsen stability. Concerning bank liability side risk, it argues that coordination problems among depositors causing bank fragility can emerge independently of competition. Also, it shows that some bank mergers can make liquidity shortages in the interbank market more likely. As regards asset side risk, it argues that there can be cases in which a concentrated banking sector would be riskier than a competitive sector. Finally, it is also pointed out that some policies, such as risk-adjusted deposit insurance premiums, could mitigate any trade-off between competition and bank risk taking.

Regarding the empirical literature, some papers support the influential 'charter-value' hypothesis claiming a negative relationship between competition and bank stability, others do not. Most studies on the diversification effects of mergers show that concentration can go hand in hand with lower individual bank risk, at least for more recent data. However, some other studies find that larger banks do not benefit from lower failure probabilities. Regarding systemic risk related to interbank linkages, at least one study argues that consolidation and increased risks have gone together in the last decade. Finally, historical analyses comparing the experiences of different countries come to different results, depending on the period and country considered. For example, it is argued that for the middle of the twentieth century Canada had both a more efficient and a more stable banking system than the US, whereas a comparison of Germany and Britain for more recent decades indicates that Germany has a less competitive but more stable and Britain a more competitive but less stable banking system.

On the basis of the theoretical and empirical survey, the idea that competition is something dangerous in the banking sector, since it generally causes instability can be dismissed. In the light of the importance of the market mechanism, allocational efficiency and growth, competition aspects need to be carefully considered, also in banking. One implication is that there should be well-defined arrangements about the relative roles of competition and supervisory authorities. And countries that have given only weak roles to competition authorities, for example in bank merger reviews may be well advised to ensure that competition concerns are not neglected. However, beyond this it is very hard to draw any strong conclusions, because both the theoretical and the empirical literature suggests that the stability effects of changes in market structures and competition are extremely case-dependent. This may also be one reason behind the diversity of institutional approaches followed in different countries. It appears that there is much room for research to bring more light into this rather opaque issue.

NOTES

*   We are deeply indebted to Charles Goodhart, who had an important impact on the intellectual and professional development of both of us. We are particularly grateful to Andrea Enria for his comments on an earlier draft of this paper and also to Clive Briault for discussions on competition considerations in a supervisory context. Further comments by our discussant Mike Artis and the other participants of the Bank of England conference in honour of Charles Goodhart, as well as by Oliver Burkart, Thomas Dietz, Christian Fehlker, Baron Frankal, Stephane Kerjean, Mark Carey, Myron Kwast, Patricia Jackson, Yoshi Nakata, Fabio Recine, Alessio De Vincenzo and Tsatsuya Yonetani were also very much appreciated. However, none of the persons mentioned above should be held responsible for any potential errors or imprecisions remaining in the paper. Any views expressed represent only the authors' own opinions and should not be associated with those of the European Central Bank or the Eurosystem.

1.   A different view on the problem is that banks are special because they represent the availability of funds, so that governments want to have a tighter control over them. See Hellwig (1991).

2. For theoretical foundations of these issues see Diamond and Dybvig (1983), Diamond (1984) and Diamond and Rajan (2001).

3. See Carletti (1998) for a survey of bank stability and De Bandt and Hartmann (2002) for a more detailed survey on systemic risk in banking and payment systems. While the sources of fragility on the liability side seem to be more specific to banking from a theoretical perspective, most of the widespread banking crises in history seem to have been associated with aggregate shocks and not with long chains of pure contagion resulting from an initially idiosyncratic problem.

4. See OECD (2000) for many examples of bank merger reviews.

5. Agreements in payment systems include uniform commissions (either interbank or to customers) and rules of admission and exclusion to networks for credit cards, euro-cheques and automated teller machines (ATMs).

6. Agreements of tie-ins generally refer to a firm selling (buying) a product or service to (from) another firm under the condition that the acquiring (selling) firm also has to buy (sell) another product or service from (to) the selling (buying) firm or, at least, that it commits not to buy (sell) it from (to) another seller (buyer). For example, a bank could try to oblige a customer to buy another financial service before getting a loan. However, there seems to be some tendency to allow tying between traditional commercial banking services, such as loans, deposits and trust services.

   Two further forms of agreements are reciprocal agreements and exclusive agreements. The former refer to linking the sale (purchase) of a product to the purchase (sale) of another product by the respective counterparty. For example firms that acquire intermediate goods from a company could favour this company when selling their final products. Exclusive agreements include all contracts that preclude a customer of an undertaking to buy products or services from competitors.

7. The two main general competition laws, the Sherman Act (agreements and monopolistic practices) and the Clayton Act (price discrimination, tying and exclusive dealings, mergers and acquisitions, interlocking directorates), were enacted in 1890 and 1914, respectively.

8. Competition considerations were integrated in the Bank Holding Act of 1956 and the Bank Merger Act of 1960, even if the application of competition laws to bank mergers was clearly stated only with the Philadelphia National Bank case in 1963 and subsequently in 1966 with the amendment of the Bank Merger Act. However, important checks and balances include for example the attribution of the competence for the merger reviews to the supervisory bodies (see Section 3) and the general rule that an anticompetitive merger can be authorised if its anticompetitive effects are clearly outweighed by special benefits for the convenience and the needs of citizens and community in its whole. This particular exemption seems however to apply only to mergers with failing institutions.

9. Article 85 refers to agreements, mergers and acquisitions. Article 86 addresses abuses of dominant positions. Germany was probably the first large European country adopting a full-scale competition law domestically, the 'Gesetz gegen Wettbewerbsbeschränkungen (GWB)' coming into force in January 1958, which grew out of the American antitrust law experience, the war allies' de-cartelisation practices in the occupied Germany and the German ordo-liberal school. In contrast to the Community law defined by the Rome Treaty, the GWB contained an explicit mentioning of banking and insurance as exceptional sectors in which special rules would apply.

10. The European Court of Justice confirmed the full application of these two articles to the banking sector only in the Zuechner sentence of 1981.

11. Whereas in Sections 2 and 4 of this chapter we discuss competition and competition policies and their relation to financial stability more generally, for reasons of space we have to constrain the discussion of institutional structures and responsibilities in this section to concentrations, more precisely to merger review procedures, which not only in the European context currently attract particular interest. Detailed cross-country descriptions of responsibilities for cartels and abuses of dominant positions in banking could be usefully addressed in another paper.

12. We will come back to this point at the end of this section, when discussing the 'failing firm defence'.
13. The information provided in this section is mainly based on the extensive country studies described in the two OECD reports (1998 and 2000). Brief summaries on merger review procedures in G-10 countries are also given in Group of Ten (2001, annex V.1). Where necessary, we clarified or complemented the information in those reports through conversations with officials.
14. In the case of banking, since a 1997 amendment of the EC Merger Regulation, income figures are used as a measure of turnovers. 'Community dimension' is reached when (a) the aggregate world-wide income of the merging banks is more than 5,000 million euro and (b) the aggregate community-wide income of each of the merging banks is more than 250 million euro. See Article 1 of the Regulation for a more detailed description of the thresholds (European Council, 1989b).
15. Note however that in special circumstances mergers with community dimension can be referred to national antitrust authorities and then reviewed under the national laws. These circumstances concern the cases when the merger produces effects only on local markets (see article 9 of the EC Merger Regulation).
16. In practice, however, in most cases the merger applicants negotiate with the supervisor(s) and the Antitrust Division a solution that is acceptable to all. So, it does not happen very often that the Antitrust Division files a suit under US antitrust law to block a bank merger that was approved by supervisory authorities.
17. However, the Antimonopoly Act stipulates that financial institutions cannot hold more than 5 per cent of the outstanding equity of a domestic corporation, whereas non-financial companies can.
18. In principle this means that if one authority blocks the merger it cannot go forward, irrespective of the decision of the other.
19. In Germany, as in most other countries, the parties of a merger request can appeal against a blocking decision to the courts.
20. However, he cannot block a merger that would not cause a threat to competition.
21. Council Regulation (EEC) No 4064/89, art. 21(3).
22. Some ambiguity may arise about the interpretation of this clause. According to Ghezzi and Magnani (1998), it implies that the member states can eventually block mergers previously authorised by the Commission but they cannot authorise mergers that have been blocked by the Commission.
23. The factors considered in this assessment of the suitability of shareholders are the same as for the licensing of a new bank. They include the reputation of shareholders, the existence of possible conflicts of interest, capital adequacy, the organisational structure of the new company and the commercial rationale behind the operation.
24. Takeover regulations are of course also relevant. Since we want to focus on the relative roles of bank supervisors and competition authorities, and not on securities regulators and regulations, we do not discuss the additional issues they raise here.
25. Danthine et al. (1999, ch. 6) for example highlighted such a risk, referring however to banks' preferences and the role of competition authorities. See Kerjean (2000, p. 16f.) for a description of the Banco Santander Central Hispano (Spain) – Champalimaud (Portugal) case of 1999 that brought the potential for conflict between EU competition policy and national interest/prudential considerations to the forefront.
26. The rationale behind such provisions is that when a failing firm is on one side of the transaction then the market structure after merger may not be worse than the market structure after the failure of the firm. For example, when the firm fails then most of its business may go to one main competitor, implying a similar increase in concentration as with a merger. Usually, the application of 'failing firm defence' provisions are subject to a number of conditions that are there to ensure that only those cases pass where any alternative (failure or alternative takeover) would be worse from a competition perspective.
27. The Japanese contribution to the 1996 OECD report on 'failing firm defence' provisions describes two bank mergers in this country that involved one party in serious difficulties;

San-in Godo Bank with Fuso Bank and Iyo Bank with Toho Sogo Bank (OECD, 1996, p. 69f.).

28. More precisely, 'charter value' is defined as the present value of future rents from holding a banking licence.

29. 'Traditional' contributions on bank runs include Diamond and Dybvig (1983), Jacklin and Bhattacharya (1988), Chari and Jagannathan (1988), Calomiris and Kahn (1991). Contributions on systemic risk include Allen and Gale (2000a), Freixas et al. (2000) and Chen (1999).

30. The link between competition and liability risk is also analysed by De Palma and Gary-Bobo (1996) in a model that focuses on the relationship between Cournot competition on the loan market and depositors' withdrawal decisions. The analysis leads to multiple equilibriums: In the safe equilibrium banks offer a small amount of loans at a high interest rate and bear no bankruptcy risk. In the risky equilibrium, banks supply a large amount of loans but are subject to a positive probability of runs when depositors receive a bad signal. Since depositors are uninsured, the results suggest that a deregulated system with imperfect markets is potentially highly fragile.

31. Covitz and Heitfield (2000) also argue that competition can lead to higher bank risk and even to higher loan rates. In a model characterised by overlapping moral hazard problems between banks and borrowers, they show that when borrowers' moral hazard is strong (as for example during times of economic recessions) and banks' moral hazard is weak, competition leads to higher loan rates, lower bank monitoring and higher bank risk. In contrast, a monopolistic lending environment may lead to lower loan rates, higher bank monitoring and lower bank risk.

32. Koskela and Stenbacka (2000) find an unambiguous positive relationship between competition and stability but their framework is somewhat different. Banks compete in the loan market but, absent any moral hazard problem, stability refers to bankruptcy risk of borrowers. Under the assumption of a mean-shifting investment technology, it is shown that a monopoly bank charges higher lending rates than competitive banks, which leads to lower investments and thus a higher probability of bankruptcy.

33. The z-score used in this chapter is a statistic derived from historical profits, equity and asset stocks measuring the number of standard deviations below the mean that a bank's profits would have to fall before its equity became negative. See Goodhart et al. (1998, p. 90) for a brief summary of credit scoring techniques more generally.

34. There is also a literature about the risk and diversification effects of commercial banks moving into other financial service areas, such as securities underwriting or insurance. See Lown et al. (2000) for a review and some new results. We do not cover this literature here, since this type of financial consolidation has a less clear link to concentration.

35. However, in private communication the author clarified to us that he regards the system with many banks at the start of the period as not very competitive either.

REFERENCES

Allen F. and D. Gale (2000a), 'Financial contagion', *Journal of Political Economy*, 108(1), 1–29.

Allen, F. and D. Gale (2000b), *Comparing Financial Systems*, Cambridge, Mass.: MIT Press.

Benston, G.J., W.C. Hunter and L.D. Wall (1995), 'Motivations for bank mergers and acquisitions: enhancing the deposit insurance put option versus earnings diversification', *Journal of Money, Credit, and Banking*, 27(3), 777–88.

Berger, A. and T. Hannan (1989), 'The price-concentration relationship in banking', *Review of Economics and Statistics*, 71, 291–99.

Besanko, D. and A.V. Thakor (1993) 'Relationship banking, deposit insurance and bank portfolio', in C. Mayer and X. Vives (eds), *Capital Markets and Financial Intermediation*, Cambridge, UK: Cambridge University Press, pp. 292–318.

Bianco, M., F. Ghezzi and P. Magnani (1998a), 'L'applicazione della disciplina antitrust nel settore bancario statunitense', in M. Polo (ed.), *Industria Bancaria e Concorrenza*, Bologna: Il Mulino, pp. 143–258.

Bianco, M., F. Ghezzi, W. Negrini and P. Signorini (1998b), 'Applicazioni della disciplina antitrust al settore bancario in Italia', in M. Polo (ed.), *Industria Bancaria e Concorrenza*, Bologna: Il Mulino, pp. 329–74.

Bolt, W. and A.F. Tieman (2001), 'Banking competition, risk, and regulation', DNB Staff Reports, no. 70.

Boot, A.W. and S. Greenbaum (1993), 'Bank regulation, reputation and rents: theory and policy implications', in C. Mayer and X. Vives (eds), *Capital Markets and Financial Intermediation*, Cambridge, UK: Cambridge University Press, pp. 262–85.

Bordo, M., A. Redish and H. Rockoff (1995), 'A comparison of the United States and Canadian banking systems in the twentieth century: stability v. efficiency', in M. Bordo and R. Sylla (eds), *Anglo-American Financial Systems: Institutions and Markets in the Twentieth Century*, New York: Irwin, pp. 11–40.

Boyd, J. and S. Graham (1991), 'Investigating the banking consolidation trend', *Federal Reserve Bank of Minneapolis Quarterly Review*, Spring, 1–15.

Boyd, J. and S. Graham (1996), 'Consolidation in U.S. banking: implications for efficiency and risk', Federal Reserve Bank of Minneapolis Working Paper, no. 572, December.

Boyd, J. and D. Runkle (1993), 'Size and performance of banking firms: testing the predictions of theory', *Journal of Monetary Economics*, 3(1), 47–67.

Calomiris, C. and C. Kahn (1991), 'The role of demandable debt in structuring optimal bank arrangements', *American Economic Review*, 81, 497–513.

Caminal, R. and C. Matutes (2002), 'Market power and banking failures', *International Journal of Industrial Organization*, 20(9), 1341–61

Canoy, M., M. van Dijk, J. Lemmen, R. de Mooij and J. Weigand (2001), 'Competition and stability in banking', CBP Document, no. 015, Netherlands Bureau for Economic Policy Analysis, December.

Capie, F. (1995), 'Prudent and stable (but inefficient?): commercial banks in Britain, 1890–1940', in M. Bordo and R. Sylla (eds), *Anglo-American Financial Systems: Institutions and Markets in the Twentieth Century*, New York: Irwin, pp. 41–64.

Carletti, E. (1998), 'Competition, stability and regulation', Italian translation in M. Polo (ed.), *Industria Bancaria e Concorrenza*, Bologna: Il Mulino, pp. 67–136.

Carletti, E., P. Hartmann and G. Spagnolo (2002), 'Bank mergers, competition and liquidity', paper presented at the CEPR/Fundación BBVA conference on 'Will Universal Banking Dominate or Disappear? Consolidation, Restructuring and (Re)regulation in the Banking Industry', in Madrid, November.

Chari, V.V. and R. Jagannathan (1988), 'Banking panics, information and rational expectations equilibrium', *Journal of Finance*, 43, 749–61.

Chen, Y. (1999), 'Banking panics: The role of the first-come-first-served rule and information externalities', *Journal of Political Economy*, 107, 946–68.

Cordella, T. and L. Yeyati (1998), 'Financial opening, deposit insurance and risk in a model of banking competition', CEPR Discussion Paper, no. 1939.

Covitz, D.M. and E.A. Heitfield (2000), 'Monitoring, moral hazard, and market power: a model of bank lending', paper presented at the Center for Financial

Studies Conference on 'Competition among Banks: Good or Bad?' in Frankfurt, April.

Craig, B. and J.C. Santos (1997), 'The risk effects of bank acquisitions', *Federal Reserve Bank of Cleveland Economic Review*, 33, 25–35.

Cruickshank, D. (1999), 'Review of Banking Services in the UK; Competition and Regulation: An Interim Report the Chancellor of the Exchequer', The Stationery Office, London, July.

Danthine, J.-P., F. Giavazzi, X. Vives and E.-L. von Thadden (1999), 'The Future of European Banking', London: Centre for Economic Policy Research, January.

De Bandt, O. and P. Hartmann (2002), 'Systemic risk in banking: a survey', in C. Goodhart and G. Illing (eds), *Financial Crises, Contagion, and the Lender of Last Resort – A Reader*, London: Oxford University Press, pp. 249–98.

De Nicolo, G. and M. Kwast (2001), 'Systemic risk and financial consolidation: are they related?', mimeo, Board of Governors of the Federal Reserve System and International Monetary Fund, April.

De Palma, A. and R.J. Gary-Bobo (1996), 'Coordination failures in the Cournot approach to deregulated bank competition', THEMA Working Paper.

Diamond, D.W. (1984), 'Financial intermediation and delegated monitoring', *Review of Economic Studies*, 51, 393–414.

Diamond D.W. and P. Dybvig (1983), 'Bank runs, deposit insurance and liquidity', *Journal of Political Economy*, 91, 401–19.

Diamond, D.W. and R. Rajan (2001), 'Liquidity risk, liquidity creation and financial fragility: a theory of banking', *Journal of Political Economy*, 109, 287–327.

Edwards, F. and F. Mishkin (1995), 'The decline of traditional banking: implications for financial stability and regulatory policy', *Federal Reserve Bank of New York Economic Policy Review*, 1, 27–45.

European Council (1989a), Second Council Directive 89/646/EEC of 15 December 1989 on the coordination of laws, regulations and administrative provisions relating to the taking up and pursuit of the business of credit institutions and amending Directive 77/780/EEC.

European Council (1989b), Council Regulation 4064/89/EEC of 21 December 1989 on the control of concentration between undertakings, corrected and amended in 1990 and 1997.

Freixas, X., B. Parigi and J.C. Rochet (2000), 'Systemic risk, interbank relations and liquidity provision by the central bank', *Journal of Money, Credit, and Banking*, 32(3), 611–38.

Ghezzi, F. and P. Magnani (1998), 'L'applicazione della disciplina antitrust comunitaria al settore bancario', in M. Polo (ed.), *Industria Bancaria e Concorrenza*, Bologna: Il Mulino, pp. 259–328.

Goodhart, C. (1987a), 'Why do banks need a central bank', *Oxford Economic Papers*, 39, 75–89.

Goodhart, C. (1987b), *The Central Bank and the Financial System*, London: Macmillan.

Goodhart, C., P. Hartmann, D. Llewellyn, L. Rojas-Suarez and S. Weisbrod (1998), *Financial Regulation: Why, How and Where Now?*, London: Routledge.

Group of Ten (2001), *Report on Consolidation in the Financial Sector*, BIS, IMF, OECD.

Hanweck, G. and B. Shull (1999), 'The bank merger movement: efficiency, stability and competitive concerns', *The Antitrust Bulletin*, 44(2), 251–84.

Hellman, T.F., K. Murdock and J. Stiglitz (2000), 'Liberalization, moral hazard in banking and prudential regulation: are capital requirements enough?', *American Economic Review*, 90(1), 147–65.

Hellwig, M. (1991), 'Banking, financial intermediation, and corporate finance', in A. Giovannini and C. Mayer (eds), *European Financial Integration*, Cambridge, UK: Cambridge University Press, pp. 35–63.

Hoggarth G., A. Milne and G. Wood (1998), 'Alternative routes to banking stability: a comparison of UK and German banking systems', *Financial Stability Review*, 5, 55–68.

Jacklin, C.J. and S. Bhattacharya (1988), 'Distinguishing panics and information-based bank runs: welfare and policy implications', *Journal of Political Economy*, 96, 568–92.

Keeley, M. (1990), 'Deposit insurance, risk and market power in banking', *American Economic Review*, 80, 1183–200.

Kerjean, S. (2000), 'Le secteur bancaire européen à l'epreuve du contrôle des concentrations', *Banque & Droit*, no. 69, janvier–février, 14–26.

Koskela, E. and R. Stenbacka (2000), 'Is there a tradeoff between bank competition and financial fragility?', *Journal of Banking and Finance*, 24, 1853–74.

Lown, C.S., C.L. Osler, P.E. Strahan and A. Sufi (2000), 'The changing landscape of the financial services industry: what lies ahead?', *FRBNY Economic Policy Review*, October, 39–55.

Matutes, C. and X. Vives (1996), 'Competition for deposits, fragility and insurance', *Journal of Financial Intermediation*, 5(2), 184–216.

Matutes, C. and X. Vives (2000), 'Imperfect competition, risk taking and regulation in banking', *European Economic Review*, 44(1), 1–34.

Nagarajan, S. and C.W. Sealey (1995), 'Forbearance, deposit insurance pricing and incentive compatible bank regulation', *Journal of Banking and Finance*, 19, 1109–30.

Niinimäki, J.P. (2000), 'The effects of competition on banks' risk taking with and without deposit insurance', Bank of Finland Discussion Papers, no. 21, December.

OECD (1996), 'Failing Firm Defence', CLP Report, (96)23, Paris.

OECD (1998), 'Enhancing the Role of Competition in Bank Regulation', DAFFE/CLP Report, (98)16, Paris, September.

OECD (2000), 'Mergers in Financial Services', DAFFE/CLP Report, (2000)17, Paris, September.

Parigi, B. (1998), 'Competition in banking: a survey of the literature', Italian translation in M. Polo (ed.), *Industria Bancaria e Concorrenza*, Bologna: Il Mulino, 19–66.

Paroush, J. (1995), 'The effects of mergers and acquisition activity on the safety and soundness of a banking system', *Review of Industrial Organisation*, 10, 53–67.

Perotti, E. and J. Suarez (2001), 'Last bank standing: what do I gain if you fail?', mimeo, University of Amsterdam and CEMFI, June.

Shy, O. and R. Stenbacka (1998), 'Market structure and risk taking in the banking industry', Bank of Finland Discussion Papers, no. 22.

Smith, B.D. (1984), 'Private information, deposit interest rates and the "stability" of the banking system', *Journal of Monetary Economics*, 14, 293–317.

Staikouras, C. and G. Wood (2000), 'Competition and banking stability in Greece and Spain', *Journal of International Banking Regulation*, 2(1), April.

Discussion of 'Competition and stability: what's special about banking?'

Michael Artis

I should like to say, for a start, how much I appreciate being able to participate in this celebratory conference for Charles Goodhart. Unlike many others here I have not been a student of Charles's nor even a colleague in the narrow sense, whether in a University department or Central Bank. But I have been a close colleague in a professional sense, sharing with Charles – albeit from a different starting point – the highly educative vicissitudes of British monetary experience. These include the experience of a variety of monetary regimes in the policy sense – from the 'monetarily constrained' Keynesianism of the 1960s to Mrs Thatcher's monetarism, via exchange rate targeting and membership of the ERM to today's inflation targeting. In addition – and relevant to the chapter under discussion – they include the experience of the British monetary system (and policy) in adapting to a more competitive framework, beginning with the startling move, under the heading of 'Competition and Credit Control'. This was a (then) revolutionary move away from a highly cartelized system with a symbiotic monetary policy which played on rationing effects, towards a much more open and competitive system. As we followed together all these twists and turns in British monetary experience I never found Charles's judgment to be other than sound, his academic merit less than first-rate or his sense of fairness less than perfect.

One of the – at first sight, strange – results of the creation of the euro-area is that whilst in various dimensions the integration of the European capital market has been visibly strengthened, in one area, that of banking, the result so far has been on the contrary a consolidation and concentration of the market *within* national boundaries. The widely expected institutional arbitrage (which would for example reveal whether 'universal banking' was the best model or not) has not occurred; and this is a market, moreover, in which wide disparities in efficiency are not only apparent to the casual observer but can be documented by careful analysis (as, for example in Hasan et al., 2000).

The chapter under discussion provides some background for an explanation of this curiosity. It takes a fresh look at the long-standing tension – or supposed tension – between stability and competition in banking. It first looks at the issue from a theoretical standpoint, and from the viewpoint of academic empirical work; and then it examines the division of responsibility and the allocation of powers of supervision and surveillance on the one hand and the control of competition and mergers on the other. This last section is particularly interesting.

Banks are multi-product firms with many peculiar features:

1. Some of what they do falls under the heading of public goods supply. Clearing systems are a basic example as is co-ordination over the availability and compatibility of ATM systems. These public good elements in banking are a peculiar feature arguably underplayed in the authors' analysis.
2. There is a strong element of 'trust' involved in banks' activities: fractional reserve banking requires it. There is asymmetric information everywhere. But then some awkward features follow: bank runs demonstrate contagion effects. Bank size can be desired for itself: it demonstrates risk-pooling, success and soundness. The bad side of this is the 'too big to fail' syndrome. Large size brings with it a moral hazard which the authorities may not be able to avoid.
3. In some countries bank deposits are a significant proportion of the personal wealth of large numbers of people. Equally, in some countries, large numbers of small to medium sized businesses (including the self-employed) are significantly dependent on bank finance (this is the source of the 'Grapes of Wrath' effect, where banking instability leads to loan foreclosure on a socially significant scale).
4. The multi-product nature of banking has some other, perhaps less 'special' but nonetheless important, features too: it means that bank output is hard to define and so also concentration. In some locales for some products the industry may be extremely competitive, in others nearly monopolistic.

All this certainly complicates matters. The public interest element poses the probability of moral blackmail. Banks can reasonably say that if they are being asked to collude in some respects (for example to ensure a banking service in rural areas) and to refrain from exploiting monopoly power in others then they should not also be asked to deconcentrate, pay fines, reveal true accounts and so on. This element has been historically quite important in helping to bolster bank concentration. Central banks like to think that one of their jobs is to 'speak for the banking community'. This is only half a step from 'capture' and already cuts against the likelihood that the central bank will enforce competition (though it will listen to arguments that the banking community must be helped to 'save itself', especially from competition from outside). It is not too surprising that societies find it difficult to treat banking 'like any other industry'. It's not just the stability issue that's involved, though this is the most important.

Reluctance to treat banking 'like any other industry' for competition purposes is reinforced by critical historical episodes and the folk memory that they provide. Here is a canonical story for such episodes. It starts with a shock which sharpens the competitive environment. Banks begin to compete in markets they are not accustomed to. The younger generation of bank managers enjoys putting the older one in the shade with stories of rapid increases in market share. The unexpected ease with which these gains are made encourages more aggressive moves into the still-new area of business. The sociology is that of Lavington's ice-skaters: the suitability of the lake for skating on is judged by the number of skaters already there (Lavington, 1921). As more people venture onto the surface, earlier inhibitions are cast away: eventually the weight of people on the lake becomes too great, the ice breaks and the skaters drown. In other words, eventually the bottom falls out of the market. Some of the smaller banks approach bankruptcy; this is a point at which some of the bigger banks are able to buy up their erstwhile competitors with the grateful approval of the central bank for whom the 'consolidation' of the banking sector is a welcome solution to a messy problem. The empirical papers reviewed by the authors perhaps do not convey the flavour of this type of episode which I believe to be canonical; at any rate such episodes are illustrations of the way in which competition is believed to lead to instability.

Banks are special in a number of ways, as argued above. Their claim to be treated in a special way, if not logically always tied to issues of stability and competition, nonetheless finds a handy expression in the way in which the competition and the supervisory authorities are related.

It is time to get back to the present European scene. The pace of cross-border merger activity, as we noted earlier, has disappointed those who saw the formation of the euro-area as the trigger for the completion of the European capital market. One reason may reside in the fact that the central bank is able, as the supervisory authority, effectively to supplant the competition enforcer. At any rate it is hard to avoid the impression that this is what has been happening in Italy. In numerous speeches (the following quotes are taken from his *Statement to the Joint session of the Sixth Committees of the Italian senate and Chamber of Deputies*, April 1999) Governor Fazio has urged the Italian banks to consolidate, and a number of domestic mergers have been approved: 'The Bank of Italy has . . . indicated . . . that the indispensable strengthening of Italian banks would have to be achieved through an increase in their size' (ibid., p. 11). Hostile take-over bids are discouraged – 'The information asymmetries typical of banking make it difficult to assess hostile takeover bids . . .' (ibid., p. 16). The tone is that of a protector, with considerable power to examine each and every merger proposed. It is not difficult to imagine that if banking were to be treated 'like any other industry', there would be more foreign and successful bids.

Schull and Hanweck (2001) have indeed already concluded that in the European Financial Area 'cross-border mergers are further confounded by the current institutional framework of EMU' (ibid., p. 141), by which they mean to refer to the fact that the EMU framework delegates supervision to the national level.

The authors are to be thanked for providing a careful description of the way in which the institutions promoting competition and supervision inter-ract in the world and for examining carefully what the empirical evidence says about the relationship between stability and competition in banking. For Europeans their exposition helps explain how it is that the European capital market remains so incomplete.

REFERENCES

Fazio, A. (1999), 'The restructuring of the Italian banking system', *Statement by the Governor of the Bank of Italy to the Joint Session of the Sixth Committees of the Italian Senate and Chamber of Deputies.*

Hasan, H., A. Lozano-Vivas and J.T. Pastor (2000), 'Cross-Border Performance in European Banking', *Bank of Finland Discussion Papers*, 24.

Lavington, F. (1921), *The English Capital Market*, London: Methuen and Co.

Schull, B. and G.A. Hanweck (2001), *Bank Mergers in a Deregulated Environment: Promise and Peril*, Westport, CT: Qorum Books.

9. Is there a Goodhart's Law in financial regulation?

Andrew Sheng and Tan Gaik Looi[*]

1. INTRODUCTION

I am very grateful to be invited to this Festschrift in honour of Professor Charles Goodhart. As another doyen of central banking, Gerry Corrigan likes to say, a man may leave central banking, but his heart never leaves central banking. As a young central banker who learnt his craft in the developing world under the late and legendary Tun Ismail Mohd Ali of Bank Negara Malaysia, I met Charles at one of the Commonwealth Central Bankers' meetings in the late 1970s. This used to be hosted by the Bank of England in the Oak Room just before the BIS Annual Meetings. I remember asking Charles one of those naïve questions on interest rate policy, for which I got a clear thoughtful answer that provoked my thinking for the rest of the trip.

My next encounter with Charles was reading his book on Money, Information and Uncertainty. Our paths crossed again in Hong Kong in 1993, when I assumed duties at the Hong Kong Monetary Authority. Charles was not only a member of the Exchange Fund Advisory Committee, but was also one of the founders of the Hong Kong Link to the US dollar, commonly called 'the peg'. He was asked by the Bank in the dire days of 1983 to advise on what to do to stabilise the Hong Kong dollar in the politically volatile period of Anglo-Chinese discussions on the future of Hong Kong. I have learnt much from Charles in his frequent visits to Hong Kong, which he used to combine with his duties as Visiting Professor at the City University of Hong Kong and en route to Beijing to lecture to the Graduate School of the People's Bank of China.

Like many other central banks throughout the world, I am sure the Hong Kong Monetary Authority and the People's Bank owe no small debt to Charles for his sound advice and training provided to many young staff members. All of us benefited hugely from both his sharp theoretical insights, as well as practical solutions to real life situations, delivered in a sincere manner that reflected his humanity and deep care for the welfare of the student as well as the emerging markets and central banks.

On behalf of emerging market central banks and financial supervisors, I want to pay tribute today to Charles the teacher, the theoretician and practical banker, and friend.

2. FINANCIAL REGULATION

As far as I am aware, Charles came into financial regulation relatively late in his career, and his papers on the subject appeared in the beginning of the 1990s. Charles's approach to supervisory issues is as insightful as his approach to monetary policy, in spite of the fact that he was never himself a bank or securities supervisor. He grasped clearly the question of regulatory objectives, the need for quality of information and transparency, and brought a sense of proportionality in a field where common sense was not always common. As far as I am aware, he was the first monetary economist to devote attention to the economic analysis of regulation in financial markets. He understood that economists tended to take the legal underpinnings of the economy for granted, sometimes a fatal flaw in analysis (Goodhart, 1997). More important, he understood that the market was shaped by behaviour of market participants in response to regulations, incentives, and uncertainty over property rights.

Many a bank regulator would be grateful for his sympathy for the asymmetric rewards for regulators:

> ... the conduct of supervision is a thankless task which is all too likely to tarnish the reputation of the supervisor. ... The best that a supervisor can expect is that nothing untoward happens. A supervisor is only noticed when either he/she angers the regulated by some restrictive or intrusive action, or when supervision 'fails' in the sense that a financial institution collapses or a customer gets ripped-off. One can talk oneself blue in the face about the desirability of allowing some freedom for banks or other financial institutions to fail, etc., but supervisors will always tend to get a bad Press when that does happen, come what may.
>
> (Goodhart, 2000, p. 28)

Even this statement was made in the context of conflicts in the pursuit of price stability and financial stability policy goals of central banks. It was a good reflection of Charles's deep appreciation of the inter-locking issues surrounding central banking, monetary, financial and systemic stability. He understood that in deciding when to provide lender of last resort (LOLR) facilities, central bankers did not find it easy to distinguish between liquidity and solvency problems.

By the early 1990s, it became relatively clear that the three key objectives of central banks were monetary stability, financial stability and safety of the payments system. But in the lead up to Goodhart's Law, where does the central bank draw the line in providing LOLR particularly where problems in non-banks pose a threat to systemic stability? Like the difficulty in drawing the boundary between monetary aggregates to M3 or M4, what is a bank and how far should the safety net be cast?

This highlights the conflict between monetary policy and financial stability objectives. Charles was the first to debate the issue of central bank independence to pursue a single objective of price stability, and whether the regulatory and supervisory function should be undertaken by institutions other than the central bank.

I will not try to summarise his many insightful and persuasive contributions on the why, how and where now of financial regulation. Much of the insights are listed in the conclusions in *Financial Regulation: Why, how and where now?* (Goodhart et al., 1998), reproduced in the Annex to this chapter. From these diverse conclusions, I would like to attempt to infer a Goodhart's Law of Financial Regulation.

3.   GOODHART'S LAW

The earliest form of Goodhart's Law on monetary policy was 'Any observed statistical regularity will tend to collapse once pressure is placed upon it for control purposes.' (Goodhart, 1984). This was paraphrased into 'As soon as the government attempts to regulate any particular set of financial assets, these become unreliable as indicators of economic trends' (*Pears Cyclopaedia*, 1990) or 'When a measure becomes a target it ceases to be a good measure' (Strathern, 1997).

But how different is a financial regulatory rule from a monetary rule? Can we differentiate regulatory credibility from monetary credibility? Or monetary discipline from financial discipline?

As Charles perceptively pointed out, financial markets involve a complex structure of contracts between market participants, and regulation is about changing the behaviour of regulated institutions (Goodhart et al., 1998). If so, monetary or financial behaviour involves a complex game between the regulator and the regulatees. In the same way that physicists cannot assume that the observer is independent of the observed, can the behaviour of regulators be assumed independent of the regulatees?

Charles also keenly observed that regulatory services are not provided by a market process, but largely imposed, which causes a variety of problems. In particular, 'If the perception that regulation is costless is combined with risk-averse regulators, there is an evident danger that regulation will be over-demanded by consumers and oversupplied by the regulator' (Goodhart et al., 1998, p. 190).

In the 25th Chorley Lecture, Charles said:

> The public does not realise that ultimately they themselves mostly bear the costs of regulation; they often see it as a free good that ought to be operated so perfectly and efficiently by the regulators that failure should never be allowed to occur. Given such standard preconceptions, it is all too easy to understand how excessive regulation can be introduced after well-publicised failures, and how all such financial failures are treated by the media as examples of regulatory mismanagement and failure. (Goodhart, 1997, p. 21)

On the other hand, a typical asymmetric reward system for financial regulators in emerging markets is the tendency to 'over-regulate and under-enforce'. This is because regulators are underpaid and have all incentives to engage in regulation, which generates power, and under-enforcement, since no one likes the laborious and often thankless task of investigation, prosecution and sanctions.

Since all financial regulation rules have a cost, the setting of any particular regulatory rule will invite regulatory arbitrage or encourage innovation to circumvent the rules. For example, the capital adequacy rules caused banks to expand off-balance sheet activities or move offshore. Regulated entities may also establish non-regulated entities to escape the regulatory net.

Hence, Goodhart's Law of monetary policy applies also to financial regulation. Since regulators are in the same game as regulatees, the behaviour has feedback mechanisms, not unlike Soros's concept of reflexivity.[1] In rational expectations theory, the policies alter economic behaviour. The result is that economic agents anticipate and neutralise the systematic component of each policy. The exception occurs when economic agents are surprised by purely random events or shocks (Sargent and Wallace, 1975).

4. MONETARY AND FINANCIAL DISCIPLINE

In essence, both monetary policy and financial regulation are conducted with the goal of influencing the behaviour of economic agents and financial intermediaries so that the policy objectives of monetary and financial stability are achieved. Whether the policy outcome achieves the policy objectives would depend on the credibility of the monetary or regulatory authority. In other words, the ability and track record of the authorities to exercise monetary and financial discipline.

The behavioural nature of the regulator and the regulatees can be seen as a series of repeated games between both parties. The policy objective of the regulator or monetary authority is to maximise social welfare through monetary and financial stability and to minimise social costs through minimisation of market misconduct. If the rules are unclear or the incentives encourage moral hazard, it is not surprising that some private sector participants may exploit these opportunities. The private sector attempts to maximise private gains and minimise enforcement costs and sanctions.

The credibility of the authority depends on its ability to reinforce monetary and financial discipline through undertaking surveillance, investigation and enforcement action. A transparent and credible series of independent and professional regulatory action (free of political and vested interests) would enhance the reputation of the market and command the respect of market participants, particularly investors.

Such market interaction clearly influences each party's behaviour and the development of the market depends on the quality of a relationship that is based on trust, fairness, and consultation. Lack of trust could result in inadequate information disclosure to regulators. A high level of transparency, accountability and reputation for fairness by the regulator would result in better information disclosure and co-operation by market players. A Pareto optimal situation arises whereby the 'regulatory contract' that is reached allows the market to operate with high transparency, efficiency and liquidity, without compromising the larger public goal of stability.

5.   WHO SHOULD REGULATE?

In various recent publications, Charles addresses the issues of who, what and how of financial regulation. Firstly, should the agency that conducts monetary policy also be responsible for financial regulation?

The main argument for the separation of monetary policy and bank supervision is to avoid policy conflicts and enhance central bank credibility. Reducing the concentration of power in central banks is another powerful argument, given their independence without necessary accountability to the legislature. Thus, recent OECD reforms have tended to separate central banks from the financial supervisory role by concentrating the latter in a financial supervisory agency independent from the central bank. However, Charles has argued that an exception could be made for developing countries where the central banks have shown relatively more independence than other agencies and have greater expertise and skills (Goodhart, 2000).

A global survey of current structures indicates that there is no ideal model on who should regulate: be it the central bank or a separate regulatory body or a combination of both. The choice would depend on the historical, political and cultural circumstances and stages of financial development of countries. The US, the UK and Europe have different models and these have served the respective regimes well.[2]

A point to note is that monetary or macroeconomic stability and financial stability are two sides of the same coin. Neither objective can be pursued in isolation. The separation of monetary policy and supervision is also not as simple and clear-cut, and it is essential that the central banks and regulatory authorities share information and co-ordinate their policies and actions.

This is particularly evident in the LOLR function, as central banks need good and timely information on the health of banks to determine their liquidity and solvency. The Asian crisis revealed that raising interest rates when the corporate sector is excessively leveraged undermined the solvency of the banking system. Thus, illiquidity can very rapidly lead to a problem of insolvency for market participants.

Consequently, central banks need to understand the micro aspects of monetary action, and regulators need to understand that the soundness of individual institutions has larger implications on macro-economic and systemic stability. In many countries, mistakes in supervisory action or macroeconomic policy occurred frequently because of information gaps or overlaps. These sometimes stem from jurisdictional disputes or neglect between regulatory agencies, creating problem sectors, such as unregulated deposit-taking institutions, excessive leverage by corporations and other classic cases of fallacy of composition.

6.   WHAT IS COVERED UNDER FINANCIAL REGULATION?

The dangers of looking at financial markets in segmented silos becomes more apparent in dealing with cross-border and cross-jurisdictional products and transactions. With greater consolidation of financial institutions offering cross-border products, national regulators are forced to cooperate or at the minimum exchange information with different regulators. Increasingly, banking, insurance, securities and asset management products are being offered by large financial conglomerates. Risks can be rapidly shifted within these complex institutions outside the jurisdictional reach of some regulators.

Just as targeting the monetary aggregate M1 can cause behavioural changes as broader aggregates such as M2 or M3 evolve, so are the regulatory nets being stretched as financial products evolve across borders and jurisdictions. The concentration of risks in derivative transactions and over-the-counter exposures are no longer easily apparent or transparent to either regulators or market participants. In essence, global systemic stability is only as strong as the weakest link in the chain of national financial systems.

No regulatory agency can therefore afford to operate in isolation, and no economy can ignore the need to co-operate. Otherwise, the effectiveness of regulation and monetary policy would be undermined. In many financial markets, institutional failures or large regulatory costs have occurred because regulatory agencies have tended to be more myopic and inflexible because of turf battles. In Asia, for example, one common reason for the inertia in developing deep and liquid bond markets is the jurisdictional battle between central banks and securities commissions on who should take the lead. Such parochialism often results in deadlock, as each agency vies for its own interest, with no agreement on what is needed for the interest of the system as a whole.

A solution for such market consolidation is to combine regulatory powers in a mega-regulator model. But there is as much danger with regulatory monopoly as with other monopolies, with economies of scale at the expense of competitive innovation. Whether one jurisdiction opts for a mega- or multiple-regulator model has tended to reflect the political realities of financial regulation, as financial scandals and crises give rise to calls for change to the existing model.

What is critical, as argued by Charles, is that objectives are clearly defined to promote better accountability, and any conflict in policy measures of different agencies on achieving objectives should be handled at the political level. This applies also in the case of a single regulator as it would also face conflicting objectives that need to be resolved internally or at the political level (Goodhart et al., 1998).

A pragmatist would argue that, irrespective of who should regulate, the importance is the effectiveness of policy outcome relative to the policy objective. In some cases, mixed models have advantages over mega-regulators. As Deng Xiaoping used to say, 'It does not matter whether the cat is black or white, as long as it catches mice'.

7.   HOW TO REGULATE EFFECTIVELY?

Despite vigorous regulation and supervision in many of the developed markets, why are financial scandals and crises still endemic?

Charles views laws and regulations as contracts that carry important incentive structures (Goodhart et al., 1998). If properly designed *and enforced*, they induce financial institution managers to act in ways that avoid or reduce systemic risk, without unintended side effects. On the other hand, badly designed regulations could generate moral hazard behaviour that increases systemic risk, such as open-ended deposit insurance schemes or policy lending directives.

Hence, Charles shrewdly recommends that the incentive structure of all intended regulations be examined before implementation. Such incentive structure clearly involves not only the *threat* of sanctions or rewards, but also *enforcement action* to ensure that the rules have credibility.

The contractual nature of financial markets make the role of information and the behavioural response to informational changes (expectations and incentives) important aspects of market behaviour. Asymmetric information makes regulation more difficult and complex, while the principal–agent relationship of the regulator and the financial institution raises moral hazard and adverse selection problems for the regulator.

First, *timely, accurate and comprehensive information is a market fundamental* that enables financial agents to make good decisions and undertake sound risk management. Markets reward and punish corporations through decisions on whether to buy, sell or hold on to the stocks and bonds of the corporations. Information disclosure is therefore a strong incentive for management to establish controls to manage risk, improve performance and be more transparent in their actions. Conversely, in regimes where disclosure requirements are not rigorous or stringent, management may well get away with bad behaviour and not be accountable for the way they behave and manage their business.

Clearly the quality of information depends on the existence and implementation of accounting and auditing standards. In addition, disclosure requirements under company and securities laws and rules would ensure that the markets and regulators have timely and accurate information to assess market performance.

Some accounting and regulatory rules amplify trends. *Current loan loss provisioning rules* in many countries, for example, recognise losses only when they occur, and do not allow banks to take a forward-looking view of their risks when the loans are granted. Thus banks pull back on their lending as loan-losses increase, thereby worsening cash flows of their borrowers and create a vicious cycle of deteriorating asset quality and a credit crunch that could lead to a recession (Banque de France, 2001).

Secondly, *regulatory avoidance or arbitrage occurs where bad regulations pose a barrier to profit opportunities* (Joao Cabral dos Santos, 1996). Financial institutions simply create new products or change their jurisdictional coverage structure to circumvent such regulations.[3] Such behaviour is being aided by technology that lowers transactions costs and erode traditional franchises.

Most regulators are more conscious of the behaviour of their regulatees, but less aware of the feedback mechanism of the market on their own policies and responses. For example, policy lags and lags in impact of regulatory action could not only become pro-cyclical but also could create unintended consequences.

Charles, in recent work on Central Bankers and Uncertainty (Goodhart, 1998a, p. 108), has observed that central bankers have been cautious in making bold interest rate moves. Such behaviour by central banks is because uncertainty is more 'complex, insidious and pervasive' than commonly assumed. He points out that it is the multiplicative nature of uncertainty and the long lags in the effects of monetary policy that constrains and complicates the action of central banks. A parallel case can be made in the 'inertia' of regulatory authorities to take dramatic enforcement action, just as central banks are hesitant for fear that reversals of policy, changes of mind, are castigated as evidence of error, irresolution and general incompetence.

Thirdly, incentive structures clearly influence financial market behaviour. For example, *pay structures affect risk taking.* Staff have the incentives to gamble for resurrection, if there is the risk of being fired for poor performance. Where bonus incentives are given, employees are likely to take on more risk in order to generate the revenue to earn the bonus (Goodhart, 1998b). Limited liability and 'option-like' bonus contracts provide the incentive for staff to take on bigger risks, as they will enjoy the upside from profitable trading outcomes without the need to compensate the firm in the event of losses (Davies, 1997).

Internal controls provide checks and balances in the organisation and promote discipline and encourage proper behaviour by management and employees. Yet, this is an area that has often been neglected to the peril of financial institutions.

Regulations that minimise moral hazard are important in promoting greater market discipline and better governance. These would include instituting a system of *ex ante* prompt corrective measures, which clearly state the obligations of financial institutions and the penalties for non-compliance with these regulations. This rules-based approach enhances the discipline both of regulators and regulatees.

Alternatively, instead of 'fixed rate rules', such as standard capital ratios, regulators can consider rules that allow grading of risks.[4] Another approach is to have clear commitment rules, with clear enforcement outcomes so that regulatees know the up and down sides of their action (Goodhart, 1998b).

In short, incentive structures have to be right for rules and regulations to be observed or to have the desired effect. In addition, regulations should:

- Be clear, transparent and explicit in objectives;
- Have legitimacy – that is have public consultation and approval;
- Promote market efficiency and a level playing field;
- Have due regard to regulatory burden on market participants;
- Appropriately protect small market participants, for example consumers and investors;
- Have transparency and due process in enforcement.

Financial regulation is but part of the discipline that can be exercised on market participants to ensure that they play by market rules. The markets are changing far too fast through innovation and technology for regulators to cover all the risks without excessive regulatory costs. Sound financial markets require three sets of disciplines to work:

- *Self-discipline* provides the best defence against imprudent or improper exposures and actions. Good corporate governance helps market and corporate efficiency;
- *Regulatory discipline* reinforces self-discipline through enforcement to promote compliance and good governance. Regulators have to provide level playing fields, and be fair, consistent and even-handed to be credible; and
- *Market discipline* separates the strong from the weak through transparency, healthy competition and accountability (Crockett, 2001).

Finally, *markets are driven by expectations*. Modern finance theory is predicated on 'rational investors'. However, behavioural researchers find that investors are seldom rational and may make inefficient investment decisions. It was found that investors use mental shortcuts or heuristics to make quick and sound decisions out of masses of information. The outcome can be misleading as they tend to over-emphasise information that is minimally relevant while minimising important information, thus magnifying the impact of the errors in decision-making. Worse, investors tend to predict the future from the past, and confuse short-term cycles with long-term trends.[5]

Average opinion is typically stable for long periods, being lulled by the perception that markets are relatively stable. Hence, a sudden shift in average opinion or sentiment results in over-adjustments that could severely disrupt the functioning of the real economy.

Should regulators act on the basis of stable markets or on the basis of low probability but catastrophic events? Charles has led the way into the realm of psychology of investors, on their collective change of mind arising from their beliefs on future events, to explain excess volatility in prices. It is an area where economists and lawyers alike are generally uncomfortable in analysis.

8.   CONCLUSION

To sum up, Goodhart's Law also helps to explain why financial regulation can fall short in regulatory targets to achieve financial stability. Regulations, incentive structures, expectations and market dynamics feed back on one another in a loop, altering the conditions of risks that have the potential to destabilise the system.

Because incentives, rules and their enforcement are all part of market behaviour, there is scope for more collaboration in research among the various disciplines of law, economics, psychology and finance to resolve the challenges posed by behavioural dynamics on financial stability.

In his pioneering work on financial regulation, Charles taught us that common sense is not too common. This is the same conclusion that a regulatory specialist, Harvard Professor Malcolm Sparrow also came to in his book, *The Regulatory Craft* (Sparrow, 2000). The essence of good regulation is to 'Pick important problems and fix them'. This calls for a systematic approach to risk management that prioritises the problems and organises the tools around the work. One must identify the regulatory issue, and then select the tools to fix the problem.

We owe Charles considerable debt for his intellectual contribution to the important task of financial regulation. To me, he has demonstrated that the issues surrounding Goodhart's Law of monetary policy has equal applicability to the issues surrounding financial regulation. The issues he pioneered will be the work of many studies in the years to come.

We wish Charles a very happy and productive retirement. I know that many of his students, colleagues and friends will still call on his time, so I am not sure that he is ready to retire. Once again, on behalf of all financial regulators, and especially those from the Far East, I want to pay tribute to a wonderful teacher, friend and intellectual mentor, who has pointed the way into these complex issues where few have gone before.

ANNEX 1

Goodhart's Policy Conclusions on Financial Regulation: Why, How and Where Now?[6]

A Main analytical themes

1. Distinction is made between *regulation* (the establishment of specific rules of behaviour), *monitoring* (observing whether the rules are obeyed) and *supervision* (the more general observation of the behaviour of financial firms.

2. The primary concern of banking regulators is to protect the financial system against systemic instability.

3. Because of the nature of contracts between financial firms and their customers (e.g. many are long term and involve a fiduciary obligation), there is a need for continuous monitoring of the behaviour of financial firms.

4. Financial transactions involve a complex structure of explicit and perceived implicit contracts between firms and their customers, firms and the regulator, and the regulator and society. Given different (asymmetric) information between regulators and firms, two dangers arise:

   - First, the effective (implicit or explicit) contract may not be the optimal one ('adverse selection') when the regulator is misinformed about the characteristics (such as the effectiveness of internal controls) of a firm.
   - Second, even with the most well designed regulatory contract, a firm may sometimes have incentives covertly to break the contract ('moral hazard').

5. Regulatory agencies (central banks or other bodies) are viewed as supplying regulatory, monitoring and supervisory services to various stakeholders, including financial firms, consumers and government.

6. If regulation is perceived as being a free good, the issue is how to guard against over-regulation.

7. Regulation is not costless, but imposes a range of costs (institutional, compliance and structural) which are ultimately reflected in the price of financial services.

8. There is no 'ideal model' (of institutional structure of regulatory agencies) that can be universally applied. Institutional structures should be designed to maximise the likelihood that the objectives will be met in the most effective and efficient manner.

9. In the final analysis, regulation is about changing the behaviour of

regulated institutions. A major issue, therefore, is whether regulation should proceed through externally imposed, prescriptive and detailed rules, or by the regulator creating incentives for appropriate behaviour.

10. Financial systems are changing substantially, to an extent that may undermine traditional approaches to regulation, most especially the balance between regulation and supervision.

B   Policy conclusions

I   *The basis of regulation*
(i)   The objectives of regulation need to be clearly defined and circumscribed.
(ii)   Expectations about what regulation, monitoring, and supervision can achieve need to be kept to realistic levels.
(iii)   Regulation should not impede competition, but should support it; by addressing information asymmetries, it can enhance competition in the marketplace.
(iv)   Regulation should reinforce, not replace, market discipline.
(v)   There must be practitioner input into the regulatory process.
(vi)   Regulatory agencies should be staffed with well-qualified people.
(vii)   The extent of deposit insurance should be limited.

II   *The general approach: incentive structures*
(i)   Regulation should be seen as a set of contracts.
(ii)   Less emphasis should be placed on detailed and prescriptive rules and more on internal risk analysis, management and control systems.
(iii)   There should be appropriate internal management incentives.
(iv)   Regulators should be publicly accountable through credible mechanisms.
(v)   Time-inconsistency and credibility problems should be addressed through pre-commitments and graduated responses, with the possibility of overrides.
(vi)   The incentive effect of pay structures should be a regulatory issue.

III   *Policy differentiation*
(i)   The form and intensity of regulatory and supervisory requirements should differentiate between regulated institutions according to their relative portfolio risk and efficiency of internal control mechanisms.
(ii)   In some areas the regulator could offer a menu of contracts to regulated firms, requiring them to self-select into the correct category.
(iii)   There should be a reconsideration of the differences in the regulatory treatment of banking and trading books.

(iv) With respect to conduct of business regulation, a major distinction should be made between wholesale and retail business.

(v) In some limited areas, consumers can be offered a choice between institutions subject to different levels of regulation.

IV Issues in developing countries

(i) The need for regulation is even greater in developing countries than elsewhere.

(ii) It is important to begin creating a legal environment in which property rights to collateral on defaulted loans are clear; and a more open and arm's-length equity market can function (e.g. by building a legal structure to protect minority shareholder rights).

(iii) The process of liberalisation must be managed carefully.

V Management of financial crises

(i) There should be a clear bias (although not a bar) against forbearance when a bank is in difficulty.

(ii) Intervention authorities need to ensure that parties that have benefited from risk taking bear a large proportion of the cost of restructuring the banking system.

(iii) Prompt action should be taken to prevent problem institutions from extending credit to high-risk borrowers, or capitalising unpaid interest on delinquent loans into new credit.

(iv) Society must establish the political will to make restructuring a priority in allocating public funds, while avoiding sharp increases in inflation.

(v) Intervention agencies should not support the values of broad classes of non-bank financial assets in a crisis.

VI The international dimension to regulation

- Harmonisation need not cover all aspects of regulation in order for the objectives of regulation to be achieved.

C Key perspectives

- Regulation is essentially about changing the behaviour of financial intermediaries. This needs to be seen and analysed in terms of a set of incentive contracts.
- Financial systems have been changing substantially in a way that is undermining traditional approaches to regulation. More weight will now have to be placed on internal risk analysis, management and control systems, with an appropriate incentive structure introduced to this end.

- Whereas regulatory services, if properly structured, are beneficial, the fact that they are not provided by a market process, but largely imposed, causes a variety of problems. In particular, if the perception that regulation is costless is combined with risk-averse regulators, there is an evident danger that regulation will be over-demanded by consumers and oversupplied by the regulator.

NOTES

*   The views expressed in this chapter are solely those of the authors and do not reflect the views of the Securities and Futures Commission, Hong Kong
1. Soros sees this as a two-way feedback mechanism in which reality helps shape the participants' thinking and the participants' thinking helps shape reality in an unending process in which thinking and reality may come to approach each other but can never become identical (Soros, 1994). Krugman simplifies this to mean that human perceptions both affect events and are themselves affected by them. See 'Soros' plea, http://web.mit.edu/krugman/www/soros.html.
2. National situations are diverse: in the UK, New Zealand, and in three eurozone countries (Belgium, Finland and Luxembourg), the central bank has no role in bank regulation. In the US, and in the remaining eight eurozone countries, the central bank is broadly or exclusively (Spain, Italy, Netherlands and Portugal) engaged in bank regulation. See Plihon (2000).
3. An example of regulatory arbitrage is the emergence of the Eurodollar market to circumvent US regulation Q.
4. There could be differentiation between financial institutions that have robust risk management systems and those who do not have such capabilities (in which case they may opt for standard capital requirements).
5. See Evensky (2000).
6. Extracted from Chapter 9 in Goodhart et al. (1998).

REFERENCES

Banque de France (2001), 'Financial Cycle: Factors of Amplification and Policy Implications', Discussion Paper, March.
Crockett, Andrew (2001), 'Market Discipline and Financial Stability', *Financial Stability Review*, June.
Davies, Daniel (1997), 'Remuneration and Risk', *Financial Stability Review*, Spring.
Evensky, H. (2000), 'Understanding Investors' Behaviour – A Primer for Practitioners', *Asia Financial Planning Journal*, at http://www.afpj.com/2000/profileapr2000.htm.
Goodhart, C.A.E. (1984), *Monetary Theory and Practice*, London: Macmillan.
Goodhart, C.A.E. (1997), 'Economics and the Law: Too Much One-Way Traffic?', *The Modern Law Review*, Volume 60, No. 1, January.
Goodhart, C. (1998a), 'Central Bankers and Uncertainty', Annual Keynes Lecture, British Academy, 29 October 1998, published with permission in *Bank of England Quarterly Bulletin*, February 1999.

Goodhart, C. (1998b), 'An incentive structure for financial regulation', in Goodhart C.A.E. (ed.), *The Emerging Framework of Financial Regulation*, UK: Central Banking Publications.

Goodhart, C. (2000), 'The Organizational Structure of Banking Supervision', LSE Financial Markets Group, Special Paper No. 127, October.

Goodhart, C., Hartmann, P., Llewellyn, D., Rojas-Suarez, L. and Weisbrod, S. (1998), *Financial Regulation: Why, How and Where Now?*, published in association with Bank of England, London: Routledge.

Plihon, D. (2000), 'What Prudential Surveillance for the Financial Services Industry?', *Revue d'Economie Financière – Special Edition on Security and Financial Regulation*, No. 60.

Pears Cyclopaedia (1990–91), 99th edition, pp. G27, G31.

dos Santos, Joao Cabral (1996), 'Glass-Steagall and the Regulatory Dialectic', *Federal Reserve Bank of Cleveland*, 15 February.

Sargent, Thomas and Neil Wallace (1975), 'Rational Expectations, the Optimal Monetary Instrument and the Optimal Money Supply Rule', *Journal of Political Economy*, April.

Soros, G. (1994), 'The Theory of Reflexivity', MIT Department of Economics World Economy Laboratory Conference, 26 April.

Sparrow, M.K. (2000), *The Regulatory Craft: Controlling Risks, Solving Problems, and Managing Compliance*, US: The Brookings Institution Press.

Strathern, M. (1997), 'Improving Ratings: Audit in the British University System', *European Review*, 5, 305–21.

10. Working with market forces

Michael Foot[1]

1. INTRODUCTION

I have much for which to be grateful to Charles. Our careers in the Bank of England overlapped by many years, our interests often required close collaboration and for two years I had the pleasure of working directly for him.

The biggest single impact this had for me was to strengthen an already deeply held but poorly articulated view of the importance of working *with* markets rather than against them. Not surprisingly, therefore, when I was asked to take part in this conference (and being in my eighth year as a financial regulator, which equals 20 years in many other professions) I immediately thought of drawing on Charles's extensive work on financial regulation.[2]

More specifically, I decided to pick up and try to take forward from my perspective some of his work on how the regulator might work with market forces. This has been given added impetus by the fact that the Financial Services Authority took this subject as one of its themes for detailed analysis in 2001. What follows is an early and personal contribution to that sizeable task.

I should make clear from the outset that the FSA's work and my own interests stretch across the regulation of all financial services and to both prudential and conduct of business aspects. Charles, in contrast, has always been particularly concerned with the *prudential* aspects of *bank* regulation.[3] For the purpose of this chapter, I too will focus on bank prudential regulation but would just make the observation that many of the issues raised have equal relevance elsewhere in the field of financial regulation.

I'm sure Charles would have put it more kindly, but it always seemed to me that he felt it rather sad that markets needed regulators at all. Certainly, I fear that he felt that much of what financial regulators did in practice was of little or no added value. Of course, he accepted the argument that there are numerous areas (such as the asymmetries of information between the large supplier of retail financial services and the many individuals who may buy that service) where imperfections in the market may justify some form of prudential and conduct of business regulation.

Even more readily, he accepted the arguments for prudential surveillance of anything that could threaten the stability of the financial system. But he argued that – with the breakdown in the traditional barriers between banking, securities and insurance and the growing complexity and dimensions of risk-taking in these areas – the regulator was in serious danger of being left behind, even in areas which might reasonably be within his purview.

Instead, Charles argued that internal management controls of risk were potentially superior to what the regulator could do by himself. Charles felt that what was needed was to find ways in which the regulator could rely on these internal mechanisms. 'In view of the growing importance of such internal control mechanisms, the question needs to be addressed whether there are steps, structures, that can be put in place to reinforce the incentives for all the parties involved . . . [including the regulators] to play their own roles efficiently in order to limit improper behaviour, excessive risk and systemic instability.'[4]

By the time Charles was writing this, the banking supervisors' treatment of *market risk* for the sophisticated banks had already been developing along these lines. Now, three years later we *may* be within a few years of doing the same with *credit risk*. But there had also been a long line of academic work on other forms of 'working with the market' in areas such as deposit insurance, 'pre-commitment' and the like. Charles would also have been only too aware – at the other end of the spectrum – of what to the regulator is an irritating aspect of almost any major failure: namely the 'we in the market knew there was something wrong' syndrome. This has had two good outings in recent years in the UK with Barings and more recently Independent Insurance; but of course those 'outings' begin after the event, not before, which sadly reduces their value to the hapless regulator.

2. WHAT IS THE REGULATOR AIMING FOR?

Before we can go further, we need to be clear just what the banking prudential regulator ought to be trying to achieve. Only then can one judge the relevance of 'market forces' to the regulator because only then can one say what use he might be able to make of what the market can provide.

Unfortunately, the question is not an easy one to answer. Although the first UK legislation on banking supervision took effect in 1979, it was not until 1997 that the Bank of England published a full statement on the objectives of that supervision.[5] There, to summarise ruthlessly the following key points were made about the regulator's primary objective:[6] 'fulfil the responsibilities, relating to the safety and soundness of *individual* authorised banks' placed on it by the 1979 Act (emphasis added); to act in the interests of depositors, defined as mainly 'individuals and non-bank corporates to support sound banking practices in other countries'.

In words of which Charles I'm sure would have approved, the Bank also had this to say about *systemic risk*. 'While the provisions of the Act relating to the supervision of banks do not address systemic risk, nevertheless banking supervision makes a major contribution to the wider central bank task'.

The creation of the Financial Servies Authority (hereafter FSA) shortly afterwards, of course, led to a different allocation of responsibilities – best summarised (in terms of the relative roles of HMT, the Bank of England and the FSA) in a *Memorandum of Understanding* published in October 1997. Here it is made clear that the Bank is among other things 'responsible for the overall stability of the financial system' while the FSA's tasks include 'the authorisation and prudential supervision of banks' and other financial institutions. The FSA's responsibilities have since been set out in statute[7] and a number of public statements have appeared outlining how it intends to interpret these objectives.[8]

One common thread through this process has been the relevant authorities' desire to make it clear that a 'no failure' regime is neither possible nor desirable. A second common theme has been the desire by the regulators to avoid overburdening the banking industry with unduly protective/conservative regulation. The FSA, for example, will be required to explain specifically how it meets requirements laid down in the Act (these are generally known as 'the principles of good regulation') which go the heart of this point. These include requirements to facilitate innovation and competition and to ensure that a regulatory burden or restriction is 'proportionate to the benefits, considered in general terms, which are expected to result from the imposition of that burden or restriction'.[9]

It follows from this that the FSA should be regularly seeking ways in which a given desired level of 'prudential soundness' of a bank can be achieved through less burdensome regulatory arrangements. It is clearly possible that the effect of some current regulatory requirements could be achieved more cheaply through better use/development by the regulator of market forces. It is in that spirit and with that aim that the FSA project on harnessing market forces is being started, and, as I made clear earlier, being applied to all the FSA's responsibilities in respect of firms, not just the prudential supervision of banks.

3. A SUMMARY OF MARKET SIGNALS

Let me move on to what these market signals might be and how they might be useful. But before we do so one final preliminary point needs to be made. We need to recognise that a statutory framework complete with regulators *does* exist and that market signals as we see them today reflect that fact. This makes more complex the analysis of these signals.

This can be illustrated with two rather different examples.

First, however open regulators claim to be with the information that they have available to them, the fact is that the market is always going to assume that they have 'confidential, privileged' information on top of that. Exactly how the market participants factor that in to their own workings need not bother us here but it is something that a regulator has to bear in mind when trying to assess the significance of a 'market signal'.

In a rather different vein, it is widely recognised that aspects of the statutory framework can have a significant effect on the perceptions of risk seen within the financial system. It was for that very reason, to take one of the best understood links of this kind, that many economists have opposed the creation of 100 per cent bank deposit protection, as the existence of such a regime introduces an asymmetry into the perception of risk, for both managers of the bank and potentially for the depositors.

It follows that – as will be evidenced below – the interpretation of 'market signals' may not be as straightforward as one might otherwise hope.

Let me now offer a simple taxonomy of those 'market signals'. The simplest type of market signal – which I suspect even the most traditional banking regulator is aware of and responds to – might be described as 'obvious and readily available', such as:

- the share price of quoted companies which contain/are associated with authorised entities; and
- prices of bonds issued by authorised entities (particularly useful for mutuals who by definition have no equity).

Such signals are, of course, not available for every authorised bank but typically they are for the larger players. Of the 184 UK-incorporated banks that are authorised here, for example, 72 are parts (usually large parts) of quoted companies. And all the larger players are 'captured' in the process.

These signals are also available world-wide. In Japan over the last few years, for example, I believe there has been a good deal of information to be gained from watching bank share prices – both in aggregate and between banks. Of particular interest has been the decline of any share to par (100 yen) – at which point to use a theatrical term, it would normally be 'curtains'.

To take just one example that banking supervisors used at the time,[10] Figure 10.1 shows the relative performance of Yamaichi, Nomura and Nikko Securities shares in the months up to the failure of Yamaichi at the end of November 1997. The Tokyo market throughout had much more faith in Nomura than in the others and it is evident that the percentage fall in Yamaichi's shares was often the most rapid. Certainly from our point of view, the plan to facilitate an orderly wind-down of the UK subsidiary bank of Yamaichi was rolled out of the drawer once the share price had fallen below 200 yen.

Bond prices, likewise, can be very useful guides – both for listed companies and for mutuals. I shall return later to the idea that one could build upon this indicator – as with suggestions of requiring the regular issue of subordinated debt.[11]

Further highly visible market signals come from the ratings agencies. Someone will no doubt one day write an interesting article studying the symbiotic relationship between regulators and ratings agencies, particularly in developed economies. Regulators undoubtedly take a ratings downgrade as one possible trigger for a more in-depth review of the firm while agencies for their part regularly quiz companies on the view their regulators take of them. To put it no higher, there is the danger of undue reliance on each other's views. That said, on our side of the fence we are conscious that the agencies don't always speak with a single voice when rating banks or insurance firms.[12] Still, I would rather have them around than not.

None of this is to suggest that markets always get it right. There are plenty of cases where downgrades have come late in the struggles of an authorised firm to avoid bankruptcy or where the stock market has been caught blissfully unaware of fatal problems.

Equally, one can readily find examples of the other kind of error, where markets have overestimated the size of problems, though this is perhaps less likely because market signals are endogenous variables which can therefore themselves influence future events. Thus, when markets mark a share price heavily down (even if 'mistakenly'), that fact can and does have an adverse implication for the survival of the company. In particular, a bank struggling to raise new capital to remain afloat is going to find it even harder after a downgrade. This is particularly so if the downgrade is to a level (BBB at S&P and Baa3 at Moody's) – which excludes certain classes of investors from holding the asset. These kinds of 'errors' thus probably have more chance of leading to failure even if this is somehow 'unjustified'. But I am convinced that there is information in such signals for the regulator and no regulator should turn his nose up at free, easily obtainable information!

The second categorisation of market forces I would offer moves on to

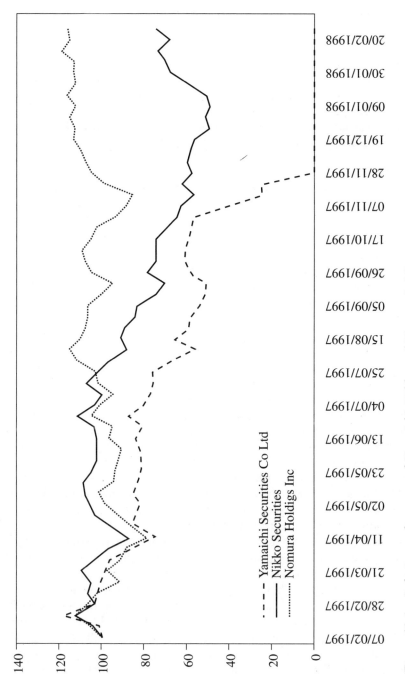

Figure 10.1   Relative performance of Yamaichi, Nikko and Nomura holdings

what you might call the 'less obvious signals'. Classic cases of what I mean would include:

- The liquidity of a bank's Certificates of Deposit in the market.
- The price at which a bank can raise funds, particularly outside its home market (remember the so-called 'Japanese premium' that has arisen periodically in recent years).
- The willingness of counterparties in foreign exchange and elsewhere to take a particular bank's name.

All of these can really only be picked up through participation in the relevant markets or a close working relationship with those who do participate. In the case of the UK, the FSA certainly expect to hear from the Bank of England and Her Majesty's Treasury of relevant information that comes across in their foreign exchange, cash or gilt operations. It is also a subject we raise discreetly with other market participants as the need arises.

I am a great believer also in asking firms outright what they fear – 'fear' in two senses. First, how do they rate their main rivals – what worries them about the strategies of their strongest rivals? Second, are they concerned about certain practices in their industry and certain firms? Answers to both sets of questions can be very revealing. Sometimes the first set of questions tell you quite a lot about the adequacy of the management strategy of the firm and the ability (or otherwise) of its staff to get their 'heads up'. Occasionally, the second set reveal deep-seated worries about particular practices or firms. That may, of itself, tell you no more than that some brash newcomer – such as Direct Line a few years ago in car insurance – has upset a cosy pricing structure in the industry. But it could indicate something much more worrying and thus is an indicator that a regulator would be foolish to ignore, given that – provided he has firms' trust – he is in a uniquely good position to get the information.

My third set of market disciplines takes advantage of many of the signals described above but yet goes rather further. I would describe this set under the heading of market constraints on behaviour.

Capital in aggregate and composition is one such constraint. If the banking regulator did not exist, then banks would still keep sizeable capital to satisfy their market and other counterparties. They also – at least in the UK – tend to keep much more than the regulator sets as the minimum.[13] Companies supply information on their capital position: ratings agencies and others analyse it. But what they are looking for and how they judge what they find is perhaps best described as a complex algorithm arising out of all these various pieces of information, together with long-standing experience of what past behaviour has been consistent with soundness and stability. Unfortunately for present purposes, of course, these judgements are often formed against the background of knowledge of the regulator's existence and the minimum standards he sets in assessing, for example, what minimum capital his banks should hold.

Another market constraint is provided by banks' reluctance to appear accident-prone. In some respects, particularly in the area of conduct of business, it is the desire of firms that jealously guard their reputation that will often lead them to put right and compensate customers for their errors without the need for intervention by the regulator. Less encouragingly, it can lead to less positive behaviour in other areas. For example, most banks like other firms are loath to admit when they have systems problems or where they have been defrauded. Banks then are typically reluctant to help prosecute their own staff or to publicise frauds – sometimes even those that have failed against *them* but which it would be helpful for other banks to be warned about.[14]

4. IMPROVING DISCLOSURE

My fourth and final categorisation of market forces covers a huge, multi-layered topic, '*additional disclosure*'. The easy part is to recognise that, other things being equal, markets work better with fuller information. The difficulty – certainly in an area like prudential regulation where it is regularly proposed that the regulator should require or encourage banks to provide additional information – is to know:

- what information would be of interest and to whom,
- to try and assess the relative costs and benefits of getting the firms to provide the information (it can be costly to provide and costly to analyse); and
- to draw a line between what is reasonable to regard as confidential because commercially sensitive and what could be published without such risk.

Banks have provided increasing amounts of prudential information about themselves over the years; and once every few months at least one international study seems to call for more. The biggest change in the last decade has no doubt been in the disclosure of market risk, where the Basel/EU requirements provided a framework in which somewhat greater disclosure could be made. The new Basel Accord proposals suggest we are in for something similar in the area of credit risk and, if the true believers have their way, the same will be true eventually of operational risk.

Quite how credit and operational risk disclosures will be disseminated and digested is a large, open question. Greater disclosure can be forced by either the market or the authorities (in various guises in different countries – as regulators, taxation authorities, setters of accounting standards or whatever). Where the authorities do it, it is nearly always on the proposition that the market will like it and want more of it when they have got used to it. The success of that proposition has been, to put it politely, mixed.

Such initiatives by the authorities are frequently a response to a crisis. Typically, a problem emerges (let us say an LTCM or an Asian debt crisis) and within a year proposals for additional disclosure by the banks or their counterparts appear, usually from several different international groups, each set of proposals more elaborate than the last.

The authors of such work are, of course, aware that there are considerable dangers in pressing for additional information, because of the need to tackle the questions set out in the bullet points above. There is also the worry that extra information may, inadvertently, mislead. This is much less of a problem in the professional/wholesale area than it is on the retail side. But, even so, it is worth asking oneself from time to time for example what, after all, do all the Value at Risk numbers on which we have placed so much emphasis in the analysis of market risk really tell you? Are they really providing an accurate profile of value at risk in extreme market conditions in the banks concerned? Or are they actually telling you more about the market conditions that those banks have faced in the last couple of years and proving of little use in markets such as those which followed the terrorist outrage in September? My view is that they represent the latter and that it can – as in September – come as a real shock even to professionals that their 'best in class' models can seriously mis-state the value actually at risk in markets where one or more external shocks causes liquidity to dry up, huge gapping of prices and no way out at reasonable cost from anything other than the strongest government bonds.

From this it is but a short step to asking whether the authorities should be mandating (or at least encouraging) greater disclosure – a seemingly attractive option since, rightly or wrongly, it appears a cheap, market-based solution to a number of sins. Moreover, despite good reasons not to assume that increased disclosure makes for a healthier financial system, many observers do indeed appear to assume that 'more is better' – as of course it *can* be.

But surely, for this to be the case, disclosure initiatives have to have one of two measurable outcomes at a reasonable cost. Either they provide a better picture of an individual financial institution for others than is currently possible and/or, if presented consistently by a range of financial institutions, they help reveal threats to the financial system.

The benefits of pursuing these twin objectives are demonstrated in the Multidisciplinary Working Group on Enhanced Disclosure's (MWGED) cogent report.[15] But no one would claim they are easily achieved.

The second objective, using disclosure to buttress systemic stability, is even harder to achieve than the former since it will usually require concerted action, or, at the least, a common view on a potential (or actual) systemic risk. As LTCM proved, it may be hard to attain a common view because the disclosures necessary to identify systemic problems simply do not exist – and even if they do, these disclosures may be insufficient.

Even so, many would reasonably argue that regulated firms (or at least the biggest of them) have a collective responsibility to ensure that the information they provide is adequate for these markets to operate in an efficient and orderly manner. And that certainly could not be said of the information received by credit departments of most of those lending to LTCM, let alone others who might have wished to know for their own protection how leveraged these funds were and where they had got the money.

Pillar III of the new Basel Capital Accord will articulate this expectation. And in their day-to-day work regulators can encourage effective involvement in markets by ensuring that firms' risk management systems and controls are appropriate, that credit controls are effective and counterparty assessments are soundly based. But regulators cannot compel firms to obtain and use information in a manner beneficial to the financial community. Those operating in markets need to be able to convince themselves (and not just after a 'scare' like LTCM) that they have some common collective interests in doing so, that it is not costly and that it will not hinder their predominant driver, individual corporate gain.

5.   DEVELOPING MARKET DISCIPLINES

Given the attractions of improving/building upon existing disclosure set out above, regulators have begun to catch up with academics. They, for some years, have been thinking about a number of possible ways of harnessing/developing market disciplines. The FSA theme looks at a wide range of these ideas.

One long-standing academic suggestion has been risk-based pricing of deposit-insurance. This allows a signal to depositors of the risks (as seen by the regulators or however else arrived at) attached to particular firms. It also has the pleasing additional market effect of increasing the costs of doing business for those rated poorly (just as already in the wholesale markets poorer risks have to pay up for funds).

A second is pre-commitment where a public commitment is made by the bank not to suffer market risk losses of more than a pre-stated amount. This is argued to strengthen market discipline because of the reaction of regulators, who have agreed a set of penalties with the firm, and the reaction of markets if the bank fails to meet its commitment.

A third on which I should like to dwell for longer is the required regular issue of subordinated debt to provide an assured market signal. Such debt has been mooted as a potential regulatory tool in the United States for a number of years, most recently in the discussions around Gramm–Leach–Bliley.[16]

Intuitively the proposal is attractive, with the market empowered to monitor and, by various means, manage the risks of banks. This would not be *ersatz* supervision, rather an adjunct to supervision using one of the 'obvious and easily available market signals' described earlier. However, the results of a US study for Congress concluded that the evidence for a mandatory policy was not, for the moment at least, compelling.[17] The same might be said of evidence from Argentina, the only country that requires banks to issue subordinated debt. One study touching on the Argentine experiment declares it a partial success, although I am not convinced that the rules of the game have been rigorous enough, or the required disclosures sufficiently comprehensive, to judge it a success, partial or otherwise.[18] Indeed the study does not persuade me that the proper conditions exist outside the banking system for external discipline to be effective. This may be a criticism of the study. Equally, it could reflect a reality that even in 'mature' markets, as Robert Bliss and David Flannery (2003) put it, 'day-to-day market influence remains, for the moment, more a matter of faith than of empirical evidence'.[19]

But although there may be good grounds for scepticism, the next step is to address the difficulties of subordinated debt measures rather than retreat from complicating factors. Is it realistic, for example, to assess the riskiness of banks using spreads that are affected by factors that are not correlated to the *actual* risks of the bank (such as the liquidity of debt markets, general sectoral or macroeconomic factors)?

In Europe we would have to assess the feasibility of subordinated debt issues into markets that are less homogenous than they are in the US. In the US, retail investors hold meaningful portions of such debt and it is also the case that European regulatory capital rules might hinder banks from investing in subordinated debt issued by their peers.[20] In the UK, more work needs doing on the mechanics of subordinated debt spreads – the only study available suggests that UK bank's subordinated debt spreads are not risk sensitive.[21] Would that perhaps change if an experiment of this kind were begun?

A rather different tack is to ask why regulators don't make more public use of the information to which currently only they have access? Why not require publication of a bank's individual capital requirements on a real-time basis? Why not reveal when examiners are put into a bank for a non-routine investigation? Why not publish the results of an 'unsatisfactory' examination?

Of course many regulators already disclose the results of certain enforcement actions against both firms and their employees. But beyond that, most regulators are generally reluctant to go.[22] On this view, for example, it would be undesirable, say, to publish the regulatory capital requirements of regulated firms or to report on action to close a firm until that action has gone through whatever rights of appeal and due process are available and has been found to be warranted.[23]

It was on arguments like these that I declined in the run-up to Y2K to name the large financial firms that were in our 'red' traffic light category, despite coming under heavy media pressure to do so. It seemed to me that the damage publication could do to the continuing interests of depositors, investors or policy-holders (because of the possibility of panic runs) was outweighed by the prospect that the problem could be fixed in time (as they were in every case) or worked around.

If used imaginatively, however, it can be argued that the information regulators hold *could* enhance market discipline or alter the behaviour of firms for the better in ways that even the cautious regulator could probably live with. It is indeed with exactly that aim in mind that we at the FSA are committed to publishing the results of an increasing amount of 'horizontal regulation' – that is projects that address risks on a particular theme or across a sector or sectors.

The 'results' of this approach will vary. Sometimes they will come in the form of a public warning, like the one given some months ago on the risks associated with certain forms of lending to the 'high-tech' sector. Sometimes, data will be used to illustrate possible improvements in services. One such project recently used firms' own but anonymised information on complaint volumes and handling to identify areas where the treatment of retail customers might be improved. But, wherever we tackle a regulatory problem at a sufficiently high level of generality, we shall be trying to use the information supplied (often from the firm to regulator) to identify best practice, without invalidating the confidentiality of that information.

To many, of course, that is nothing like far enough. 'Why bother to keep firms' confidentiality?' I can hear some of you cry: 'let people decide for themselves or if they are not capable of deciding for themselves (value at risk might be a good example), let those who can make sense of it do it and sell their output to the rest'. I think there is a perfectly good answer to this but I shall leave it to my colleagues' theme work to argue the case in detail.

I have touched several times on the fact that it is not only the regulator who may impact upon disclosure. The tax man and the auditor both have their part to play too and where, as in the UK, the private sector plays a large role in determining accounting standards there are indeed many hands stirring the pot. One particularly heated and extensive recent debate – over fair value accounting – illustrates that well enough. Both those in favour and those against think it could have major implications for the way in which market, credit and interest rate risk would be reflected in company accounts and viewed by the market. More analysis, I fear, for my colleagues in the market discipline debate because while as a lapsed economist I find the concept of fair value accounting an attractive one, it is also clear to me that there are a number of key features of the present proposals that require extensive testing and 'dual running before one could sensibly contemplate their adoption.[24]

6.   TO WHOM ARE MARKET SIGNALS RELEVANT?

For reasons set out at the beginning, nearly all of the above has been focused on prudential (rather than conduct of business) issues and upon wholesale rather than (save for deposit-insurance and greater self-publicity by regulators) retail counterparts. This does no more perhaps than reflect the reality of this debate to date and the fact that:

- prudential data is often easier to get hold of than data on a firm's conduct of business (cob) record;
- wholesale players have both the resources and the incentive to analyse the material available while by and large retail players do not.

However, certainly from the point of view of the single regulator with responsibility for the whole range of financial service industries, this is far from the whole story. In areas such as the provision of personal investment products and advice, the quality of a firm's conduct of business record is very often more important than its prudential position in determining whether the firm will survive or whether its customers get a fair deal. The most obvious example of this, of course, is in the area of 'pensions mis-selling', where righting the wrongs of the period 1988–94 is going to cost the pensions industry something of the order of £15–20bn in compensation and administration costs. Although one can never be sure of the exact knock-on effects, it is apparent that – while the stronger firms have readily managed to meet their extra liabilities – the shape of the industry today is very different from how it might have been had these problems not arisen.

I should also like, as an aside, to note that that compares with a net cost to the UK bank deposit-protection fund of around some £25 million in the period of its existence since 1987. (Even the gross cost to the fund at the worst, that is before the BCCI Liquidator started to make payments, was less than £100 million.) If you add in losses made by the Bank of England on the taxpayer's behalf in respect of the 1991–92 small banks' crisis, you still have trouble making the total more than £150 million.

7.   THE YARDSTICKS FOR CHANGE

How will the FSA order the collection of interesting partly baked ideas set out above? In particular, how will we decide what change will be worth attempting and what might fall in the 'nice to have' or 'looks pretty dubious' categories? Fortunately, here our statute and our usual practices provide some fairly robust guides to the process involved. There are perhaps three key issues.

First, is there a reasonably clear cost–benefit analysis that shows the likely benefits of the change exceeds substantially the likely costs? These are benefits as defined in meeting our new statutory objectives, which include the objective that has been close to Charles's heart in much of his writing – namely the maintenance of market confidence – and the *principles of good regulation*.[25]

Second, within this, will any change make it cheaper to achieve the same regulatory effect as now?[26] This could either be by virtue of the regulator doing his job more smartly or by, for example, engineering a disclosure framework that seems to make some of his previous work unnecessary.

Third, what could be done within a UK context – that is without carrying the rest of the developed world with us? For example, many would argue that something radical like the adoption of fair value accounting – even if fully justified on a theoretical basis – would have to be done across the G10, not just in the UK, if British companies were not to suffer in international competitive terms.

Whatever the outcome of the FSA's market forces study, I don't expect to see the disappearance of the financial regulator in my working lifetime (if only to ensure that there is always someone to blame!). But I *do* think that there are better, more focused and cost-effective ways to harness market forces both on the prudential side but also in respect of our conduct of business work. In some ways, the conduct of business area will be easier ground to till. It just has to be possible to present information better to consumers that at present to improve their decision-making process, and to harness market forces to help us do it. We start in a world in which 40 per cent of the UK population say they do not know the meaning of a percentage. And, to adapt one of Eddie George's most quoted jokes, most of the other 70 per cent aren't completely sure either!

NOTES

1. I am indebted to a number of colleagues at the FSA, notably Jonathan McMahon and Lyndon Nelson. Needless to say any remaining errors are mine.
2. Notably, 'An incentive structure for financial regulation' in a collection of papers published in 1998.
3. A typical example is provided by *Financial Regulation: Why, How and Where Now*, which Charles co-authored with Philipp Hartmann, David Llewellyn, Liliana Rojas-Suarez and Steve Weisbrod (1998). As early as page 10 comes a section entitled 'Why banks are special'.
4. 'An incentive structure for financial regulation', p. 96.
5. *The Objectives, Standards and Processes of Banking Supervision*, Bank of England, February 1997.
6. Subsidiary objectives noted included 'protecting against illegal deposit taking' and 'tackling financial crime'.
7. *The Financial Services and Markets Act 2000*, Section 3.
8. See for example 'A new regulator for the new millennium', FSA, January 2000.
9. *The Financial Services and Markets Act 2000*, Section 2.
10. All three of the companies described had banks in the UK.
11. A number of studies have examined this question, including Donald P. Morgan and Kevin J. Stiroh, 'Bond market discipline of banks: is the market tough enough?', Staff Report FRBNY – No. 95, 20 December 1999 and 'Using subordinated debt as an instrument of market discipline', Staff Study 172, Washington, DC, December 1999.
12. See Donald P. Morgan, 'Rating banks: risk and uncertainty in an opaque industry', FRBNY, April 2000.
13. The tendency of UK incorporated banks to hold capital in excess of the FSA's regulatory capital requirement is looked at briefly in Jeremy Richardson and Michael Stephenson, *FSA Occasional Paper 7: Some Aspects of Regulatory Capital*, March 2000, pp. 41–5.
14. Trade association intervention can help in such circumstances and I am grateful that, for example, in the UK the BBA offers exactly this service.
15. Multidisciplinary Working Group on Enhanced Disclosures (MWGED). 'Final report to Basel Committee on Banking Supervision, Committee of the Global Financial System of the G-10 central banks, International Association of Insurance supervisors', *International Organisation of Securities Commissions*, 26 April 2001.
16. 'The feasibility and desirability of mandatory subordinated debt', Report by the Board of Governors of the Federal Reserve System and the Secretary of the US Department of the Treasury, submitted to the Congress to section 108 of the Gramm–Leach–Bliley Act of 1999, December 2000.
17. Ibid., p. vii.
18. Charles W. Calomiris and Andrew Powell, 'Can emerging market bank regulators establish credible discipline? The case of Argentina, 1992–1999', May 2000.
19. Robert R. Bliss and Mark J. Flannery, 'Market discipline in the governance of US bank holding companies: monitoring vs. influencing', September 2000.
20. See Andrea Sironi, 'An analysis of European banks SND issues and its implications for the design of a mandatory subordinated debt policy', October 2000.
21. David Bennett, 'Are primary market subordinated debt spreads for UK banks risk sensitive?', unpublished MSc thesis, April 2001.

22. The reasons are discussed in the FSA's 'response to the Cruickshank report's recommendations on the use of disclosure', December 2000, 27–31.
23. Multidisciplinary Working Group on Enhanced Disclosures (MWGED), 'Final report to Basel Committee on Banking Supervision, Committee of the Global Financial System of the G-10 central banks, International Association of Insurance supervisors', *International Organisation of Securities Commissions*, 26 April 2001.
24. The use of exit prices for non-easily traded assets, the impact on some aspects of commercially necessary hedging, and the approaches to 'own credit risk' are just three such considerations.
25. Again, Charles would welcome nearly all of the *principles* – including as they do the encouragement of innovation and competition.
26. In the context of this chapter, 'regulatory effect' equates to 'number of prudential failures' but in practice we shall be thinking much more widely in line with our statutory objectives.

REFERENCES

Bank of England (1997), *Objectives, Standards and Processes of Banking Supervision*, Bank of England, February.

Bennett, David (2001), 'Are primary market subordinated debt spreads for UK banks risk sensitive?', unpublished MSc thesis, April.

Bliss, Robert R. and Mark J. Flannery (2000), 'Market discipline in the governance of US bank holding companies: monitoring vs. influencing', *European Economic Review*, forthcoming.

Board of Governors of the Federal Reserve System and the Secretary of the US Department of the Treasury (2000), 'The feasibility and desirability of mandatory subordinated debt', report submitted to the Congress to section 108 of the Gramm–Leach–Bliley Act of 1999, December.

Calomiris, Charles W. and Andrew Powell (2000), 'Can emerging market bank regulators establish credible discipline? The case of Argentina, 1992–1999', World Bank Working Paper No. 14, May.

Financial Services Authority (2000a), 'A new regulator for the new millennium', January.

Financial Services Authority (2000b), 'Response to the Cruickshank report's recommendations on the use of disclosure', December.

Goodhart, Charles A.E. (1998), 'An incentive structure for financial regulation', Financial Markets Group Special Paper No. 13, London: London School of Economics.

Goodhart, Charles A.E., Philipp Hartmann, David Llewellyn, Liliana Rojas-Suarez and Steve Weisbrod (1998), *Financial Regulation: Why, How and Where Now*, London and New York: Routledge.

Morgan Donald P. (2000), 'Rating banks: risk and uncertainty in an opaque industry', FRBNY, April.

Morgan Donald P. and Kevin J. Stiroh (1999a), 'Bond market discipline of banks: is the market tough enough?', Staff Report FRBNY No. 95, 20 December.

Morgan Donald P. and Kevin J. Stiroh (1999b), 'Using subordinated debt as an instrument of market discipline', Staff Study FRBNY 172, Washington, DC, December.

Multidisciplinary Working Group on Enhanced Disclosures (MWGED) (2001),

'Final Report to Basel Committee on Banking Supervision, Committee of the Global Financial System of the G-10 central banks, International Association of Insurance supervisors', *International Organisation of Securities Commissions*, 26 April.

Richardson, Jeremy and Michael Stephenson (2000), *FSA Occasional Paper 7: Some Aspects of Regulatory Capital*, March, pp. 41–5.

Sironi, Andrea (2000), 'An analysis of European banks SND issues and its implications for the design of a mandatory subordinated debt policy', Finance and Economics Discussion Series 2000-41, Board of Governors of the Federal Reserve System, October.

Discussion of 'Is there a Goodhart's Law in financial regulation?' and 'Working with market forces'

Dirk Schoenmaker

1. INTRODUCTION

I started to work with Charles on financial regulation at the LSE Financial Markets Group in the Summer of 1991, just after the collapse of BCCI. Charles has always been very mindful of the fact that failures can (and should)[1] happen and that supervisors will be criticised for it, rightly or wrongly. Both Andrew Sheng and Michael Foot seem to acknowledge this point from practical experience.

The origin of Charles's work on regulation is twofold. First, in his masterpiece 'The Evolution of Central Banks' Charles showed that central banks started off in their micro-capacity as crisis managers (lender of last resort) and that only later the macro-monetary policy side of central banks came to prominence (Goodhart, 1985, 1988a). Second, with the establishment of the SIB, the legal predecessor of the FSA, in the mid eighties, Charles became involved in the regulatory debate on the economics of regulation and started to write on issues such as the costs of regulation (Goodhart, 1988b).

I have learned much from Charles about the central bank roots of regulation and will finish my discussion with some unsettled issues in that domain.

In Chapter 9, Andrew Sheng argues that Goodhart's Law helps to explain why financial regulation can fall short in its target to achieve financial stability. In Chapter 10, Michael Foot shows how the regulator may work with market forces. The supporting arguments are well articulated and I fully agree with the main message from both chapters. However, as Charles has shown on many occasions, the role of a speaker or discussant is to be provocative and I will try to adopt that role.

2.   DOES GOODHART'S LAW APPLY TO CAPITAL RATIOS?

Andrew Sheng applies Goodhart's Law, 'that any observed regularity will tend to collapse once pressure is placed upon it for control purposes' (Goodhart, 1984, p. 96) to financial regulation. He provides a few interesting examples. In one of these, Sheng argues that capital adequacy rules are circumvented by expanding off-balance sheet activities, moving offshore or establishing non-regulated entities. I would like to explore this example further. The Basle capital ratios – or Cooke ratios named after its founding father – have become the centrepiece of prudential supervision, and have almost reached the status that monetary aggregates once had during the heydays of monetarism. Have the ratios of the Basle Capital Accord of 1988 served their purpose, or have they collapsed? The purpose of the Capital Accord – which was designed as a broad-brush framework – was twofold: i) bringing more capital in the banking industry; and ii) creating a level playing field for internationally operating banks.

In a recent BIS working paper (BIS, 1999), it is shown that the average capital ratio of the major banks in the G-10 countries rose from 9.3 per cent in 1988 to 11.2 per cent in 1996, an increase of almost 2 per cent (see Figure 10.1D).[2] The BIS study concludes that the Basle Accord has served its first purpose.[3] At the margin, of course, the capital adequacy rules have been circumvented: investment bankers have been innovative with 'capital' instruments that are no real equity to count as Tier I or II capital and semi-government bodies have lined up at regulators' doorsteps to argue that their paper should get a zero risk-weight. The major loophole is securitisation: assets are taken from the balance sheet and capital is accordingly reduced, while banks often keep, formally or informally, the top slice of the risk of the securitised assets. Nevertheless, the available evidence shows that capital on the whole has been increased in the banking industry since 1988 and that the capital ratio framework has not collapsed.

Incidentally, Michael Foot observes that banks have tended to keep much more capital than the regulator sets as the minimum. The question is whether this is due to pure market forces, as Foot seems to argue, or because regulators have been leading the way. By putting emphasis on the Basle capital ratio, I believe that regulators have been instrumental in making capital an important policy variable (this is the first part of Goodhart's Law). Next, market forces have joined the bandwagon and all banks disclose prominently their Basle capital ratio in their annual report. Market discipline serves thus as a useful complement to regulation.

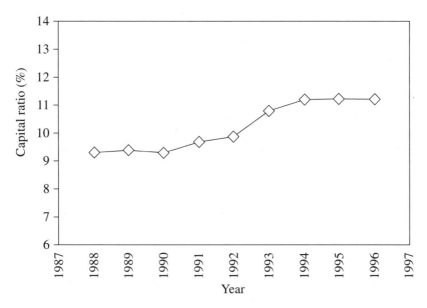

Source: BIS (1999).

Figure 10.1D Average capital ratios in G-10 countries

3. RULES VERSUS DISCRETION

Andrew Sheng draws an interesting parallel between monetary policy and financial supervision. Both aim to influence the behaviour of economic agents. The policy outcome depends on the credibility of the monetary or regulatory authority (that is the ability and track record of the authorities to exercise monetary and financial discipline). The key issue is how to avoid time inconsistency. In the monetary economics literature, there has been a long and intensive debate on whether monetary authorities should follow a rule or exercise judgement in deciding on interest rate changes (*rules vs. discretion*). On the literature on financial supervision, Andrew Sheng refers to the system of ex-ante prompt corrective action measures. Prompt corrective action was promoted by Benston and Kaufman (1994) in the aftermath of the savings and loans debacle and was subsequently implemented in the FDICIA legislation in the US. Sheng favours this rules-based approach as 'enhancing the discipline both of regulators and regulatees'.

I agree with the disciplinary working of such prompt corrective action rules, in particular in disciplining individual financial institutions in difficulties. However, I wonder how such rules would work during a system-wide crisis. A foreboding of that was the recent response of the FSA to the declining stockmarket prices in the wake of the 11 September terrorist attack in the US. To avoid forced sales of equities and a further drop in equity prices the FSA suspended part of its capital rules for insurance companies. Under a prompt corrective action mechanism, this suspension would not have been possible. Of course, it could be argued that such a mechanism should include a discretionary override for exceptional circumstances such as a system-wide crisis.[4] However, this raises several questions. How would one define a system-wide crisis (for international banks)? Would such an override undermine the mechanism? Or, even worse, would such an override create moral hazard? For example, if price-swings are on the border of the system-wide crisis definition, capital constrained financial institutions may have an incentive to force prices down further to let the override kick in.

4.   PRO-CYCLICAL NATURE OF CAPITAL RULES

This leads us to the wider debate on the pro-cyclical nature of capital adequacy regulations. Charles has been an early observer of the problem that 'most measures aimed at encouraging more prudent bank behaviour are liable to be pro-cyclical in the short run . . .' (Goodhart, 1995, p. 292). This is the case with Basle I, where capital regulations become more binding. During periods of falling asset prices and bad debts, bank profits are down and thus lower the amount of available capital. Basle II will be worse: not only *available* capital may drop during bad times, but *required* capital will also increase because the Basle II proposals are more risk sensitive (capital will be based on, for example, stock market volatility or default risk which are likely to rise during bad periods). The increased risk-sensitivity of the Basle II capital rules is from a micro-prudential perspective a good thing, but the increased pro-cyclicality could have a destabilising effect. This latter aspect is worrisome from a macro-prudential perspective (see, for example, Danielsson et al., 2001). At the time of writing, this issue is largely unresolved. Incorporating a discretionary override in the capital adequacy framework (or other forms of macro-managing the capital rules) is fraught with problems and may enhance moral hazard, as argued above.[5] Charles, Andrew Sheng and Michael Foot stress in their papers the importance of the interaction between micro-prudential supervision and macro-systemic stability.

5.   THE CONCEPT OF RISK

When designing risk-sensitive capital rules, one needs to adopt a risk concept. In Chapter 10, Michael Foot wonders what Value at Risk numbers really tell us about market risk. Are they actually telling us more about the market conditions in the last couple of years and proving of little use in markets such as those following the terrorist attack in September 2001? This outcry reminds me of another regulator's warning: *Returns in the past are no guarantee for the future.* Academics, including Charles and his colleagues at the LSE (Danielsson et al., 2001), have argued that supervisors should be interested in what happens beyond the confidence interval (for example 99 per cent) chosen by the supervisors for capital purposes. Other risk management tools, such as extreme value theory, and longer horizons (for example 10 years) could be useful. This will increase forecast precision and may also reduce the pro-cyclicality, as risk is measured over the business cycle. Finally, risk (market volatility) is partly the outcome of interaction between market players and thus endogenous (a well-known example of the 1987 stock market collapse is programme trading), while existing risk models treat risk as an exogenous process. In sum, the concept of risk is still evolving.

6.   WORKING WITH MARKET FORCES

Michael Foot gives an overview of market signals that supervisors can use. In particular Figure 10.1 in his chapter, which contrasts the share price of Yamaichi with the share price of its competitors in the months up to Yamaichi's failures, illustrates the usefulness of market signals for supervisors. Towards the end of his chapter, Michael explores how market discipline may be further developed. He refers to the proposal that requires banks to issue subordinated debt to provide an assured market signal. He argues, correctly, that such forms of market discipline would not replace supervision, but rather would complement it. I agree and would add a further argument for the complementary nature of market discipline. Markets only care about the private cost of failure. Public authorities also care about possible externalities of a failure (Schoenmaker, 1996). Hence, markets would under-supply the monitoring of financial institutions. This concern of the wider implications of failure is the origin of the development of the lender of last resort function and the subsequent development of the supervisory function by central banks (Goodhart and Schoenmaker, 1995).

It is important to foster market forces and to reduce moral hazard effects of public intervention. Market discipline will only work insofar as market participants can reasonably expect to lose money in case of a failure. Bailouts of secured and unsecured creditors would undermine these expectations. Authorities could follow a mixed strategy of bailout to reduce moral hazard. See Freixas (1999) on constructive ambiguity.

7.   DISCLOSURE BY SUPERVISORS?

Again, I will refer to the evolution of central banks. By acting for the public good rather than driven by profit motives, central banks started their role of crisis manager of the banking system (Goodhart, 1988a). Banks facing problems would solicit funds from the central bank and provide the central bank with confidential information about their problems. Given their non-profit orientation, the central bank would use this information discretely to form its judgement to provide lender of last resort funding to individual banks or not. This view contrasts with that of Goodfriend and King (1988), who argue that markets can provide this monitoring function. They assert that monitoring enables the commercial lender to distinguish illiquidity from insolvency in case of a request for funds. Reviewing the literature, they further conclude that there is no analysis that establishes the relative advantage of the central bank in monitoring and evaluating credit risks. It is sufficient for the central bank to conduct open market operations to maintain the liquidity of the banking system as a whole.

It would be beyond the scope of this short paper to give a full discussion of the market view versus the central bank view.[6] It seems to me that Michael favours markets and disclosure, but still sees a role for the supervisor acting for the public good. This would explain his reluctance for supervisors to publish private information (such as the required capital requirement) about firms under their supervision. Once a supervisor starts to disclose such private information, it may lose its role as confidant in good times as well as in times of crisis.

8.   CONCLUDING REMARKS

I would like to finish with a few unsettled issues in financial regulation. Although Charles has not argued against the establishment of a single regulator outside the central bank, he has raised the implication of crisis management by committee (that is supervisor, central bank and treasury).[7] The recently established structures with a single regulator have not yet been tested on their capacity for crisis resolution.

Next, Charles has been an early observer of the pro-cyclical nature of capital rules: banks reduce business in bad times. By designing risk-sensitive capital rules, the Basle II proposals are more pro-cyclical and could have destabilising effects. This problem has not yet been resolved. Both authors acknowledge this point.

Finally, the above problems lie in the grey zone where micro- and macro-economics interact. Combining the two domains seems to be key to solving them. The trend towards separate supervisors outside the central bank is, in that respect, worrying. In a recent survey on the skill profile of supervisors, Charles and I find that stand-alone supervisory agencies are more micro- and legally-oriented and may risk losing sight of the broader macro-picture.[8]

NOTES

1. As an economist, Charles has always argued that the optimal ratio of bank failures is larger than zero.
2. See also earlier work of Berger, Herring and Szegö (1995). They show that the aggregate equity/asset ratio of US commercial banks rose from 6.2 per cent in 1989 to 8.0 per cent in 1993, an increase of almost 30 per cent in four years.
3. At the conference, Brian Quinn (former Director of the Bank of England) noted that Basle has also achieved its second purpose of an international level playing field. After 1988, Japanese and French banks toned down their international strategy of expanding market share.
4. Charles has been in favour of the instrument of a discretionary override both in banking supervision (Goodhart, 1995) and in monetary policy (Begg et al., 1993).
5. Remember, for example, that Keynesian policies sometimes worked pro-cyclically due to implementation lags.
6. In addition, the free banking view argues that the banking system will be stable if left alone (that is no central bank intervention at all).
7. See, for example, Goodhart (2000). In the European context, Charles has argued that up to $(3n+3)$ parties can be involved in a crisis that hits n countries. Apart from the supervisor, central bank and ministry of finance of each country concerned, the European Central Bank (checking on monetary consequences), a putative EFSA (European System of Financial Services Authorities) and the European Commission (checking on state aid) will be involved.
8. Goodhart, Schoenmaker and Dasgupta (2002). Hellwig (1995) also stresses the importance of system-wide aspects in prudential supervision.

REFERENCES

Bank for International Settlements (BIS) (1999), 'Capital Requirements and Bank Behaviour: The Impact of the Basle Accord', Working Paper, no. 1, Basle: Committee on Banking Supervision.

Begg, David, Terence C. Daintith, Leonhard Gleske, Charles A.E. Goodhart, Philippe Lagayette, Peter Middleton, Mario Monti, Richard Portes, Eric Roll, David Walker and Charles Wyplosz (1993), *Independent and Accountable: A New Mandate for the Bank of England*, London: CEPR.

Benston, George J. and George G. Kaufman (1994), 'Improving the FDIC Improvement Act: What Was Done and What Still Needs to Be Done to Fix the Deposit Insurance Problem', in George G. Kaufman (ed.), *Reforming Financial Institutions and Markets in the United States*, Boston/Dordrecht: Kluwer.

Berger, Allen N., Richard J. Herring and Giorgio P. Szegö (1995), 'The Role of Capital in Financial Institutions', *Journal of Banking and Finance*, 19, 393–430.

Danielsson, Jon, Paul Embrechts, Charles Goodhart, Con Keating, Felix Muennich, Oliver Renault and Hyun Song Shin (2001), 'An Academic Response to Basel II', Special Paper, no. 130, London: LSE Financial Markets Group.

Freixas, Xavier (1999), 'Optimal Bail-Out, Conditionality and Constructive Ambiguity', Discussion Paper, no. 327, London: LSE Financial Markets Group.

Goodfriend, Marvin and Robert King (1988), 'Financial Deregulation, Monetary Policy, and Central Banking', *Federal Reserve Bank of Richmond Economic Review*, 74, 3–22.

Goodhart, Charles A.E. (1984), *Monetary Theory and Practice: The UK Experience*, London: Macmillan.

Goodhart, Charles A.E. (1985), *The Evolution of Central Banks: A Natural Development?*, Suntory–Toyota International Center for Economics and Related Disciplines, London: LSE.

Goodhart, Charles A.E. (1988a), *The Evolution of Central Banks*, Cambridge, Mass.: MIT Press.

Goodhart, Charles A.E. (1988b), 'The Costs of Regulation', in A. Seldon (ed.), *Financial Regulation – or Over-Regulation*, London: Institute for Economic Affairs.

Goodhart, Charles A.E. (1995), 'Price Stability and Financial Fragility', in K. Sawamoto, Z. Nakajima and H. Taguchi, *Financial Stability in a Changing Environment*, London: Macmillan Press.

Goodhart, Charles A.E. (2000), 'The Organisational Structure of Banking Supervision', Special Paper, no. 127, London: LSE Financial Markets Group.

Goodhart, Charles A.E. and Dirk Schoenmaker (1995), 'Should the Functions of Monetary Policy and Banking Supervision be Separated?', *Oxford Economic Papers*, 47, 539–60.

Goodhart, Charles A.E., Dirk Schoenmaker and Paolo Dasgupta (2002), 'The Skill Profile of Central Bankers and Supervisors', *European Finance Review*, 6.

Hellwig, Martin (1995), 'Systemic Aspects of Risk Management in Banking and Finance', *Schweizerische Zeitschrift für Volkswirtschaft und Statistik*, 13, 723–37.

Schoenmaker, Dirk (1996), 'Contagion Risk in Banking', Discussion Paper, no. 239, London: LSE Financial Markets Group.

Some concluding comments

Charles Goodhart

I am delighted to be given the last words in these volumes. Let me turn to a few issues that were raised earlier, especially those subjects on which, despite official retirement from the LSE faculty, I hope that I will go on doing work as a member of the Financial Markets Group.

The first is related to the chapter presented here by Richard Payne and concerns the micro-structure of the foreign exchange market. One of the stylised facts in this field is that volatility in financial markets is autocorrelated. When there is a major jump, a sharp fluctuation, in markets, markets tend to remain volatile for some time, and when markets are calm, they tend to remain calm for some time. This has been modelled by various GARCH (Generalised Auto Regressive Conditional Heteroskedasticity) or SV (stochastic volatility) type models. But these GARCH and SV models are simply mechanical ways of fitting observations. There is neither institutional knowledge nor theory behind it. The work that Richard and I are doing indicates that if you get a major shock in a market, what happens is that liquidity is absorbed; the limit orders have all been taken up. Moreover, liquidity providers have had something of a shock, and are not necessarily quite sure where things are going. So they become much more reluctant to enter new limit orders. So the limit order book, instead of being nearly horizontal over the relevant range, tends to become much steeper, thinner and attenuated. Then, once the limit order book has become thin, usually accompanied by higher bid-ask spreads, what occurs is that any small shock will bring about a large change in price. It is bound to do so, because there is no deep limit order book there to stop it. And that is, by nature, self-reinforcing.

But eventually volatility will tend to die away, and when it does so (and, as Richard Payne was saying, when there is a balance in the market with the buy side equalling the sell side), then there will be market makers out there competing for the business, and what you get is a big, deep book, and the spread will be small; and it will then take a large shock to move prices very much. So, unless you do get a massive shock, what will happen will be that prices will remain within a small range. In other words, one can look at the micro market structure to give a theoretical, institutional basis to GARCH.

Second, let me move on to a difference of opinion between myself and

Lars Svensson over the authorities' utility functions. Again this is work I hope to do in future, perhaps with Daniel Thornton. Let me remind you that one of the major concerns in financial intermediation is the interaction between principals and agents. Almost all financial intermediaries are agents, including central banks. Now how do you make your agents accountable, whether they are a central bank or a fund manager? What you tend to do is to give them benchmarks. There is the current legal case of Unilever versus Mercury Asset Management. Now what are the benchmarks for a central bank? The usual benchmarks for a central bank nowadays are that either they have introduced for themselves quantitative bands, or they accept bands, or they negotiate bands for inflation. Anyhow, these bands of, say, 0–2, or $2\frac{1}{2}$ with 1 per cent either side, or whatever, are there. I appreciate that they are not strictly regarded as an exact measure of success or failure, anymore than that fund managers' benchmarks are regarded as a strict measure of success or failure, but they tend in that direction. When the Bank of England goes through the 1 per cent band and has to write a letter, the likelihood is that people would claim that this is an indication of (comparative) failure. The existence of such a benchmark, a trigger, is going to change the way that people think about things. Once you have overshot that benchmark trigger (or it may be an area), then in effect you have failed. Once you have failed, it does not really matter that much how far you have failed, because failure is a zero one exercise; there is an English phrase, 'You might as well be hung for a sheep as for a lamb.' The quadratic utility function totally ignores the reality that there are trigger points or trigger areas, which distinguish success from failure.

Consider the rate of inflation. Assume that the rate of inflation in this country becomes 10 per cent, and we want to consider the disutility of a further rise from 10 to 11 per cent. And contrast that with a rise in the rate of inflation from 3 to 4 per cent. Under a quadratic utility function, if the inflation rate rises from 10 to 11, it is three times as bad as when the inflation rate rises from 3 to 4. Now, in fact, the trigger point comes at about $3\frac{1}{2}$. I am prepared to claim that in terms of, if you like, the effect on central bank officials or Monetary Policy Committee members, and anyone else responsible as agents under these circumstances, that the shift in inflation from 10 to 11 per cent is *much* less bad in marginal terms than a shift from 3 to 4. In other words, in terms of the slope of such a loss function, when you get out to the point where you are already a bad failure, it does not actually matter any more to the agent. The loss function then becomes virtually flat; whereas when you are near to your failure point, your loss function is very steep indeed, so that the loss function is not quadratic over its whole length. The loss function has a very clear point of inflection at that point where, as an agent, it has been decided that this divides success from failure. I know that the division between success and failure can be fuzzy, but even so, you can have a fuzzy area and an inflection point.

The final subject that I want to discuss briefly involves an area where more work needs to be done, though I have not even begun to do so myself. This goes back to the historical matters that Mervyn King was talking about in the first session, relating to the Bank of England Act in 1844 and the question of what the Bank of England should be doing. The first set of central bank reaction functions that ever became specified were formulated about that time, which were known as the Palmer rules, named after Horsley Palmer, a Governor of the Bank; and Horsley Palmer was the John Taylor of his day. The objective then was to maintain the gold standard, and this was done by lowering (raising) interest rates as the Bank's gold reserves increased (decreased). It operated as an interest rate adjustment function, very much like John Taylor's. The rules were simple; the Bank raised interest rates when its gold reserves were declining, in order to bring about a capital inflow. That relationship between interest rates, or interest differentials, capital inflows and the desire for reserves, has generally remained one of the key elements, the key constants, of central bank ideas and thinking about the world, more or less ever since.

The point that I want to bring to your attention is that in the last four or five years, such relationships between interest rates and capital flows have broken down. Let me put it this way, I do not think that any central banker now in any major country has any idea of the effect of changing interest rates either on capital flows or on the exchange rate. The relationship between interest rate differentials (interest rate changes) and capital flows, and what is likely to happen to the exchange rate, has simply collapsed; it has evaporated. What we thought we knew has gone. We do not know why it has gone. There have been suggestions that capital flows have shifted from being related to fixed interest flows to being related to equity market flows. So the argument now goes that, if you raise interest rates, you damage growth, and if you damage growth you damage your equity market, and therefore capital flows go in the 'wrong' direction. But this means that one of the key elements in a central bank's armoury for operating on the trans- mission mechanism, which is to affect the exchange rate via interest rates, has just dropped out of our hands entirely. This is a huge change, given how important the interest rate/exchange rate nexus is for small open econo- mies, including the UK. For the interest rate/capital flow/exchange rate channel to become unreliable is a matter of great concern. While much of this is discussed widely in the press, I have seen no serious good academic research over the last few years about why it has occurred, and what to make of it, and how best to react in response.

I will end there. I have much enjoyed this collection. I greatly appreciate all your kind words, and apart from undue praise for my own work, I agree with almost everything that has been written, with one exception. That was Ben Friedman's comment in the first session that I was prone to eccentricity; surely not! Moi, eccentric; never!

Index

Public–Private Partnerships for Sustainable Development